ASSOCIATED SYSTEMS THEORY: A SYSTEMATIC APPROACH TO COGNITIVE REPRESENTATIONS OF PERSONS

Advances in Social Cognition, Volume VII

ASSOCIATED SYSTEMS THEORY: A SYSTEMATIC APPROACH TO COGNITIVE REPRESENTATIONS OF PERSONS

Advances in Social Cognition, Volume VII

Edited by
ROBERT S. WYER, Jr.
University of Illinois, Urbana–Champaign

Lead Article by
Donal E. Carlston

LEA
LAWRENCE ERLBAUM ASSOCIATES, PUBLISHERS
1994   Hillsdale, New Jersey   Hove, UK

Lawrence Erlbaum Associates, Inc., Publishers
365 Broadway
Hillsdale, New Jersey 07642

Cover design by Kate Dusza

Library of Congress Cataloging-in-Publication Data

Associated Systems Theory: A Systematic Approach to Cognitive
    Representations of Persons
Advances in Social Cognition, Volume VII

ISSN: 0898-2007
ISBN: 0-8058-1473-6 (cloth)
ISBN: 0-8058-1474-4 (paper)

Books published by Lawrence Erlbaum Associates are printed
on acid-free paper, and their bindings are chosen for strength
and durability.

Printed in the United States of America
10 9 8 7 6 5 4 3 2 1

Dedicated to the memory of
Thomas M. Ostrom

Contents

Preface

This is the seventh volume of the *Advances in Social Cognition* series. From its inception, the purpose of the series has been to present and evaluate new theoretical advances in all areas of social cognition and information processing. An entire volume is devoted to each theory, allowing for its evaluation from a variety of perspectives and examination of its implications for a wide range of issues.

The series reflects two major characteristics of social cognition: the high level of activity in the field and the interstitial nature of the work. Each volume contains a target chapter that is timely in its application, novel in its approach, and precise in its explication. The target chapter is followed by a set of companion articles that examine the theoretical and empirical issues raised by the target. These latter chapters are written by authors with diverse theoretical orientations, representing various disciplines within psychology and, in some cases, entirely different disciplines. Target authors are then given the opportunity to respond to the comments and criticisms of their work and to examine the ideas conveyed in the comparison chapters in light of their own. The dialogue created by this format is both unusual and, we believe, extremely beneficial to the field.

In the initial volume of this series (published in 1988), Marilynn Brewer presented a general formulation of person impression formation integrating numerous theoretical and empirical issues that had not previously been considered in the field of social cognition. The present volume returns to this area with an even more detailed conceptualization of person impressions and the processes that give rise to their construction. In the words of its author, Donal Carlston, the target chapter provides "a comprehensive account of the representational systems that underlie people's exposure to social stimuli and their ultimate production of memories, judgments, and behaviors. The theory attempts to explain where different kinds of representations come from, how they are related to each other, and how they relate to important cognitive and behavioral activities." In pursuing this ambitious objective, Carlston identifies four fundamental systems—visual, verbal, behavioral, and affective—and postulates the manner in which the systems interact. Carlston's fresh and imaginative approach is likely to be a major stimulant to research and theory for years to come.

The scope of Carlston's formulation is reflected by the diversity of the companion chapters, written by researchers whose work cuts across cognitive psychology, social psychology, and psychophysiology. These articles provide additional insights into the phenomena to which the theory pertains and suggest ways in which the theory can be extended and refined. Considered in combination, the target and companion chapters are a timely and important contribution to the field of social cognition.

In addition to the authors themselves, we acknowledge the invaluable assistance of Lawrence Erlbaum Associates. Larry's continued support and encouragement of the *Advance* series, and the commitment of his staff to ensure the publication of a high quality series of volumes, is deeply gratifying. It is a genuine pleasure to have the opportunity to work with them.

A final acknowledgment and expression of gratitude is in order. Many of the theoretical and empirical advances that have been made in social cognition in general, and in person impression formation in particular, were stimulated either directly or indirectly by Thomas Ostrom. Tom, who is considered one of the founders of the field of social cognition, was among the first to recognize the importance of conceptualizing the content and structure of mental representations in developing a theoretical and empirical framework for understanding person impression formation. His own research and theorizing and his more general counsel to his colleagues have been major stimulants to the field. His influence is apparent in many of the articles contained in this volume. We are all in his debt, and so it is to him that this volume is dedicated.

—Robert S. Wyer, Jr.

1 Associated Systems Theory: A Systematic Approach to Cognitive Representations of Persons

Donal E. Carlston
Purdue University

> *What is all Knowledge too but recorded Experience . . . of which, therefore, Reasoning and Belief, no less than Action and Passion, are essential materials?*
> —Carlyle (1907, p. 84)

People's impressions of other people have been extensively studied within the areas of impression formation, attribution, person perception, and social cognition (Fiske & Taylor, 1991). Within these realms, research has seemingly equated impressions with trait ascriptions, group memberships, or interpersonal attraction. A central theme of the current chapter is that impressions embody these cognitions and more. As Carlyle said about knowledge more generally, impressions are "recorded experience," and what they record is arguably a wide range of cognitions that represent "reasoning and belief," as well as "action and passion."

In current parlance, impressions potentially may incorporate appearance images, categorizations, trait inferences, liking evaluations, affective reactions, relationship orientations, habitual responses, and episodic memories. Most of these constructs have been individually studied within social cognition, or within psychology more generally. However, little attention has been paid to the manner in which these diverse impression-related contents are organized, how they evolve or interact, or how they ultimately influence various interpersonal responses. One exception, Associated Systems Theory (AST; Carlston, 1992), seeks to integrate these different cognitive constructs within a single, organized structure, and suggests both the origins and consequences of impressions differing in representational form.

1

The overarching goal of AST is to provide a comprehensive account of the representational systems that mediate people's exposure to social stimuli and their ultimate production of memories, judgments, and behaviors. The theory attempts to explain where different kinds of representations come from, how they are related to each other, and how they relate to important cognitive and behavioral activities. In doing so, it attends to a fundamental assumption that sometimes gets neglected in social cognition research: that "thinking is for doing" (Fiske, 1992). In other words, cognitive representations serve a purpose, and that purpose relates to the different things that our cognitive systems do. At the same time, the theory incorporates a second assumption of psychology: that "doing causes thinking." This means that every activity lays down cognitive traces, and that these traces, or representations, are the building blocks of the cognitive system. At a general level, then, AST is a theory of the interrelationships between activities and associations, between responses and representations, and between behaviors and beliefs.

AST focuses on forms of impression-related (or "impressional") representations, rather than on their contents. In other words, the theory does not directly specify when one is likely to feel positive or negative about others, when one will think this or that about them, or whether one will act one way or another toward them. Instead, AST focuses on the ways in which those feelings, thoughts, and actions are generated, stored, and retrieved during various kinds of activities. In essence, the concern is not with *what* people think about others, but *how* they think it. Moreover, the concern is not with representations of people in general, or even with groups of people, but with impressions of single individuals. However, the nature of the theory suggests that it may be extensible to groups and even to nonsocial objects, as noted later in the chapter.

The first section of the chapter describes the forms of representation posited by AST and how they are hypothesized to relate to each other and to the basic mental systems involved in "doing" one thing or another. The second section of the chapter examines the processes underlying people's formation of different kinds of representations. The underlying theme that "doing causes thinking" is unveiled in subsections dealing with situational exposures, automatic processes, and communication. The third section examines the processes involved in the utilization of impressional representations in memory retrieval, social judgment, and interpersonal behavior. In other words, it considers the "doings" that thinking is for. The fourth section covers several additional factors that can influence the generation or utilization of impressional representations: the engagement of processing systems, and individual differences. The chapter then concludes with some general characterizations of the basic principles underlying AST.

Theories may satisfy a variety of different functions, including the integration and organization of existing knowledge, the explanation of previously unexplained phenomena, and the suggestion of hypotheses or avenues for additional research. Like most theories, AST serves some of these functions better than others. Initially, I conceived of it primarily as a rational framework for integrating the myriad forms of representation that were being explored by different social cognition researchers. As it evolved, the theory seemed increasingly to mesh with theoretical and empirical work in a variety of areas of psychology, providing a somewhat broader integration than I originally envisioned. I now find myself tempted to view AST as an explanatory and heuristic theory, rather than as simply an integrative scheme. In this spirit, I venture some modest accounts of related research and advance some plausible, though often untested, hypotheses for future examination. The reader is forewarned of the tentative and speculative nature of some of these ideas.

A STRUCTURAL MODEL OF REPRESENTATION

One hallmark of the social cognition approach to social psychology is the assumption of continuity between the cognitive processes operating in social and nonsocial domains (Schneider, 1991). A logical extension of this assumption is that there is also continuity in the mental systems operating in social and nonsocial domains. In other words, social cognition processes necessarily derive from the same perceptual, language, and response systems that govern other human activities. The nature of these systems has been detailed by research in cognitive psychology and human neuropsychology, and though the former work has had a great deal of impact in social cognition, the latter has had only a haphazard influence. This is unfortunate because the physical nature of mental systems almost certainly influences the nature and role of the cognitive representations that come into play during interpersonal relations. To quote Gardner (1985): "[A]dequate models of human thought and behavior will have to incorporate aspects of biological systems. . . . Cognitive science will have to incorporate (and connect to) neurobiology as much as to artificial intelligence" (p. 388). Following Gardner's suggestion, AST connects to neurobiology primarily in an attempt to discern the kinds of mental systems that may underlie person representations.

The Theory of Mental Systems

The basic mental processes covered in neuropsychological texts (e.g., Kolb & Whishaw, 1990; Walsh, 1978) typically include sensory/perceptual processes, the motor system, language, emotion, and memory. These processes are basic to human mental activity and are distinguishable from each other both in cognitive function and in biological structure (as discussed later). Similar processes are included in Martindale's (1991) "neural-network" approach to cognitive psychology. Martindale discussed sensory and perceptual analyzers, conceptual (semantic and syntactic) analyzers, an episodic analyzer, and an action system. However, he mentioned an emotion system only in passing, characterizing it as a subcortical system that provides inputs to higher level analyzers.

Consistent with these approaches, AST posits the existence of four primary mental systems: (a) a visual/sensory system, (b) a verbal/semantic system, (c) an affective system, and (d) an action system. Each of these individual systems is thought to be hierarchically organized, as characteristically assumed by many theories of brain function (e.g., Hebb, 1980; Kolb & Whishaw, 1990; Konorski, 1967; Martindale, 1991). The lowest levels of such systems consist of highly specialized physical structures that are involved in the reception of stimuli and the production of responses, and the highest levels consist of abstract concepts that relate to these perceptual or response processes. In between is a hierarchy of midlevel units that progressively shifts from the specific concepts necessary for the execution of system functions to more and more general representations of material relating to those functions. An example of such a hierarchical structure is provided by Martindale's description of the action system. At the lowest level, this system connects the motor system to specific action units (e.g., "walk" and "open door") that, in turn, are related at a more global level to script units. These, in turn, are related to goal units, and these are linked, at the most abstract level, to aspects of the self-concept (for related conceptions, see Shallice, 1978; Vallacher & Wegner, 1987).

These four hierarchical systems might be represented as four overlapping cones, to use a metaphor suggested by Scott Phillips (personal communication, January 20, 1993). As depicted in Fig. 1.1, these four cones are independent of each other at lower levels, where they connect with basic physical structures involved in perception, language, emotivity, and motor responding. Moving up through the cones, cognitive material becomes more abstract and elaborated; eventually, as the cones merge together, it begins to blend with cognitive material relating to other systems.

The overall structure is consistent with neurological models in which the products of different processing systems project onto common association areas, or "convergence zones," where they combine, interact, and influence each other (see Damasio, 1989b; Hebb, 1949, 1980). According to neuropsychologist A. Damasio (1989a), these interactions produce new material with some characteristics of each contributing system, as depicted on the upper surface of the cones in Fig. 1.1.

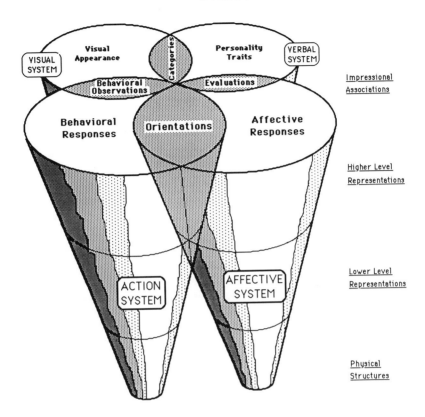

FIG. 1.1. Graphical representation of the overlapping hierarchical structures of the primary mental systems.

Mental Systems and Cognitive Representation

According to J. R. Anderson (1978), "well designed systems tend to have special representations for the kinds of information they have to process frequently" (p. 273). In other words, mental systems utilize, and are associated with, particular forms of cognitive representation. Some researchers (e.g., Damasio, 1989a; Farah, 1989) have suggested that when people access a cognitive representation, they may actually reactivate structures within the primary system that was involved in the initial perception or production of this material. Thus, for example, utilization of mental images may cause the activation of structures in the visual system, producing an experience that mimics the original experience of visual perception (Kosslyn & Pomerantz, 1977; Shepard & Podgorny, 1978). Similarly, verbal representations may involve low-level activation of speech centers ("subvocal speech"), affective responses may partially engage the physical systems involved in emotional experience, and action representations may involve incipient motor responses (see, e.g., Englekamp, 1991; Farah, 1988, 1989). Thus, cognitive representations are integrally linked to the systems they relate to, and are likely to reflect characteristic features of those systems.

AST assumes that each primary mental system involves special, abstract forms of cognitive representation that have features corresponding to the inputs or outputs with which each ordinarily deals. With regard to person perception, the characteristic representation for the visual system is hypothesized to be a visual image of a person's *appearance*.[1] Appearance is here defined broadly to include physical expressions and mannerisms, as well as static features such as height and attractiveness. The characteristic representation for the verbal system is assumed to be words and propositions; in the case of person perception, these are likely to involve *personality trait* labels. The characteristic representation for the affective system is presumably an *affective response*—that is, an abstract representation of affect that is linked to physiological structures involved in the primary experience of emotion. Finally, the characteristic representation for the action system is the *behavioral response*—an abstract representation of a meaningful sequence of acts that, in the interpersonal context, are directed at another human being.

These primary representations correspond somewhat to the four representational codes discussed by Fiske and Taylor (1991; see also Holyoak & Gordon, 1984). These are a propositional code involving traits, an analog code involving appearance, an affective code, and a temporal code involving memory for behavior. The last of these probably departs most from the present scheme, in that it involves episodic memory for other people's behavior, whereas *behavioral response* is defined here as the cognitive representation of an explicit behavioral act by the perceiver. AST treats episodic memories for others' behaviors as a closely related, but secondary, form of representation.

Each mental system presumably utilizes specialized procedures and knowledge bases to execute its functions. Moreover, each system may rely on unique principles of organization and representational codes, although

---

[1]Other sensory systems presumably have their own characteristic representations, but because the visual system has been most emphasized in both cognitive and social cognitive research, it is also given a more prominent role in AST. As discussed later, neuropsychological evidence suggests that the visual, auditory, and somatosensory systems are connected in similar ways to the secondary motor cortex and to the prefrontal lobe, implying considerable parallelism in the organizational characteristics of these systems (Kolb & Whishaw, 1990). Consequently, the conclusions drawn here regarding the visual system should generalize to these other sensory systems.

this has been somewhat controversial (see, e.g., J. R. Anderson, 1978; Pylyshyn, 1981). However, as depicted in Fig. 1.1, these separate systems ultimately merge together, and at the level where they do so, common principles of organization and process are assumed to operate, so that representations from different systems can interact with each other. Nonetheless, these representations are assumed to retain characteristic features that derive from their systemic origins.

When the separate systems merge together, the products of these systems are hypothesized to combine with material relating to other systems. J. R. Anderson (1978) suggested that the resultant combinations of representations may be viewed as new representations, and this convention is adopted here. AST identifies four forms of combined, or "hybrid," representation, each of which embodies characteristics of the different primary systems to which it is related. Both the hybrid and primary representations are depicted in Fig. 1.1, and in a simpler and more stylized fashion in Fig. 1.2.

Categorizations seemingly incorporate characteristics of both the visual and the verbal systems. In the domain of person perception, this implies that categorizations embody both appearance information and trait information. Some theorists have tended to emphasize the visual, appearance

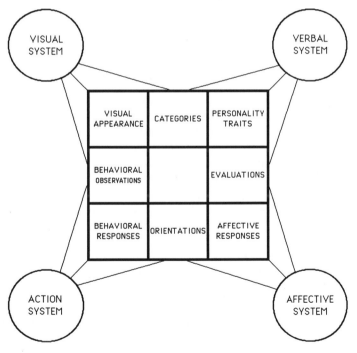

FIG. 1.2. Structural representation of the interrelationships among forms of person representation and primary mental systems.

qualities of these categorizations (e.g., Klatzky & Andersen, 1988), whereas others have emphasized the verbal, trait features (e.g., Cantor & Mischel, 1977; Rothbart, 1988), and still others have emphasized both (e.g., Brewer, 1988). As with most forms of representation, a whole range of categorical representations exist: from those that are much like visual images (e.g., one's image of a "slob") to those that are much like trait ascriptions (e.g., an "extrovert").

The term *evaluations* is used here to refer to representations that combine verbal and affective content (see Millar & Tesser, 1992). More specifically, evaluative representations employ verbal concepts to embody affective feelings. Such representations have been conceptually (Zanna & Rempel, 1988) and empirically (Breckler & Wiggins, 1989) distinguished from affective responses, as well as from personality traits (Carlston, 1980b). This category is again viewed as encompassing a range of representations: from those that are quite trait-like (e.g., "good" or "wonderful") to those that are more affective (e.g., "I really like her").

Orientations are a form of representation that combines affect and action. Consistent with early definitions of attitude (Eagly & Chaiken, 1993), orientations might be viewed as "tendencies" or "predispositions to respond to a person or object" in a particular manner. Examples of such predispositions are the approach and avoidance tendencies exhibited by most species, the dimensions of dominance orientation and dependency that Battistich, Assor, Messe, and Aronoff (1985) identified, and the four "relationship modes" specified by A. P. Fiske (1991). Evidence for the importance of such representations has been obtained by Fiske, Haslam, and Fiske (1991), who concluded that "people represent their social world in terms of the kinds of relationships they have with others" (p. 673).

Finally, *behavioral observations* are characterized as a subset of entries in episodic memory (Tulving, 1983) that incorporate both visual/sensory information and behavioral-response features of the action system. In other words, representations of others' behaviors will ordinarily be intermeshed both with perceptions of their appearance and with features of one's own role in the recorded events (see Conway, 1990; Tulving, 1972, 1983). The link between the visual system and behavioral observations is supported by Swann and Miller's (1982) finding that people who tend to form vivid images of others' appearances have better memories for others' behaviors. The link between behavioral observations and behavioral responses is suggested by the fact that both incorporate higher level action representations (such as scripts; Abelson, 1981), both have context features, and both stimulate entries in episodic memory. However, like other forms of representation, behavioral observations vary in the extent to which they incorporate features of the implicated systems. Thus, such representations may range from those that are primarily observational images to those in which one's own behavior enjoys a prominent focus.

Overall, AST suggests the importance of eight mental systems: primary systems governing vision, language, affect, and action; and secondary systems governing categorization, evaluation, orientation, and episodic memory. Moreover, in the context of person impressions, these eight systems are hypothesized to involve eight different forms of cognitive representation. For the primary systems, these are visual appearance, personality traits, and affective and behavioral responses; for the secondary systems, they are categorizations, evaluations, orientations, and behavioral observations. Additional detail regarding all of these systems and representations may be found in Carlston (1992).

Nothing in the current proposal mandates that these eight different forms of representation be independently accessible by the perceiver. As discussed later in this chapter, impressions may often be experienced as undifferentiated amalgams of representational features, rather than as discrete representational forms. Hybrid representations, in particular, may be closely integrated with other forms of representation that derive from the same primary systems. For example, a perceiver's visual image of a target person may be intimately tied to an episodic memory of that person's behavior. Such close associations between related forms of representation are explicitly predicted by the AST model.

The graphical arrangement of representations in Fig. 1.2 is more than just a convenient way to depict different representations in terms of their relationship to primary systems. It also represents the presumed relationships among different forms of representation, both in terms of the sequences in which some processes occur, and in terms of the general strength of association among individual representations. These ideas will be developed more fully later in this chapter, after several kinds of evidence regarding mental systems and representational forms are discussed.

Neuropsychological Evidence for the Basic Mental Systems

Martindale (1991) suggested that three different kinds of evidence are useful in identifying the systems (or "modules") that govern human mental activity. One of these is psychological evidence of task independence, which is the kind of material ordinarily considered in the social cognition literature (see, e.g., Fiske & Taylor, 1991). The others are anatomical and physiological studies that reveal structures devoted to certain kinds of processes, and clinical studies that show specific impairments to such processes. Although such work is rarely considered in social cognition (for exceptions, see

Anderson & Anderson, 1991; Pratto, 1991; Tulving, 1993), it does provide some support for the systems and organization proposed earlier. This work is briefly summarized here.

However, several caveats are in order. First, the tasks utilized in neuropsychology, and the brain functions examined, do not always correspond very well to the kinds of cognitive activities we are concerned with in social cognition. Second, neuropsychologists remain uncertain as to the role played by some brain structures in some activities. In some instances, the best evidence comes from studies with monkeys; in others, attempts to localize functions are complicated by the redundancy and plasticity of cortical functioning. Third, multiple pathways wind their way to and from single brain sites, so that any discussion of the sequential functions of brain structures is bound to be an oversimplification. Nonetheless, keeping these limitations in mind, neuropsychology does suggest the existence of different brain structures that are implicated in the kinds of functional systems described previously.

Brain Structure. The sensory systems include the visual, auditory, somatosensory, and olfactory systems. The first three have identifiable primary cortexes that project in similar ways through secondary association areas to the premotor and prefrontal cortex. Because visual information has been most central to social cognition work, this structure is described, keeping in mind that most senses have parallel structures.[2]

Visual information is transmitted from the optic receptors to the primary visual cortex in the occipital lobe, where basic perceptual processing takes place, and then to the parietal lobe, where the stimulus is integrated with information from other senses to form an initial percept. Following the polymodal pathway, this information is then projected to a second association area, in the superior temporal sulcus, where identification and categorization take place, and then finally to the frontal lobe, where verbal associations appear to be made. It may be noted that these perceptual, classification, and verbal association functions correspond to the perceptual, categorical, and verbal process representations shown from left to right in the top row of Fig. 1.2.

Visual information also passes via the perforant pathway to the medial temporal region, most notably the hippocampus, which is implicated in long-term memory, and via a series of parallel pathways to the prefrontal

---

[2]The exception is the olfactory system, whose sensory inputs are passed to the pyriform cortex (a relatively primitive area at the base of the brain), and then through either the thalamus or the hypothalamus to the orbitofrontal cortex. Although olfaction has not been extensively studied in human neuropsychology, this structure may imply a rather direct connection between olfaction and the social and sexual behaviors believed to be regulated by the frontal cortex (Kolb & Whishaw, 1990).

cortex, which serves to "organize behavior with the help of temporal memory" (Kolb & Whishaw, 1990, p. 468). The prefrontal cortex is connected to the frontal cortex proper, which plays an essential role in allowing people to adjust and regulate their behavior in response to environmental cues. These visual, memory, and behavioral functions closely relate to the visual (appearance), memory (behavioral observations), and behavioral (behavioral responses) representations shown from top to bottom in the left column of Fig. 1.2.

Adjacent to the hippocampus in the medial temporal region is the amygdala, a structure believed responsible for associating affective properties with particular stimuli. Evidence mentioned in the next section relates this structure to approach–avoidance behaviors. Moreover, because the amygdala is anatomically connected with the orbital-prefrontal cortex, it has been suggested that these structures together play a role in regulating emotional behavior. These affective, approach–avoidance, and regulatory effects are subsumed by the affective response, orientation, and behavioral response representations shown from right to left in the bottom row of Fig. 1.2.[3]

Finally, the speech centers in the dominant association cortex (especially Broca's area and Wernicke's area) are implicated in verbal activity, although, as already noted, higher mental processes such as verbal association seem to involve the frontal cortex. As mentioned earlier, the amygdala projects toward the frontal cortex, and this region may provide one site for the interactions between affect and language depicted in the right column of Fig. 1.2. However, there is also evidence for interplay between affect and language in the regions of the nondominant temporal lobe that are homologous to the speech centers in the dominant hemisphere. For example, Gorelick and Ross (1987) concluded that "the organization of affective language in the right hemisphere mirrors that of propositional language in the left hemisphere" (p. 553). The verbal, affective, and evaluative representations relating to such structures are depicted in the right column of Fig. 1.2.

Clinical Syndromes.   Most of the systems and subsystems represented in Fig. 1.1 and 1.2 are subject to disruption through brain damage, and clinicians have documented and labeled the different syndromes involved

---

[3]The amygdala also connects directly with the visual system, in a manner that may represent "part of a system for processing socially relevant visual information" (Kolb & Whishaw, 1990, p. 615). This direct connection is not well represented by the spatial arrangement depicted in Fig. 1.1. However, it does not appear that this particular "system" produces unique forms of representation, as do the others depicted in the figure. Instead, the effect of the amygdala appears to be to imbue all other forms of representations with emotional valence—a function accommodated by AST, although not reflected in the figure.

(for a review, see Williams, 1979). The labels for the disorders relating to each functional system are depicted in Fig. 1.3. Proceeding down the left column of the figure, *Agnosias* reflect an inability to recognize sensory stimuli that have been properly recorded by the perceptual system. One such deficit, prosopagnosia, reflects an inability to recognize acquaintances by their facial appearance. *Amnesias* are deficits in the memory system, including face amnesia (which is closely related to prosopagnosia), retrograde amnesia (the inability to remember past events, including behavioral observations), and anterograde amnesia (the inability to store new events, including behavioral observations). *Apraxias* are disruptions in the ability to carry out purposeful movements in the absence of paralysis. Such deficits are variously attributed to lesions in the parietal and prefrontal cortexes, or to subcortical structures (cf. Kolb & Whishaw, 1990). Dysfunctions in more global social and sexual behaviors appear to result from damage to the orbital-frontal cortex.

Listed in the right column of the figure are *aphasias*, which include the inability to produce or comprehend verbal content; *aprosodias*, which are disruptions in the ability to produce or interpret the affective components of language; and *affective disorders*, including anhedonia (flat affect) and

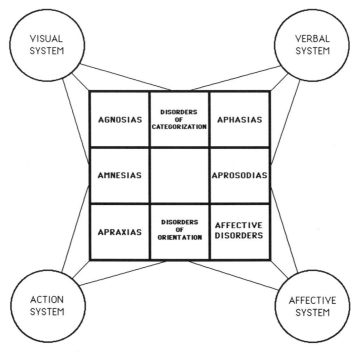

FIG. 1.3.   Clinical disorders relating to disruptions of different representational forms.

bipolar affective disorder (manic depression). The middle column of the figure includes disorders of visual categorization, which have been attributed to lesions in the superior temporal lobes, and what are here termed *disorders of orientation*, which appear to involve damage to the amygdala. For example, in monkeys, removal of this structure appears to alter approach and avoidance behaviors, as well as social involvement and aggressiveness. In humans, damage to this structure can create similar effects, which are features of the Kluver–Bucy syndrome (Jacome, 1991).

This clinical work provides additional evidence of the importance of each primary and secondary system posited by AST. Perhaps in the future, social cognition researchers can work with neuropsychologists to determine the consequences of such syndromes for impressional and interpersonal processes (see, e.g., Anderson & Anderson, 1991). Such work will be exceedingly difficult, given the pervasive nature of the deficits usually associated with brain damage, and the need for impression-assessment procedures that sidestep such deficits. However, it may be possible to learn something about the nature and role of different impression-related representations by examining those who lack the ability to produce or process such representations (Anderson & Anderson, 1991; Tulving, 1993).

The Basic Dimensions of Representation

The primary systems are arranged as they are in Figs. 1.1 and 1.2 because this provides a convenient way to depict hybrid representations in cells adjacent to the primary representations to which they are most closely related. However, this arrangement does not mean that those systems diagonal to each other in the scheme are unrelated. Visual stimuli often provoke strong affective reactions, and verbal material probably plays an important role in both the planning and representation of behavior. However, at least in the person perception domain, it is not apparent what unique forms of representation combine the features of visual and affective representations, or of verbal and behavioral representations. Moreover, there seems to be relatively little evidence for specialized visual–affective or verbal–behavioral systems, comparable to that for the other primary and secondary systems discussed.

The arrangement of representations in Fig. 1.2 also serves to highlight some systematic differences among different forms of person representation. Specifically, representations in different rows differ progressively in their degree of focus on the target or the perceiver, and those in different columns differ progressively in their degree of concreteness or abstraction. The nature and implications of such differences are discussed in the next sections.

Target Versus Self-Reference. Although all forms of representation reflect the subjective perceptions and experiences of the perceiver, some forms of representation pertain primarily to the target being perceived, whereas others implicate the perceiver to a larger extent. More specifically, the representational forms in the top row of Fig. 1.2 pertain primarily to characteristics of the person being perceived, those in the middle row implicate this person and the perceiver more equally, and those in the bottom row pertain most strongly to the perceiver. Visual appearance, categorization, and personality traits are ostensibly characteristics of a person being perceived, and they do not inherently reference the perceiver. The observed behaviors of others tend to implicate the perceiver as well as the actor because, as Tulving (1983) noted, the perceiver is generally a participant in the episodes being observed, and may actually be interactively involved with the target. Evaluations similarly implicate both the person being evaluated and the evaluator because the perceiver's evaluation or liking for another is as informative about the perceiver as it is about the target (Wyer, Budesheim, & Lambert, 1990). Finally, in the bottom row are behavioral responses, orientations, and affective responses of the perceiver, which are most clearly attributes of the perceiver, even though they are directed at the target.

These differences in focus have a number of interesting implications. For example, forms of representation depicted in the bottom row of the figure may be more likely to implicate the self-concept than forms of representation in the top row. Moreover, ascribed characteristics represented in the lower rows may commonly be viewed as more idiosyncratic to the perceiver because they necessarily reflect particular experiences, relationships, and interactions between the perceiver and the target. Characteristics represented in upper rows may be perceived as more objectively true and more consensual across different perceivers because these are ostensibly properties of the target and not of the perceiver. Finally, because representations in the lower rows implicate the self, a relatively stable structure for most perceivers (Kihlstrom & Cantor, 1984), it may be more difficult to influence or change impression content of this type than content represented in the top row.

Concreteness Versus Abstraction. The representational forms in the left column of Fig. 1.2 (visual appearance, behavioral observations, and behavioral responses) are all relatively concrete, and may include details reflecting the time and place at which they were recorded. Representational forms in the center column (categorizations and orientations) are somewhat more abstract because they typically summarize multiple instances or observations. The forms on the far right (personality traits, evaluations, and affective responses) are most abstract because they reflect general characteristics of the target person, independent of any particular time, place, or circumstance.[4]

These variations in abstraction may also have a number of consequences. For example, the greater detail and frequency of concrete forms of representation may make them relatively more difficult to recall than more abstract forms of information (see Hastie & Carlston, 1980, with regard to personality traits; Zajonc, 1980, with regard to affect and evaluations). However, when they are recalled, concrete forms of representation may be particularly influential (Nisbett & Ross, 1980). It is also plausible that more abstract forms of information will exhibit greater consistency and stability than more concrete forms. For example, a perceiver may view someone as *either* honest or dishonest, but probably will not view that person as *both* honest and dishonest, at least not without adding a qualifier that increases the concreteness of these representations (e.g., "honest in finance, dishonest in love"). Similarly, a perceiver may view someone as *either* good or bad, or as *either* affectively pleasing or displeasing, but it is difficult to simultaneously hold inconsistent cognitions at this abstract level. In contrast, a person may be perceived as sometimes well groomed and sometimes slovenly, as sometimes lying and sometimes telling the truth, or as sometimes well treated and sometimes badly treated. As bothersome as such inconsistencies sometimes seem to be (e.g., Srull, 1981), they may be less so at this concrete level than at more abstract levels.

Of course, these described consequences of the abstractness and self-reference of representational forms are mere speculation. Nonetheless, the arrangement of representational forms shown in Fig. 1.2 does capture systematic differences among these representational forms. The scheme thereby provides an organizational structure that may be useful for classifying different kinds of impression-related content, and ultimately for exploring the implications of such content for various kinds of phenomena. This possibility will be elaborated after a brief discussion of other taxonomic schemes.

Taxonomic Evidence for the Basic Representations

One simple approach to cataloging the variety of representational content composing people's impressions is to collect and content analyze people's descriptions of other people. Over the years, a number of researchers have

---

[4]As noted earlier, each representational category actually encompasses a range of representational forms. Thus, some variation in abstraction and self–other reference occurs within, as well as between, different forms of representation. To repeat an example used earlier, categorizations vary from the concretely visual ("slob") to trait-like abstraction ("extrovert"). The boundaries between representational types are "fuzzy"; at the extremes, descriptors may blend into adjacent representational categories.

done precisely this (e.g., Beach & Wertheimer, 1961; Dornbusch, Hastorf, Richardson, Muzzy, & Vreeland, 1965; Fiske & Cox, 1979; Livesley & Bromley, 1973; Ostrom, 1975; see also Park, 1986), and several others have collected and analyzed self-descriptions (Gordon, 1968; McGuire & Padawer-Singer, 1976). Before examining these data, it should be acknowledged that, for a variety of reasons, the kinds of descriptors identified in such studies may not correspond directly to basic forms of cognitive representation and may not accurately reflect the ways in which impressions are actually represented cognitively.

First, because the overall representation or impression of an individual is probably experienced as a flood of associations, rather than in terms of discreet representational components, some descriptors may actually be an amalgam of different underlying representational forms. Second, because person descriptions must be reported verbally, some "translation" of form is likely to occur in order to make representations more readily communicable. Furthermore, nonverbal forms of representation may be difficult to report using verbal labels (cf. N. H. Anderson, 1988; Zajonc, 1980), and therefore may not be reported at all. Finally, subjects are likely to believe that the description task calls for particular kinds of descriptive responses, which may result in either biased reporting or post hoc construction of suitable responses. For example, instructions to "describe someone" probably focus attention on the target person, and thus may be likely to elicit target-focused representations, rather than self-referent ones, regardless of the kinds of representations that are actually stored in memory.

Despite these concerns (see also Carlston, 1991, 1992), it seems likely that people's descriptions of others are somewhat influenced and constrained by the underlying representational forms in which this information is recorded. In other words, people cannot help but describe others in a way that reflects how they think about those others. If one's impression of Bill Clinton is that he is a gregarious Democratic president who promised change and played the saxophone on TV, these representations will surely find expression in one's descriptions of him. Therefore, if properly interpreted, these descriptions may illuminate the kinds of cognitive representations that underlie the reported impression.

Past Taxonomies.   To determine whether evidence for the major AST representations have been found in people's descriptions of others, Cheri Sparks and I examined the major taxonomies that have been proposed for the classification of such descriptions. Table 1.1 summarizes taxonomic entries that appear to relate closely to the different representational forms posited by AST. It is evident that most, though not all, of the AST representational forms recur regularly across these different taxonomies. The major exceptions are the self-referent representations of affective and behavioral responses.[5] In some taxonomies, the *affective* category is probably partially subsumed within the more verbal *evaluations* label. However, the category of *behavioral responses* seems to have been neglected altogether, except where it falls within such general rubrics as "mutual interaction." As noted earlier, descriptive tasks are more likely to elicit target-focused descriptors than self-referent ones.

Although similar content is included in these different taxonomies, each scheme tends to group the content in rather different ways. For example, Beach and Wertheimer (1961) grouped all descriptors into four major categories of person descriptors: (a) *objective information*, which includes appearance, background, and other descriptive facts; (b) *social interaction*, which includes the target persons' behavior, the subjects' reactions to the target, and others' behaviors toward the target; (c) *behavioral consistencies*, which includes temperament, morals, and values; and (d) *performance and activities*, which includes abilities, motivation, and interests. In contrast, Fiske and Cox's (1979; see also Fiske & Ruscher, 1989) system corresponds more closely to AST. Major categories include: (a) *appearance* (what people look like), (b) *behavior* (what they do), (c) *relationships* (what one does with them), (d) *context* (where one finds them), (e) *origins* (how they got this way), and (f) *properties* (what makes them up).

As a rule, these different systems are data driven, rather than theory driven, and so the classifications reflect descriptive similarities rather than important conceptual distinctions. As a consequence, the taxonomies are simply hierarchically organized lists that leave unanswered many questions about the relationships among different descriptor types. Are some major categories of descriptors more similar to each other than others? Along what dimensions do descriptors that fit one category differ from those that fit another? Is the extent to which respondents use a category related in any systematic way to the extent to which they use other categories? How are the descriptors that are used related to the ways that people perceive, think, feel, and act toward other people?

AST provides tentative answers to such questions by specifying the systematic differences and relationships among basic categories of description. As already discussed, descriptors vary progressively in their abstractness and self-reference. Moreover, they are hypothesized to vary systematically in their relationships to each other and to primary perceptual and response systems. All of these assumptions are captured within the structural arrangement depicted in Fig. 1.2.

---

[5]All self-referent representations are omitted from the Ostrom (1975) system because it emphasized forms of information that people seek about others in forming impressions. One would not ordinarily think of seeking information from others about one's own responses, orientations, or evaluations.

TABLE 1.1

Classification of AST Representations by Other Taxonomic Systems

AST Representation	Beach & Wertheimer (1961)	Dornbusch et al. (1965)	Fiske & Cox (1979)	Livesley & Bromley (1973)	Ostrom (1975)
Visual appearance	I. Objective information 1. Target's appearance	Organic variables 6. Handicap 8. Physical description 9. Physical attractiveness Norms 56. Grooming	Appearance: How they appear Body Face Voice Grooming Overall attractiveness	I. Objective information 1. Appearance III. Personal characteristics and behavioral consistencies 13. Expressive behavior	2. Physical and biological characteristics height, weight dress physical appearance attractiveness
Categorizations		Demographic variables 3. Race 4. Ethnicity 5. Religion Group status 32. Membership in a specific collective 35. Socioeconomic status	Behavior: What they do Occupation Origins: How they got this way Nationality Ethnicity Class	VIII. Social factors 21. Social roles	2. Physical and biological characteristics sex race 3. Behaviors and affiliative memberships occupation group membership
Personality traits	III. Behavioral consistencies 8. Target's enduring personal characteristics (temperament) [some of] 9. Self-concept and emotional adjustment IV. Performance and activities 11. Target's abilities	Total personality 48. Adult terms 49. Children's terms Abilities Norms 57. Honest–dishonest [some of] Modes of interaction [some of] Moods of interaction	Properties: What makes them up Traits	III. Personal characteristics and behavioral consistencies 9. General personality attributes [some of] 10. Specific behavioral consistencies [some of] IV. Attitudes and achievements	1. Character traits and general habits adjectives personality characteristics

Evaluations	II. Social interaction 7. Self's reaction to target	Total personality 50. Undifferentiated positive comments 51. Undifferentiated negative comments	Relationship: What one does with them Perceiver's reaction	VII. Evaluations IX. Target–other relations [some of] 28. Self's opinion of, and behavior toward, the target person
Affective responses Orientations	" "	Interpersonal relations 25. Relations with self Quality of interaction 16. Self to target	" Relationship: What one does with them Role	" IX. Target–other relations [some of] 27. Mutual interaction
Behavioral responses Behavioral observations	II. Social interaction 4) Target's behavior toward self 5) Target's behavior toward other people	Recreational variables Aggression	Behavior: What they do Chronic nonverbal Activities	1. Objective information 3) Routine habits and activities 4) Actual incidents 3. Behaviors and affiliative memberships present and past activities

Note. To permit easy reference, entries are shown with the appropriate superordinate classification heading, and, wherever possible, are worded and numbered as in the original text. The terms *self* (the person writing the description) and *target* (the person being described) have been substituted for various other referents to facilitate comparison across schemes. The notation "[some of]" is included where some subordinate entries or examples correspond to the relevant AST representation and some do not. Some entries are shown as corresponding to more than one AST representation because another taxonomy fails to make relevant distinctions, or provides examples that fit multiple AST classifications. Table prepared by C. W. Sparks and D. E. Carlston.

19

The AST Taxonomy.   Cheri Sparks and I have elaborated the basic structure shown in Fig. 1.2 to produce a comprehensive taxonomy of the kinds of descriptors that people use in describing their impressions of other people (Carlston & Sparks, 1992a, 1992b). The basic goal has been to classify descriptive statements in terms of the kinds of underlying representation that they most probably reflect. The resultant taxonomy incorporates the theorized interrelationships among different forms of representation, and thus addresses many of the questions left unanswered by other taxonomies. Additionally, because of the dimensional features of the structure, this taxonomy allows person descriptions to be characterized in terms of their overall abstractness and self-reference, rather than simply in terms of the different descriptors or descriptor categories that are utilized.

The taxonomic system that we have developed is based on the 3 × 3 scheme shown in Fig. 1.2, and provides explicit definitions of the descriptive contents most likely to reflect each of the basic forms of representation. Actually it goes a step further, adding two columns and two rows of descriptors between those in the basic 3 × 3, to allow finer distinctions to be made among the descriptors that people actually use in describing others. As shown in Fig. 1.4, the descriptors in the resulting 5 × 5 matrix are arranged in terms of their theorized levels of abstractness and self-reference, just as in the basic 3 × 3 depicted in Fig. 1.2.

Attempts have been made to verify and refine this arrangement of descriptors using multidimensional scaling methods similar to those described later in this chapter. However, the real objective of these efforts is not to identify 25 different kinds of descriptors, but rather to classify the kinds of descriptors obtained from subjects in a manner that reflects the likely contributions of the eight basic representational forms. It is then possible to select or combine descriptors to produce estimates of the amount of appearance, categorization, trait, evaluation, affect, orientation, behavioral response, and behavioral observation material present in a person description.

Definitional and procedural details of the taxonomy are available elsewhere (Carlston & Sparks, 1992b) and are not elaborated here. However, some advantages of this scheme over previous taxonomies should be mentioned. First, because of its systematic nature, the AST taxonomy includes some kinds of classifications (e.g., behavioral responses) that have been largely overlooked by other taxonomic schemes. Second, because it specifies the expected interrelationships among descriptors, similarities and differences in their nature and use are apparent. Third, because similar descriptors are classified in spatially proximate cells, the impact of misclassifications is minimized. Fourth, because the taxonomy specifies the dimensional characteristics of different descriptors, impressions can be summarized in terms of their dependence on different primary systems, or

	Concrete observations	Summary observations	Moderately abstract descriptors	Qualified abstractions	Global abstractions
Inherent properties of the target	VISUAL APPEARANCE at a specific time and place	General visual appearance	CATEGORY labels	Personality categories Traits with specific qualifiers	PERSONALITY TRAITS
Derived properties of the target	Target's BEHAVIORS at a specific time and place	Target's general behaviors	Personal preferences	EVALUATIONS with specific qualifiers	General EVALUATIONS of target
Properties of others in relation to the target	Others' specific behaviors regarding the target	Others' general behaviors regarding the target	Miscellaneous other content	Others' specific or qualified evaluations of the target	Others' general evaluations of the target
Properties of the target in relation to the self	Target's specific behaviors regarding the self	Target's general behaviors regarding the self	Relationship descriptors Target's orientation to self	Target's specific evaluations or affect toward self	Target's general evaluations or affect toward self
Properties of the self in relation to the target	Self's specific BEHAVIORAL RESPONSES to target	Self's general behavioral responses to target	Self's ORIENTATIONS toward target	Self's affect toward specific aspects of target	Self's AFFECTIVE RESPONSES to target

FIG. 1.4. Summary of the AST taxonomy for classifying person descriptors.

in terms of their relative abstractness or self-reference. Fifth, because the taxonomy is tied directly to a theory of underlying structure, a number of hypotheses are suggested about the generation and utilization of different person descriptors (as described elsewhere in this chapter). Sixth, because people's descriptors are linked through the theoretical structure to response systems, the implications of impressions for judgment, affect, and behavior are more apparent. Such issues are addressed in later sections.

Associative Connections Among Representations

Neural-network models generally assume that separate cognitive systems are massively interconnected in some way (see Martindale, 1991). This interconnectedness allows the representational products of different functional systems to interact with each other, as discussed earlier. It is unclear whether such interactions occur within a single area (the frontal lobe would be a good candidate), or whether different association areas are interconnected in a manner that accomplishes the same thing. Conceptually, this probably makes little difference, and it is convenient to view these linkages as occurring within a common association area, such as that depicted in the square matrix in Fig. 1.2. Within this area, AST assumes that associative links exist among all the diverse forms of mental representation that were discussed earlier.

The assumption that different forms of representation may be linked within a common associative structure has been proposed previously. Such linkages have been hypothesized for affect and episodic memories (Bower, 1981), categorical and propositional representations (Brewer, 1988), attitudes and behaviors (Fazio, Chen, McDonel, & Sherman, 1982), traits and images (Lynn, Shavitt, & Ostrom, 1985), and episodic memories and traits (Carlston & Skowronski, 1986). More generally, associative network models have been described that incorporate diverse forms of attitudinal (see Fazio, 1989) and person (Wyer & Carlston, 1979) representations.

AST utilizes the associative network metaphor to characterize the interrelationships among cognitive representations. The mechanics of such networks have been elaborated in a number of places (Carlston, 1992; Carlston & Skowronski, 1986; Collins & Loftus, 1975; Fiske & Taylor, 1991; Higgins, Bargh, & Lombardi, 1985; Wyer & Carlston, 1979), and are only briefly reiterated here. The basic conception is that cognitive concepts are represented by nodes that are linked to other nodes by pathways of varying strength. Concepts in short-term memory are activated, and they transmit excitation down connecting pathways to other concept nodes, where it accumulates. When enough excitation accumulates at a node, through all of the pathways connecting it to previously activated nodes, this new concept is retrieved into short-term memory. The activation of a concept leaves it with residual excitation, which decays slowly and facilitates its reactivation. The simultaneous activation of any two concepts tends to strengthen the associative pathway between them, facilitating the subsequent spread of activation from one to the other.

There is now some thought that the activation of a concept may produce spreading inhibition as well as spreading activation (e.g., Grossberg, 1988; Hoffman & Ison, 1980; Neely, 1976; Roediger & Neely, 1982; Wilson & Cowan, 1972). In the absence of an inhibitory process, activation might continue to reverberate among concepts that were previously relevant, causing them to activate and reactivate each other at the expense of concepts that have current relevance. For example, as someone unrecognizable approaches you from a distance, your mind presumably activates different alternatives that fit the features you have discerned — alternatives that may range from "panhandler" to possible acquaintances. Once you identify this person, perhaps as your Uncle Harry, it is important that the other alternatives not intrude on your attention because you need instead to focus on associations relevant to interacting with your Uncle Harry. Yet activation has already spread to these alternatives and perhaps to associated nodes; as it passes back and forth between these nodes, it could force immaterial concepts into consciousness.

A mechanism for spreading inhibition could prevent short-term memory from becoming overloaded with irrelevant memories by suppressing the activation of alternative concepts as soon as a relevant concept has been identified. In general, theorists have suggested that inhibition spreads from activated concepts to other concepts of the same general type. For example, Martindale (1991) suggested that concepts at one level of a system hierarchy tend to inhibit other concepts at the same level, whereas they tend to activate concepts at other levels. Thus, in terms of his characterization of the action system, a script unit would be likely to inhibit alternative script units, but to activate goal or action units to which it is linked.

In terms of the AST structure, this implies that the activation of any form of representation may be more likely to interfere with retrieval of other alternate concepts of that same form. For example, retrieving an image of an acquaintance's appearance may inhibit retrieval of alternative images of that person's appearance, although it should facilitate retrieval of other associated forms of representation. Such inhibition effects have been previously demonstrated in the empirical literature. For example, when a behavior is interpreted in terms of one trait, this seems to reduce recognition of alternative trait implications (Carlston, 1980a; see also Smith, 1989); when an ambiguous picture is interpreted in one way, this interferes with other possible interpretations (Boring, 1930); when a person is categorized in one way, this makes alternative categorizations less likely (Zarate & Smith, 1990); and so on. In each case, inhibition seems to spread primarily from the seminal stimulus to morphically similar, alternative concepts.

In summary, AST uses an associative-network model, with spreading activation and inhibition, to represent the connections among all the varied forms of mental representation discussed earlier. Actually, network models are now commonly viewed as a convenient shorthand for characterizing processes that are more elaborately represented in terms of parallel distributed processes (see Martindale, 1991). For example, in many such parallel distributed processing (PDP) models (e.g., Grossberg, 1988; Rumelhart & McClelland, 1986), concepts are not represented by simple nodes, but rather by patterns of activation across feature nodes. Impressions might then be viewed as large "waves" of activation that immerse the features associated with a variety of such concepts. This conception has some advantages when discussing some representational issues, such as the similarities between generic and specific forms of representation, or between perceived and imagined representations (see, e.g., Johnson & Raye, 1981). For most purposes, however, the simpler associative-network metaphor suffices.

From this point of view, an *impression* is a cluster of associated concepts within an associative network. As depicted in Fig. 1.5, a central concept of

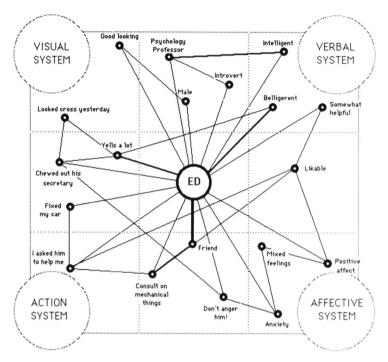

FIG. 1.5.   Sample network of associations among concepts of differing representational forms. (Although described here verbally, many of these representations would
not be stored in verbal form.)

a target person is linked by pathways of varying strength to nodes
representing visual images, categorizations, personality traits, evaluations,
affect, orientations, behavioral responses, and behavioral observations that
are associated with that person. These different specific representations
may also be linked to each other, as well as with more primitive concepts in
the systems to which they are most closely related.

It is hypothesized that the probability of associative links is somewhat
higher for specific representations that are spatially proximate in Fig. 1.2.
Thus, for example, categorical concepts should tend to be most associated
with appearance images and trait ascriptions, affect should tend to be most
associated with evaluations and orientations, and so on. Such associations
are predicted because representations reflect the operations of specific
mental systems, and different systems are differentially engaged and
utilized by different goals and activities. When a system is engaged, those
representations that relate to it are more likely to be simultaneously
activated, and are therefore more likely to become associated with each
other. Additionally, representations that derive from the same system may
have basic features in common, so that the activation of one facilitates the

activation of the other. Possible mechanisms for such featurally based associations are discussed later in this chapter.

Of course, there will be many exceptions where distant forms of representation have become closely linked through thought and use. For example, one may have strong affective reactions to people who look like close friends, or draw trait conclusions about others who behave in certain ways. The existence of such "nonproximal" associations raises the issue of how pervasive and restrictive the described representational structure really is. An analogy may help to clarify matters. Consider the midwestern states to be different forms of representation, cities to be specific items of each form, and the geographic relationships among the states to reflect the underlying representational structure of the midwest. Additionally, consider travel speeds to represent the strengths of association among the different represented items (i.e., cities).

In general, travel speeds are faster between cities in adjacent states than between cities in distant states, just as associative strengths should generally be greater for proximal forms of impressional representation. However, there are many exceptions, some of which are quite systematic and reliable. For example, one can almost always travel from Chicago to Minneapolis more quickly than one can travel from Lafayette, Indiana, to Granville, Ohio, although the latter are in adjacent states and the former are not. Such exceptions do not alter the underlying geographic structure: Indiana and Ohio remain geographically closer than Illinois and Minnesota. Even if one could generate a special map that accurately depicts travel times under some circumstances (e.g., by airplane), this would not apply under other circumstances (e.g., travel by car). Moreover, such a map would misrepresent some geographical features such as physical similarity (e.g., Indiana is more like Ohio than Illinois is like Minnesota).

Similarly, there are probably many circumstances where people build up strong and reliable associations between forms of representation that are more distant in Fig. 1.2. However, in general and on average, proximal representations should be more strongly associated than distant representations. Moreover, even when this is not true, Fig. 1.2 conveys important characteristics of representations, such as their featural similarity and relative abstractness and self-reference. The representational structure shown in Fig. 1.2 is therefore assumed to be pervasively important, although the extent to which it actually characterizes people's impressions is essentially an empirical issue. One approach to addressing this empirical issue is presented in the next section.

Multidimensional Scaling of Impression Structures

To test various aspects of AST theory, Cheri Sparks and I collected large numbers of written descriptions of person impressions. In one study, 52 subjects wrote descriptions of male and female friends, relatives, and celebrities under one of several different instructional conditions (e.g., "Tell us what you think of each person" vs. "Tell us how you feel about each person"). A variety of different instructions were also used in a second study, in which 173 subjects wrote descriptions of four different people, ranging from "very best male friend" to random selections from a long list of self-generated "real, living persons." To assess the relational structure underlying these impressions, separate multidimensional scaling analyses were done on the 312 descriptions from the first study and the 692 from the second. Each of these analyses collapses across a wide variety of different kinds of impressions in an attempt to detect a common, underlying structure that may not be discernable in any particular kind of impression.

The impressions from each study were first content analyzed using the AST taxonomy described earlier, and analyses were performed to ensure that interrater reliabilities were adequate. Then for each description, the frequency of descriptors corresponding to each of the eight basic forms of representation was computed. Next, these frequencies were correlated with each other, across the descriptions written by different subjects, producing an 8 × 8 correlation matrix. This correlational analysis was conducted separately for each of the repeated measures so that individual subjects would contribute only one pair of observations to each correlation. The resultant similarities matrices each reflect the degree of co-occurrence of different kinds of descriptors across one type of descriptions.

The similarities matrices were then used as input to INDSCAL multidimensional analyses, which compute the most probable spatial structures underlying similarity data. INDSCAL (Kruskal & Wish, 1978) permits multiple, nonindependent matrices to be analyzed at once, so that a single, best-fitting structure can be determined across all of the repeated measures in a study.

Figure 1.6 shows the two-dimensional structures obtained for each of the studies. Indexes of the overall fit between data and solution were modest, but acceptable, given that the similarities matrices that were input derived from computed correlations, rather than from subjective similarity ratings. The structure shown in Frame b has been rotated 45 degrees to facilitate comparison with Frame a and with Fig. 1.2. The orientation of axes is not totally arbitrary in INDSCAL because of the way that repeated measures are mapped onto dimensions, but the differing orientations obtained in these two studies probably just reflect the different repeated measures used in each.

It is readily apparent that the structural representations shown in both frames of Fig. 1.6 are consistent with that predicted by AST. The arrangements of individual taxonomic categories are remarkably similar to each other, and to the arrangement of representational forms suggested by

a) Study 1

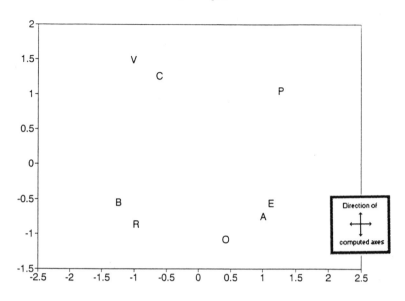

b) Study 2

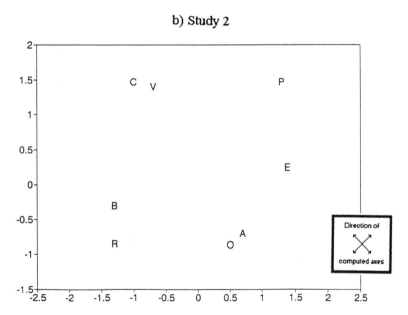

Key: A Affect   B Behavioral observations   C Categorizations   E Evaluations
      O Orientations   P Personality   R Behavioral responses   V Visual appearance

FIG. 1.6.   Two-dimensional INDSCAL plots of the similarity of different representational forms as determined from their co-occurrence in person descriptions.

Fig. 1.2. In each instance, visual appearance and affective responses oppose each other on one diagonal, and personality traits and behavioral responses oppose each other on the other. In each instance, behavioral observations lie between visual appearance and behavioral responses, orientations lie between behavioral responses and affect, and evaluations lie between affective responses and personality traits. Moreover, categorizations are located in the expected position between visual appearance and personality traits in Frame a, and very nearly in the same position in Frame b.

Both frames of Fig. 1.6 suggest close relationships between behavioral responses and behavioral observations, and between visual appearance and categorizations. It is noteworthy that these relationships were detected from actual patterns of descriptor use, not from similarity ratings. The relationship between behavioral responses and observations makes conceptual sense: Both are episodic in nature, both relate to behavioral scripts, and both involve the self to some extent, as discussed earlier.

The relationship between visual appearance and categorizations is also understandable, given that most of the categorizations obtained in our studies were visual (e.g., gender and ethnicity). Moreover, the least visual forms of categorization, personality categorizations, were not included in the categorization classification for these analyses. Preliminary INDSCAL analyses of all 25 taxonomic classifications found personality categorizations to be so similar to personality traits that these were grouped together instead (cf. Rothbart, 1988). When personality categorizations and other categorizations are lumped together, the combination tends to fall midway between visual appearance and personality traits, as depicted in Fig. 1.2.

These results are particularly striking because they not only support the structural premises of AST, but some of the process assumptions as well. In other words, these results not only suggest that different kinds of descriptors are related in the manner predicted by AST, but also that these relationships are reflected in the frequencies with which different descriptors are used in written descriptions. AST predicts that related forms of representation should tend to co-occur because they are linked to the same mental systems. The past and present operations of these systems should tend to co-activate related forms of representation, increasing the associations between them and creating correlated patterns of use. This argument is developed more fully in later sections.

Generality of the Model

Because they viewed the underlying processes of person perception and object perception as similar, Fiske and Cox (1979) suggested that taxonomies of person descriptors should be extensible to the description of nonsocial objects as well. This is probably particularly true of the AST taxonomy because it derives from a model of basic functional systems that are necessarily implicated in both social and nonsocial activities. Thus, AST seemingly implies that cognitive representations of rocks and stereos, no less than of people, should reflect contributions from the visual, verbal, affective, and action systems. In other words, we should store impressions of what such objects look like, what their properties are, how we feel about them, and what we do with them, as well as of the various hybrid forms of representation already discussed.

Within social psychology, attitude theory and research probably deals most closely with people's impressions of objects that are not individual persons (e.g., legislation and ethnic groups). The present approach relates to attitude work in several significant ways. First, the verbal, affective, and action systems correspond to the cognitive, affective, and conative (behavioral) components of the classic tripartite definition of attitude (Breckler, 1984; Katz & Stotland, 1959). AST is similar to several recent models of attitudinal representation (e.g., Fazio, 1986; Millar & Tesser, 1986; Zanna & Rempel, 1988) in characterizing these components as different sources of information that contribute to a common cognitive product. Second, the distinction AST makes between affect and evaluation has also been emphasized recently by several attitude theorists (Breckler & Wiggins, 1989; Zanna & Rempel, 1988). Like Zanna and Rempel, AST views evaluation as a more deliberative, pro–con judgment, whereas affect refers to experienced feelings or emotions. Third, AST makes a distinction between orientations (a hybrid of affect and behavior) and evaluations (a hybrid of affect and cognition), which could be characterized as two different kinds of attitudes. The orientations concept is more consistent with the definition of attitude as a response "tendency" or "predisposition," whereas the evaluations concept is more consistent with definitions of attitude as "an evaluative response" (see Eagly & Chaiken, 1993). As discussed later, these concepts also relate to Fazio's distinction between attitudes formed through direct and indirect experience.

These connections with attitude research suggest that AST may be useful in characterizing impressions of things other than individual people: Similar representational forms and structures should apply equally to impressions of objects, issues, groups of people, and perhaps even the self. Social cognition researchers are already making concerted efforts to determine the exact nature of self-representations (Linville & Carlston, in press), and AST may suggest some additional possibilities for doing so. For example, the AST taxonomy might be applied to self-descriptions to provide an unstructured assessment of underlying representational forms (see Gordon, 1968; McGuire & Padawer-Singer, 1976, for previous efforts along these lines).

Some modification of the AST taxonomy is necessary before it can be used with self-descriptions because it includes a distinction between target and self-referent characteristics that is more useful when the target is not the self. All the descriptors in self-descriptions are presumably self-referent, with the possible exception of intruded material involving impressions of significant others.[6] Thus, the top row of the AST scheme (see Fig. 1.2) might be redefined to cover the perceiver's descriptions of his or her own appearance, group memberships, and traits; the middle row might then include significant self-events and self-evaluations; and the bottom row would encompass behavioral responses toward others, global orientations, and emotional state. The advantage to such a taxonomy is that it is linked to a theory of cognitive representation, and it permits meaningful comparisons to be made between the representational forms used in self- and other descriptions.

THE GENERATION OF IMPRESSIONAL
REPRESENTATIONS: "DOING CAUSES THINKING"

AST conceptualizes impressions as an associative network among items of information that are represented in a variety of different forms. Marcel (1983) advanced the controversial suggestion that concepts come to be represented in all possible forms, but the more conservative view adopted here is that impressions are represented in a hodgepodge of forms that reflect the particular experiences of the perceiver. More specifically, it is assumed that a person's physical and mental activities leave behind representational residues (see Zajonc & Markus, 1984, regarding the physical memories underlying lower level representations of emotion). Consequently, the general nature of such past activities shapes the kinds of representations that people generate.

Figure 1.7 summarizes the AST process model, depicting the generation of initial representations, their translation into other forms, their alteration by various cognitive activities, and, eventually, their influences on various overt responses, which are discussed in later sections of this chapter. Each row across the figure relates to a different form of representation, and each column relates to a different step in the generation or utilization of impressions. Given the right kinds of experiences, which translate material into multiple representational forms, some informational content is likely to be represented redundantly. For example, one's general opinion of another may be reflected in one's evaluations, trait inferences, and behavioral responses. However, other kinds of informational content may be

---

[6]McGuire and Padawer-Singer (1976) found that such material represented about 20% of the responses of school children. Children may generally confine themselves less strictly to task demands than adults, for whom this percentage might be lower.

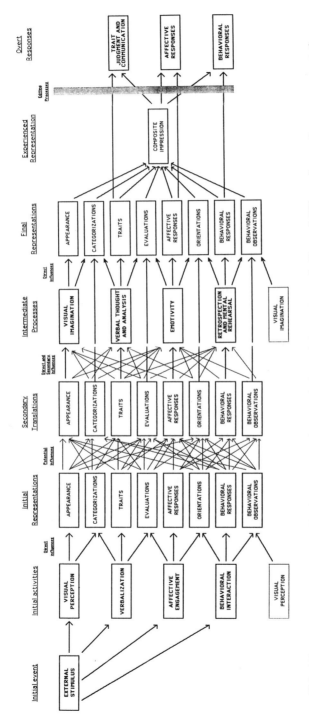

FIG. 1.7. Summary of processes affecting the generation, translation, reinforcement, and effects of different forms of person representation.

31

unique to related forms of representation. For example, the manner in which one acts out one's opinions is reflected only in one's behavioral responses, or in related hybrid forms of representation (e.g., behavioral observations and orientations). The following sections outline some of the central processes that govern the generation of different forms of representations (see also Carlston, 1992).

Involvement and Initial Representations of Others

As previously noted, AST assumes that cognitive representations reflect the operations of one or more mental systems. Thus, one way in which representations come into being is through the activity of these systems. More specifically, representations related to the visual system (especially appearance) should be produced through perception of other people, and those related to the verbal system (especially personality traits) should be produced through verbal thought and communication. The affective and behavioral response systems should also produce characteristic representations; that is, behavioral interactions with someone should produce behavioral responses, and emotional involvements should produce affective responses. Hybrid representations may result from the concurrent operation of several systems at once. Thus, evaluations may result from simultaneously thinking about and reacting emotionally to other people, and orientations from emotionally reacting to and interacting with others. In the same way, behavioral observations might reflect the simultaneous operations of the visual and action systems, and categorizations might reflect the simultaneous operations of the visual and verbal systems.

From this perspective, the nature of people's past experiences and activities with a person are likely to influence the kinds of impressional representations that are stored. The predicted effects of different kinds of involvements on representation are illustrated in Fig. 1.8. When a perceiver engages in passive observation of a target, the resultant impression should be dominated (at least initially) by visual appearance representations. Appearance representations are also likely to be produced during other kinds of interactions, provided that the perceiver can see the target.

However, activities other than passive observation should result in the generation of other forms of representation as well. When the perceiver is behaviorally involved with the target person, so that actual interaction takes place, this presumably favors the generation of representations relating to the action system. As illustrated in Fig. 1.8, initial impressions in this case should include other "concrete" forms of representation: behavioral observations and behavioral responses. When a perceiver engages in verbal thought about the target, the initial impression should include "target-based" forms of representation: categorizations and personality traits.

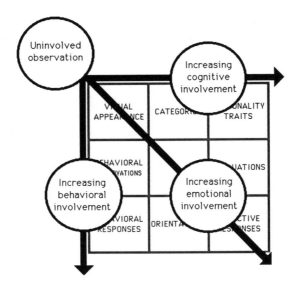

FIG. 1.8. Influence of different kinds of involvement on the generation of different forms of person representations.

Finally, when the perceiver is emotionally involved with the target, the initial impression should include affective responses.

There are many circumstances where these initial impressions may quickly prime additional forms of representation, as discussed in the next section. Nonetheless, in general, systematic relationships are expected between the nature of one's past interactions with someone and the forms of representation that one is likely to have. For example, impressions of most celebrities are formed through passive observation, with little real cognitive, affective, or behavioral involvement. On the other hand, the longer that one has known someone, the more likely it is that one will have become cognitively, affectively, and behaviorally involved, and the more likely it is that one will have formed representations related to these systems. Consistent with this expectation, Carlston and Sparks (1992a) found that the use of trait descriptors, evaluations, affective responses, and orientations progressively increased across college students' descriptions of celebrities, relatives, and friends. However, use of visually related representations (appearance, categorizations, and behavioral observations) showed a reversed pattern, or no effects at all (use of behavioral responses was too low to establish a clear pattern). Fiske and Cox (1979) similarly demonstrated that people used more trait descriptors, and wrote more overall, in describing friends than acquaintances (see also Klein, Loftus, Trafton, & Fuhrman, 1992).

Although people may frequently be involved with others in a variety of ways, there are some instances where one kind of involvement predominates. For example, impressions formed through formal, in-role interactions may often be characterized by behavioral, but not affective or cognitive involvement. Thus, we may be able to recognize the regular clerk at a nearby grocery store, we may have a repertoire of behaviors that we customarily engage in with this person, and we may have episodic memories of this person's past behaviors. However, our initial impression is not likely to involve personality ascriptions, evaluations, or affective responses unless we become cognitively or emotionally involved in some way. This may partially explain why even positive in-role interactions between different races seem to have little effect on racial attitudes (Cook, 1978).

There are also occasions where impressions may be formed through thoughtful consideration, but without feeling or behavioral interaction. This seemingly characterizes many laboratory experiments, where subjects watch videotapes, look at photographs, or observe others through one-way mirrors. Real-world analogues to such situations undoubtedly also exist, as when personnel officers evaluate applicants from forms and photographs. The cognitive representations formed in such situations should tend to be target focused, consisting of visual appearance, categorizations, and trait judgments. Behavioral observations and evaluations are also possible, but self-referent representations (behavioral and affective responses) seem considerably less likely.

In other special situations, appearance information may not be available about a target person, so that impressions must lean more heavily toward other forms of representation. For example, auditory representations, which are of some importance in most interactions (Ray, 1986), become especially so when the target person is not visible to the perceiver, as in telephone interactions. When people communicate through paper or electronic mail, no sensory data about the target person may be available at all. In such instances, nonvisual forms of representation, such as personality traits, behavioral, and affective responses, should tend to predominate.

Impressions formed through third-person communications represent a particularly interesting, and particularly common, special case. Such impressions probably underrepresent behavioral representations because the audience has no actual interaction with the person being described. In fact, the verbal nature of such communications may produce a considerable bias toward verbally related forms of representation, such as personality traits, and perhaps categorization and evaluations. In other words, impressions formed through communicated information are likely to be more target based and abstract than those formed through first-hand interactions. Given the predominant use of verbal descriptions as stimuli in social cognition research, it is not surprising that impressions have generally been characterized as trait judgments and (to a lesser extent) categorizations or evaluations (see Bassili, 1989). A fuller range of impression-related representations may become more apparent as researchers move to more interactive paradigms (e.g., Ickes, Stinson, Bissonette, & Garcia, 1990; Kenny, 1991; Park & Flink, 1989).

Translation into Secondary Forms of Representation

Representations produced through the direct operations of the primary mental systems may stimulate the generation of additional representations, including representations of altogether different forms, as depicted on the left side of Fig. 1.7. Of the various terms used to characterize such processes, *translation*, *elaboration*, and *inference* seem most suitable because these imply the generation of new representational forms without the alteration or loss of the initial form (as implied by *transformation*). Psychologists have demonstrated a variety of different translation processes that relate to person perception. For example, appearance information has been shown to precipitate categorizations (Klatzky, 1984; McArthur, 1982; Zarate & Smith, 1990) and affective reactions (Zajonc, 1980); trait concepts may be stimulated by observed behaviors (Jones & Davis, 1965; Winter & Uleman, 1984) or social categorizations (Zarate & Smith, 1990); and either trait or behavioral information may lead to the formation of mental images of a person's appearance (cf. Paivio, 1971). Wilson (1968) provided a classic example of such appearance inferences in a study showing that high-status people are perceived as having greater height. In principle, information in any form may be translated into any other form, although some kinds of translations are likely to be more common than others.

The translation of information about a particular person into new representations of that person utilizes generic knowledge structures that have been termed *conceptual social memory* (Hastie & Carlston, 1980). According to Hastie and Carlston, conceptual social memory specifies "the referential and relational 'definitions' of all important social concepts, events and generic individuals" (p. 14), and provides "procedures that generate inferences from abstract representations" (p. 26). The relational definitions among trait concepts, in particular, have been called *implicit personality theories* (Rosenberg & Sedlak, 1972). It has been suggested that such theories might extend also to behavior–trait relations (Schneider, 1973), although these have more typically been viewed from the perspective of attribution theories (e.g., Jones & Davis, 1965). Conceptual social memory extends even further, to include perceived relationships between behavior and affect, categorization and evaluation, relationships and orientation, and so on. For an even broader conception, see Cantor and Kihlstrom's (1985) concept of *social intelligence*.

Carlston and Skowronski (1988) described conceptual memory as a network of associative links between generic representations that can be used to extrapolate beyond what is already known about a particular target person. Thus, for example, the generic behavior "returning others' property" may be associatively linked with "honesty" in conceptual memory, and a perceiver who knows that "Dave returned lost money to its owner" can use that linkage to infer Dave's traits. We characterized this process as the importation of links from conceptual memory into the associative structure representing the target person. Thus, Dave is initially linked to his behavior, and a generic version of this behavior is linked to the trait *honest* in conceptual memory, so that the combination of these structures leads to an indirect pathway connecting Dave to *honest*.

Carlston and Skowronski (1986, 1988) demonstrated the utility of this network approach in several studies employing a reaction-time (RT) methodology. In one of these (Carlston & Skowronski, 1988), the strength of subjects' perceived associations between a generic behavior (returning lost money) and a trait (*honesty*) was determined some weeks before an experiment. Later in that experiment, subjects viewed a videotape in which an actor expressed his intention to return a lost wallet to its rightful owner. Afterward, subjects responded to a series of timed questions about this actor and other actors depicted in other videotaped episodes.

The strength of subjects' behavior-trait associations, as determined weeks earlier, closely related to the time taken to respond to a question about the actor's honesty. However, as predicted, this relationship held only in conditions where subjects had not previously made this trait inference, or if they had, where they were primed to think about the actor's behavior just before the critical trait question. In other words, only subjects who based their responses on the behavioral representation needed to consult conceptual memory to translate this representation into a trait response. Presumably the remaining subjects had consulted conceptual memory earlier, had already formed a direct link between the actor and the trait of honesty, and answered the timed question by accessing this direct association.

The mechanics underlying the "importation" or "combination" of associative structures may be clarified somewhat by switching to the PDP formulation mentioned earlier. Both the specific representations that constitute person impressions and the generic (or "schematic") representations that constitute conceptual social memory can be characterized as patterns of activation across nodes that reflect various visual, verbal, affective, and action features. In fact, the principal difference between a specific and a generic representation may be the number and nature of the feature nodes incorporated in these patterns. For example, compared with an actual behavior, a generic one may include less visual or episodic detail, but perhaps more features detailing motives and consequences. The pattern of feature activations representing a generic behavior may activate other patterns of features, including those that compose other forms of representation to which this behavior is linked in conceptual memory (e.g., personality traits).

The pattern of activation that represents an actual behavior may sufficiently approximate a generic pattern to cause or allow the activation of generic representations in conceptual memory. Once these new forms of representation are activated, they can become associated directly with the actor. In other words, the activation pattern that constitutes our impression of someone is likely to encompass these new feature nodes, representing material "imported" from conceptual social memory, as well as old feature nodes representing the prior impression.[7]

Automaticity in the Translation of Representations

When one cognitive representation persistently gives rise to another, the translation of the first into the second may become automatized (J. R. Anderson, 1982; Schneider & Shiffrin, 1977; Smith, 1989). In other words, the translation may tend to occur largely without effort, intent, awareness, and/or control (see Bargh, 1989). Theorists have suggested that certain social stimuli may automatically give rise to behavioral responses (Langer, Blank, & Chanowitz, 1978), categorizations (Zarate & Smith, 1990), personality traits (Gilbert, 1989; Winter & Uleman, 1984), and affective responses (Clark & Isen, 1982; Niedenthal, 1990; Zajonc, 1980), although each of these suggestions has been controversial (e.g., Bargh, 1984; Bassili, 1989; Gilbert & Hixon, 1991; Lazarus, 1982).

In principle, virtually any kind of translation can become automatized, at least in some respects, for some people, under some circumstances. However, because automaticity develops from repetition (Bargh, 1984; Smith, 1989), some kinds of translations are more likely to become automatic than others. The key consideration is whether the past experience of the perceiver has provided sufficient opportunities for the development of cognitive procedures that generate one form of representation from another (Smith, 1989). More specifically, the likelihood that a representation of Characteristic A will automatically lead to generation of a representation of Characteristic B is affected by the past frequency of several kinds of events. These include the past frequency that the perceiver: (a) has been exposed to people who have Characteristic A, (b) has inferred Characteristic B, and, more specifically, (c) has inferred that people with Characteristic A also have Characteristic B. According to Smith (1989), the

---

[7]It may be evident from this description why such processes are more commonly discussed using the simpler, associative network metaphor.

"specific" practice effect involving both the same stimulus (A) and the same inference (B), is more important than the "general" practice effects involving either the same stimulus *or* the same inference. Each kind of practice effect is considered in the following paragraphs.

A perceiver is more likely to have automatic procedures relating to frequently observed characteristics and, concomitantly, to the characteristics of frequently observed groups of individuals. Consistent with this argument, Zarate and Smith (1990) found that White subjects were able to categorize the photos of Whites faster than those of African Americans. It may also be true that characteristics that can be readily and reliably identified will be more likely to trigger automatic procedures than characteristics that are less overt or consistent. Thus, for example, visible categories (e.g., race) and behaviors (e.g., aggression) seem more likely to generate automatic procedures than abstract characteristics like traits or evaluations. As a general rule, then, automatic translations may be more likely to proceed from concrete forms of representation to abstract forms, rather than the reverse.

This same conclusion also follows from the greater diversity of concrete forms of representation. That is, because fewer abstract representations are associated with more concrete representations, the concrete ones map onto the abstract ones more reliably than the other way around. For example, the concrete act of stealing will map reliably onto the abstract trait of *dishonesty*. However, dishonesty may map onto several different concrete representations, including such behaviors as lying and cheating, as well as stealing. As a consequence, the mapping from concrete to abstract is more likely to become proceduralized than the reverse.

A second factor influencing automaticity of translations is the regularity with which the perceiver has inferred the target characteristic in the past. An important determinant of this frequency is the *chronic* tendency that people have to focus on some kinds of target characteristics rather than others. For example, Bargh and Thein (1985) have shown that people who chronically draw inferences about others' independence develop automatized routines for making such judgments. Researchers have typically viewed chronicity in terms of people's preference for a particular trait (Bargh, Bond, Lombardi, & Tota, 1986) or category (Smith, 1989) representation, but people may also have chronic preferences for one kind of representational form over others. In other words, people may differ in the extent to which they habitually form visual, verbal, action, or affective representations, and these differences should affect the extent to which they develop procedures for generating such representations automatically. Such individual differences will be discussed in more detail later in this chapter.

Situational demands may also influence the kinds of representations that are generated frequently. Different forms of representations may be generated with enough consistency in certain settings or for certain groups of people to achieve a degree of automaticity. For example, in academic settings, judgments regarding intelligence are likely to occur with considerable frequency; in conflict situations, relationship judgments (e.g., friend or foe) may become automatized; in performance contexts, talent evaluations will undoubtedly be common; and in interactions of a routinized nature, as between those acting in prescribed roles, consistent patterns of behavioral response are likely to occur. Thus, in such settings, procedures are likely to develop to handle relevant representational translations.

The most important factor influencing automaticity is the frequency with which a specific characteristic has previously led to generation of a specific inference (Smith, 1989; Smith, Branscombe, & Bormann, 1988). It has already been noted that the different kinds of involvement that a perceiver has had with a target person may influence the kinds of representations that are formed of the target (see Fig. 1.8). Similarly, the characteristic nature of involvements with different groups may affect the frequency with which different kinds of representations are generated, and thus the likelihood that such representations will be triggered by specific group characteristics. In other words, behavioral responses are more likely to occur automatically if one has repeatedly interacted with people like the stimulus person, affective responses are more likely if one has been emotionally involved with such people, and verbal representations are more likely to be generated if one has been cognitively involved with such people, as in thinking about them or in communicating about them to others.

These considerations suggest that most people may develop a degree of automaticity for those representational translations that have been emphasized by their past experiences. They do not suggest that all translations of any particular general type (e.g., behaviors to traits) will necessarily become automatic, as has been proposed by some (e.g., Winter & Uleman, 1984; but see Newman & Uleman, 1989). Nonetheless, past experiences should tend to influence the kinds of associations that people have between different representational forms, and thus the likelihood that particular translations, automatic or not, will occur.

Social Processes Affecting Impressional Representations

The preceding sections suggest that impressional representations may result from three related kinds of processes: (a) the direct operations of one or more mental systems, (b) the automatic translation of initial representations into additional forms of representation, and (c) the use of conceptual social memory. Past experiences with or regarding a given person determine the nature of the systems that have been engaged and the kinds of representations that are likely to exist. Past experiences with or regarding similar people influence the kinds of automatic translations likely to exist, as well as the nature of conceptual social knowledge.

From this perspective, people's personal and social experiences are major determinants of the *forms* of representations that compose their impressions (as well as the content of those impressions, of course). However, at present, we know little regarding the frequencies with which people engage in different kinds of interactions, are exposed to different kinds of information, make different kinds of inferences, or communicate different kinds of descriptors in real-world settings. In fact, we know little regarding the frequencies with which people encounter personal attributes or behaviors of any type (Hastie, Park, & Weber, 1984), except perhaps for the suggestion that positive attributes are encountered more frequently than negative ones (Fiske, 1980; Skowronski & Carlston, 1989). In the absence of such data, the following sections outline some of the general social processes that shape the kinds of impressional material to which people are exposed.

Information Seeking.   People may actively seek to obtain information about different characteristics of target individuals (Fiske & Ruscher, 1989; Jones, 1986), just as they do about target issues in the attitude realm (Cotton, 1985; Frey, 1986). The primary interest in AST is with efforts to selectively obtain information relating to the different representational forms, and several hypotheses are advanced in this regard. In general, people may be inclined to seek information relating to some kinds of representations more than others. For example, abstract and self-referent representations may be more important for people to know, although they are also kinds of information that others cannot reliably provide to a perceiver. Therefore, perceivers may be likely to seek out first-hand experiences that allow such forms of representation to be generated.

People may also seek information that can be used to verify the validity of representations that they have already generated. For example, subjects apparently seek information relevant to trait expectancies that they have been given (Snyder & Swann, 1978). Similarly, people may be eager to personally meet target individuals whom they have only heard described by others. After initial attempts to verify existing representations, people may then turn their attention to information that they are lacking altogether (White & Carlston, 1983). That is, they may seek to "fill out" their impressions by generating forms of representation that they are missing. Examples of this "completion hypothesis" include the tendency of fans to seek behavioral interactions with celebrities about whom they have thoughts and feelings, the desire to "figure out" the personality traits of individuals with whom one has interacted, and the need people have to define their relationships with acquaintances. Because these perceivers may have imagined the information that they are lacking, these activities might also be viewed as attempts to verify existing representations, although the representations being verified are probably relatively impoverished.

Communication.   Another particularly important issue, from a social psychological standpoint, involves the kinds of impression-related representations that are communicated in different contexts. AST suggests a variety of principles that may govern such communications, assuming that the impressions being described are complex enough to allow some selectivity. Some of these were alluded to earlier, in discussing the free description method used in taxonomic classification. One such principle is that people may be more likely to communicate verbal forms of representation, not only because these are more readily communicated verbally, but because the engagement of the verbal system during communication should tend to activate such representations. Some more specific (and speculative) principles are outlined next.

First, the nature of impression-related communications may be shaped by the audience's knowledge of the target individual and its relationship with the communicator (see, e.g., Fussell & Krauss, 1992). When an audience is unfamiliar with the target being described, person descriptions may focus on the kinds of concrete, target-based information that one would ordinarily encounter through passive observation: visual appearance, categorizations, and behavioral observations. However, when the audience is familiar with the target, social rules against communicating the obvious (Grice, 1975) may encourage communication of representational forms that are more privileged and nonconsensual (e.g., self-referent rather than target based). However self-referent descriptors are also self-disclosing, and thus may be avoided except in remarks to a well-known other, or in reciprocation for similar communications from the audience. Well-known others may already be aware of more "overt" aspects of one's impressions (e.g., ones's past behavioral responses), which may encourage more "covert" descriptions (e.g., trait inferences). Combining all of these considerations leads to the prediction that appearance should be most commonly communicated in descriptions to strangers, and affective responses should be most commonly communicated in descriptions to close acquaintances.

Second, communicated impressions are also likely to vary across different communicator and audience goals (see, e.g., Sedikides, 1990). A communicator who is trying to give a general impression is more likely to rely on abstract forms of representation, whereas one who is trying to justify an act or judgment may provide more concrete information. Similarly, communications to someone with interpersonal concerns are likely to focus more on abstract forms than communications to someone who is simply looking for the target (Fiske & Cox, 1979). Along the same lines, Carlston and Sparks (1992a) found that the inquiry "How do you feel about X?" led to greater use of affective responses, evaluations, and orientations than did other inquiries, such as "What is X like?"

Considerations such as these will obviously influence the kinds of descriptions that are communicated to an audience and, concomitantly, the kinds of representations that the audience stores. Such communications may also alter the impressions of the communicator. Communicating an impression requires some cognitive work (see Cohen, 1961) and some translation of existing representations into communicable form. Consequently the communicator's impression is likely to include more verbal forms of representation (i.e., personality traits, categorizations, and evaluations) than it did previously (see Hoffman, Mischel, & Baer, 1984). There is some evidence that such verbal representations may overshadow related visual representations, making the latter more difficult to utilize (Schooler & Engstler-Schooler, 1990). Impressions are likely to be altered in other ways as well, as the communicator attempts to convert the impression into forms appropriate for communication to a particular audience (see Higgins, McCann, & Fondacaro, 1982). In addition, the communication event is likely to be stored as an episodic representation. Thus, in one way or another, the communication of an impression may change the salience of, or associations among, representations, thereby altering the impression of the communicator.

Rumination. Thought, or "rumination," can have important consequences for representational structures (Millar & Tesser, 1986, 1989; Tesser & Leone, 1977; Uleman & Bargh, 1989). Some such consequences may be similar to the effects of communicating those representations to others. For example, suppose, that a perceiver is anticipating communicating with others (Cohen, 1961), or is rationally analyzing the attributes of a target person (Wilson, Dunn, Bybee, Hyman, & Rotondo, 1984). The kinds of verbal thought that eventuate about the target person may increase the salience of personality traits, categorizations, and evaluations, just as suggested when actual communication takes place.

Thoughts may also be directed by other goals or activities, and the result may be the generation or strengthening of other forms of representation. For example, anticipated interaction (Devine, Sedikides, & Fuhrman, 1989), behavior prediction (e.g., Griffin, Dunning, & Ross, 1990), and retrospection (Brown & Kulik, 1977) should all direct attention to behaviorally related representations, including behavioral observations, behavioral responses, and orientations. Casual daydreaming and imagination may implicate the visual system and reinforce such related representations as appearance, categorization, and behavioral observations. Romantic reflection or obsessional hatred ("emotivity") may focus the perceiver on affectively related representations, such as affect, evaluations, and orientations. Processes such as these are depicted in the middle of Fig. 1.7.

In each instance, thought should enhance the salience of certain representations and strengthen the links between these and the person being thought about. When rumination involves several different forms of representation at once, as when we think about the trait implications of behaviors, this should also strengthen the pathway between the specific representations involved (Srull, 1981). As a consequence, the activation of either representation may be more likely to activate the other.

Rumination may also change the nature of the particular representations about which one thinks. More complex and concrete representations, in particular, may be skimmed more often than they are fully recalled. In other words, certain salient features of such representations will be recalled, and other features will be neglected. In a kind of "mental base touching," people may check in fleetingly with representations just long enough to derive the information that they need (Carlston, 1992). For example, when we visualize someone's appearance, we ordinarily "see" an impoverished image that omits many relevant features (Kosslyn, 1981). Moreover when we only think of them in passing, we may get only a fleeting glimpse of this impoverished image. If each fleeting glimpse reinforces those features that we do retrieve, the image may eventually become a caricature that exaggerates the most dominant features and obscures the others. Such "caricaturization" might similarly occur with episodic memories, and perhaps other forms of representation as well. Such possibilities are discussed more fully in Carlston (1992; see also Linton, 1982).

Impression Change

The preceding sections have numerous implications for the manner in which impressions can be changed. First, impressions may change when new representations are generated. As illustrated in Fig. 1.7, new representations may be stimulated by exposure to an external stimulus (as depicted on the far left), or by various kinds of ruminative processes (as depicted in the middle). New representations presumably are added to the associative network relating to a target individual; if they are strongly associated with that individual, and salient, they should effect subsequent impressions of the target.

Second, impressions may change due to changes in the associative strength or salience of representations. Thus, if a target's behavior is most salient one day, but the target's personality traits are most salient the next, then a change has effectively occurred in the impression of that target. The nature and importance of that change logically depends on the degree of congruity between the behavioral and trait representations, as well as on the nature of the impressional response. In principle, however, fairly dramatic changes may occur in impressions simply due to changes in the relative salience of component representations.

Of course, when new representations are added to a network, as described earlier, this effectively changes the salience of component representations. For example, if an affective response already exists, and a new, different affective response is generated, the new response is likely to be relatively more salient than the original one. Moreover, given the principle that retrieving one representation spreads inhibition to alternative representations of the same form, retrieval of the original affective response may be effectively suppressed. In a sense, then, the new representation may "replace" the old one.

How then do we recognize that our feelings about someone have changed? Often we may not (see Goethals & Reckman, 1973), but when we do it may be through noncompeting forms of representation, such as episodic memories. For example, although we now feel negative toward someone, we may be aware that we once liked them because we can remember episodes where we acted as if we did. However, it would probably be quite difficult to actually retrieve a positive affect, with associated visceral responses, once it has been superceded by a negative one.

Finally, impressions may change due to changes in the features of existing representations. As suggested in the preceding section, repeated retrieval and use of representations may result in the enhancement of prominent features at the expense of less prominent ones, resulting in a caricatured representation. Thus, an attractive acquaintance may tend to become increasingly more attractive in our minds. It is also possible that representations will increasingly come to resemble related, generic representations that are stored in conceptual social memory (cf. Tesser & Leone, 1977). This may occur because the target-specific representation activates features of generic representations, causing these features to attach to the specific representation.

THE UTILIZATION OF IMPRESSIONAL
REPRESENTATIONS: THINKING IS FOR DOING

According to AST, the cognitive representations associated with each mental system are projected onto a common association area where they become linked together within a single associative network. An impression is essentially a subsection of this network that contains different representations associated with a single individual. When a perceiver engages in any activity relating to that individual, representations within this impression are accessed and provide the material necessary for that activity. The various activities that people engage in necessarily involve the same basic mental systems that are implicated in the formation of impressions, as illustrated in Fig. 1.9. For example, the verbal system is involved in the production of judgments and communications, the affective system in the production of emotional responses, the action system in the production of behaviors, and the visual system in the production of images. The possibility that representations reflect partial activation of the systems that generated them (e.g., Damasio, 1989a; Farah, 1989) makes them ideal mediators between higher level impressional networks and lower level production mechanisms. Thus, if the mental representation of a behavioral response involves activation of the same basic features as the execution of the response, then not only will the representation be generated by the behavior, but the behavior will be facilitated by activation of the representation.

Consequently, cognitive representations serve as both the product of inputs from mental systems and the source of outputs to them, as illustrated in Fig. 1.9. This arrangement seemingly bestows a special role on the representations that are most closely allied with each system. This is

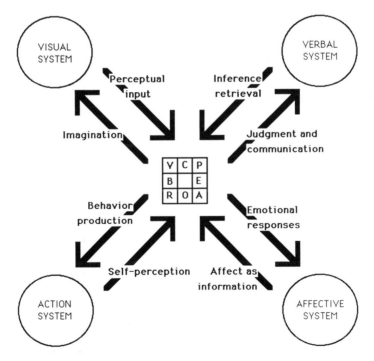

FIG. 1.9.   Processes involving input from, or output to, different primary system.

illustrated by the earlier suggestion that verbal representations may play a special role in the production of written descriptions of other people. Similarly, behavioral representations should play a key role in the production of behavior, affective representations in the production of emotional responses, and so on. Such direct influences are illustrated by the horizontal arrows on the right side of Fig. 1.7, such as the arrow leading from *traits* to *trait judgment and communication.*

However, these direct influences may underestimate the central role that the overall associative network plays in the representation of stimuli and the production of responses. Regardless of representational form, every concept relating to a person is potentially linked to every other concept. Where direct connections do not exist, the more general system of associations constituting conceptual social memory may nonetheless provide for indirect connections. For example, although verbal representations may be most closely linked to the communication system, virtually any kind of representation can be translated into verbal form (albeit crudely) and then communicated to others. All of the representations embodied in a composite impression represent possible contributors to different kinds of responses (see Fig. 1.7). The nature of these contributions is likely to depend on a variety of factors, including the strength of connections to the pertinent response systems and the current levels of activation of all associated concepts (including goal concepts).

The general implication is that all of the different kinds of activities we may engage in with regard to a person are products of the same impressional structure. Retrieval, judgment, emotion, and behavior all derive from the same network of associations among representations, although each may be more closely associated with some representations than with others. The spread of activation through the network to the proper recipient systems produces memories, judgments, emotions, and behaviors. Some of the implications of this proposal are detailed in the following sections.

Memory for Impressional Material

In spreading activation variants of associative network models, memory search involves the spread of excitation from one or more originating cues through connecting pathways to related concepts. When enough excitation accumulates at one of these, from all connecting pathways, the concept becomes activated and a "memory" occurs. As previously noted, impression networks may involve a variety of different kinds of concepts, from visual images to affective responses, and searches for information about an individual may therefore activate a host of different kinds of representations. Moreover, the different kinds of representations that are retrieved may not be readily discriminable to the perceiver who is searching memory. Instead, the memories may surface as an amalgam of representational features that blend together, with no clear demarcation between one representation and another. For example, a memory of a particular event may be a composite of images, verbalizations, feelings, and even incipient motor responses.[8]

The contamination of episodic memory by other salient material has been termed *reconstruction*, and examples abound. Research suggests that memories for specific events can be colored by salient appearance (Miller, 1988), category (Sagar & Schofield, 1980), trait (Hastie & Kumar, 1979), affect (Laird, Wagener, Halal, & Szegda, 1982), evaluation (Hartwick, 1979), and orientation (Harvey, Yarkin, Lightner, & Town, 1980) information. Similarly, trait inferences may be influenced by observed behaviors (Carlston & Skowronski, 1986; Jones & Davis, 1965) or categorizations (Cantor & Kihlstrom, 1987), as well as by other trait representations (Carlston, 1980b; Rosenberg & Sedlak, 1972). Additionally, emotional responses to one individual may be contaminated by memories of another acquaintance whose appearance was similar (S. T. Fiske, 1982). Such interrepresentational influences may be the inevitable results of a memory system that mixes different kinds of representations within a common pool.

From the current perspective, the anomaly is not that individual memories are contaminated as much as they are, but that they are not contaminated more. Alba and Hasher (1983) cited a great deal of research showing that memory for events is often quite accurate, and that reconstructive biases may be an exception, rather than the rule. People are sometimes able to recount events without apparent contamination by their own feelings and inferences (R. C. Anderson, 1971) or by material that others have communicated to them (Dodd & Bradshaw, 1980). Moreover, people are generally able to respond to personality inquiries with trait descriptions and to episodic inquiries with event descriptions, rather than getting confused and doing it the other way around. If representations are jumbled together in the manner suggested here, how are people ever able to disentangle their features and respond with material appropriate to a given task?

Possibly three related processes contribute to the disentanglement of different forms of representation. First, the search process may sometimes serve to selectively activate the most appropriate representations. Remember that retrieval is a function of the spread of excitation from all

---

[8]Whether multiple representations are "blended" together, or merely aggregated, is a matter of some debate in cognitive psychology (Schooler & Tanaka, 1991). The key distinction is whether people are able to separate the composite into its constituent components. As suggested later, there may sometimes be features that allow for "dis-aggregation," though it is unclear how attentive people ordinarily are to such features.

activated sites (as well as of the prior state of activation of all associated material). When the task, context, objectives, or prior retrievals are most closely associated with a given form of representation, the convergence of excitation from these sites may tend to favor that form of representation. For example, inquiries about a target person's behavior may cause one to think of particular settings and activities, as well as of the target; the confluence of excitation from all of these concepts may favor behavioral representations, particularly when other kinds of representations are neither salient nor closely linked to these same settings and activities.

Second, because different forms of representation comprise different kinds of features, people may be able to disassociate different representations by attending to these featural characteristics. For example, observational memories are marked by visually detailed features, which include situational context and which incorporate one's own perspective and role in the episode. These markers distinguish observational information from other forms of representation, such as affect or categorization. If the perceiver is sensitive to such markers, they may help in sorting out observations from other forms of representation. A similar process of distinguishing different kinds of representations through their featural markers has been explored in research on reality monitoring (e.g., Johnson, Raye, Foley, & Foley, 1981). Those forms of information that lack appropriate features can be selectively ignored or edited from the retrieved material. Such editing processes have been characterized as a final stage of information processing that mediates between retrieval and the production of overt responses (Carlston, 1992; Holyoak & Gordon, 1984; Tourangeau & Rasinski, 1988). To illustrate, an inquiry about a close friend's traits may bring certain emotional events to mind, but because these lack the characteristic features of traits, they may be edited from one's description.

The most difficult representations to distinguish and edit out are likely to be those that relate to the same primary systems, because these will have similar experiential markers. This seems obvious for representations such as evaluations and affect, which both include the visceral experience of emotion. But it may be equally true for other forms of representation that are depicted as adjacent in Fig.1.2. For example, visual appearance, behavioral observations, and categorizations should be confusable because each of these generally involves imagery. Evidence for this is provided by a recent study that showed the recognition of stereotypic figures to be affected by both attributed behaviors and gender categorization (Katz, Silvern, & Coulter, 1990). Along the same lines, other studies have suggested that categorization in terms of gender (Frable & S. Bem, 1985), age (Rodin, 1987), or race (Malpass & Kravitz, 1969) can interfere with the recognizability of a target's appearance. Phenomena such as the internalization of others' behaviors (Thompson & Kelley, 1981) or the attribution to others of one's own may similarly reflect the confusability of behavioral observations and behavioral responses—two representations that involve equivalent episodic markers (action and context).

A third method of overcoming the confounding of various forms of representation that are retrieved together is to cognitively compensate for the potential contamination. Such adjustments have been observed among subjects aware of previously primed material that could influence current efforts to generate trait impressions (Lombardi, Higgins, & Bargh, 1987; Martin, 1986; Skowronski, Carlston, & Isham, 1993). For example, in describing a disliked acquaintance, one may be aware of the negative affective tone that permeates one's retrievals, and one may try to compensate by describing the acquaintance in more positive terms than those actually retrieved. Like selective reporting, such compensation would represent an editing process.

These editing processes require a fair amount of effort, and may therefore characterize what people are capable of doing more than what they actually do. When people recall or report an event socially, do they often care whether affective or evaluative features are mixed in with more objective facts? When they are describing someone's personality, do they mind whether appearance or affective information intrudes? The mishmash of associations that ordinarily pop into mind when thinking about a target person may serve as a perfectly adequate memory under everyday circumstances. Perhaps in the research laboratory there is somewhat more pressure to sort out the concrete from the abstract, the observed from the inferred, or the objective from the subjective, resulting in the nonreconstructive accuracy noted by some researchers (e.g., Alba & Hasher, 1983).

Judgments Regarding a Target Person

People are often called on to verbally describe or judge the personalities of others. As illustrated in Fig.1.9, AST characterizes such activities as outputs from the impressional structure to the verbal system. Thus, the same structure and spreading activation processes are presumably involved in judgment as in retrieval, although linkages to the verbal system assume special importance. One implication is that those forms of representation most closely related to the verbal system (i.e., personality traits) may be particularly likely to influence the judgments that people make. This possibility is consistent with Ebbesen and Allen's (1979) suggestion that, in making trait judgments, people search memory first for pertinent trait representations; if none is found, they proceed to relevant observational memories (see also Klein et al., 1992).

More generally, AST may imply a sequential search that begins with personality traits, then moves to other closely related forms of representation, such as evaluations and categorizations, before progressing to less related forms, such as visual appearance or behavioral observations. In other words, when asked whether a friend is honest, I may first search my memory for such a trait, and then, if necessary, consider the implications of general evaluations ("I like him, so he must be") or categorizations ("He's a policeman, so he should be"), followed by appearance ("He looks honest") or affect ("I have good feelings about him"), and finally by behavioral observations ("I once saw him return a lost purse"), orientations ("We've had a pretty trusting relationship"), and behavioral responses ("I just loaned him $5, so he must be honest"). However, this progression assumes that all of these different forms of representation are equally salient, and that past experience has not led to the selective strengthening of associations between distant forms of representation (e.g., between certain behaviors and honesty). Because this will almost never be true, the sequentiality of such searches may only be apparent across a wide variety of judgments about different kinds of people.

The role that salience and pathway strength play in judgment processes was demonstrated in several studies by Carlston and Skowronski (1986, 1988). In these studies, subjects watched a videotape of an actor named Dave as he persuaded friends that they should return money they found in a professor's laboratory. Some subjects were led to infer Dave's honesty early in the experiment, and others were reminded of his behavior later in the experiment, just prior to a timed judgment about his honesty. The response times in both studies suggested that subjects relied on their existing trait inferences to make the trait judgment unless they were reminded of the behavior just beforehand, in which case they relied on it. In other words, trait judgments were influenced by the most directly related form of representation, except when a more distant form of representation had become particularly salient.

In principle, each of the different forms of representation could be sufficiently salient, or sufficiently associated with a particular judgment, to have a dominant influence on that judgment. Table 1.2 characterizes the possible representational bases for different kinds of judgments. Event-based judgments, which are derived from behavioral observations, have been extensively studied within both social cognition (Sherman, Judd, & Park, 1989) and attribution theory (Harvey, Ickes, & Kidd, 1976). Judgments may also be affected by the visual salience of the target person (Taylor & Fiske, 1978) or the target person's features (McArthur, 1982). Considerable research has been done on stereotypical judgments, which are based on categorizations (e.g., Hamilton, 1981); on analytic or implicit personality theory (IPT) judgments, which are based on other trait attributes (Rosenberg & Sedlak, 1972); and on halo effects, which reflect the effects of general evaluation on specific trait judgments (Thorndike, 1920).

TABLE 1.2
Forms of Human Judgment Delineated by Associated Systems Theory

Form of Judgment	Representational Basis	Definition
Event-based	Behavioral observations	Judgments based on the implications of recalled events.
Salience-based	Sensory representations	Judgments determined by current sensory inputs.
Stereotypical	Categorizations	Positive or negative inferences from a target's group membership.
Analytic	Trait attributes	Attributes inferred from other attributes of the target.
Halo	Evaluations	Judgments based on general evaluations.
State-dependent	Affect	Judgments influenced by the perceiver's current emotional state (including mood).
Egocentric	Orientations	Judgments based principally on the nature of the perceiver's relationship with the target (e.g., loyalty, rivalry, etc.).
Justificatory	Behavioral responses	Judgments that justify one's own behaviors (e.g., derogation of a victim, dissonance-based attitude change).

Note. Although it is assumed that most judgments are stimulated by a whole complex of associations of various forms, some common types of judgments may be principally stimulated by one or another form of cognitive representation. Such "pure" types are included here.

The effects of current emotional states, such as mood, are characterized here as state-dependent effects on judgment (Clark, Milberg, & Erber, 1988). Egocentric judgments are based principally on the nature of the perceiver's relationship or involvement with another person (e.g., judging someone to be *fun* because one enjoys doing things with him or her). Finally, Table 1.2 uses the term *justificatory* for judgments based on one's own behaviors toward the target. Such judgments tend to justify the perceiver's own behaviors, as in the derogation of a victim by an assailant.

Earlier, parallels were noted between the components of person impressions and the components of attitudes as these are characteristically studied in social psychology. Many of the forms of human judgment listed in Table 1.2 could be characterized as attitudes of one sort or another. For example, Millar and Tesser (1992) suggested that attitudes might be equated with either affect or evaluation. Fishbein's (1963) approach is more consistent with the notion that attitudes are a feature of perceived attributes (e.g., traits), and the classic "predisposition to respond" definition (see Eagly & Chaiken 1993) is more consistent with the notion that attitudes are orientations. In self-perception theory (D. J. Bem, 1972; Fazio, 1987), attitudes are viewed as influenced by past behavioral responses (Fazio & Cooper, 1983); in stereotyping, they are viewed as influenced by categorizations (Hamilton & Trolier, 1986).

An important implication of the AST approach is therefore that measures of attitudes may have somewhat different characteristics, depending on which form of attitudinal judgment they elicit. For example, Millar and Tesser (1989) showed that attitudinal measures that tap into affect relate to different sorts of behaviors than measures that tap into evaluations. Moreover, Wilson and his colleagues (e.g., Wilson and Schooler (1991) demonstrated that "reasons analyses" may focus subjects' attention on the more cognitive components of their attitudes, diverting their attention away from more optimal mental representations. Such attitudinal work raises more general issues about the relationship between judgments and behaviors, which are addressed in a later section of this chapter.

The various kinds of judgments listed in Table 1.2 are obviously ideal types that are likely to occur in pure form only when one form of representation dominates the judgment process. More often, a variety of different representations will become activated and spread excitation through the associative network, until representations within the verbal system are activated and produce the judgmental response. In other words, judgments, like memories, may generally reflect an amalgam of different representations, rather than merely one dominant form (Park, 1986). Cohen, March, and Olsen (1972) called this the *garbage can model* of decision making: One finds bits and pieces of salient memories and puts them together to make the best composition one can.

Interpersonal Behavior

AST assumes that behaviors reflect output from the same impressional structure as do memories, judgments, and emotions. Essentially, excitation can spread through this associative network to representations of behavioral responses, and from these through a multilevel hierarchy of associated units that culminates in the motor system and produces behavior. This *action system* has been described by Shallice (1978), and Martindale (1991), among others. Vallacher and Wegner's (1987) action-identification theory deals with different upper level representations of behavioral acts, and with how the perceiver's reliance on representations at one level or another has consequences for the manner in which people think about and execute these behaviors.

The major concern here is with the connections between the action system and other forms of representation. As depicted in Fig. 1.1 and 1.2, the action system is linked most directly to cognitions that we have termed *behavioral responses*, as well as to related forms of representation, behavioral observations and orientations. These representations may be linked, in turn, to the other forms of representation in the perceiver's associative network. When a perceiver is interacting with a target person, a number of concepts in this network will become activated, including concepts representing that target, the situational context, the demands of the interaction task, and the perceiver's goals or objectives. Excitation spreading from these various points of origin may activate concepts within the action system, and behavioral acts may then be produced. Which behavioral acts are produced should depend on the salience of different kinds of representations, and on the nature and strength of the associations among them.

Millar and Tesser (1986, 1992) identified two different kinds of behavioral acts, which they termed *consummatory* and *instrumental*. They defined consummatory acts as those performed for reasons intrinsic to the act itself, such as hedonistic pleasure, and instrumental acts as those performed in the pursuit of other goals. Moreover, they argued that consummatory acts are driven by affect, and that instrumental acts are driven by cognition. Expanding on this framework, AST suggests that there are eight different kinds of behaviors, each of which is associated with a different kind of cognitive representation (see Table 1.3). Generalizing from principles described earlier, AST suggests that these different kinds of behaviors should occur when one particular kind of representation is so salient that it predominates.

The AST framework preserves Millar and Tesser's distinction and associates consummatory behaviors with affect, as they did. However, AST associates instrumental behaviors with evaluations, which are both affective and cognitive, rather than merely with cognition. The logic here is that instrumental acts are intended to produce desired consequences, even if they are not executed for their own enjoyment, and thus they have some affective features as well as the more rational or analytic features on which Millar and Tesser focused. Behaviors that are shaped entirely by those rational features are characterized here as *reasoned* behaviors; in the interpersonal context, these would derive from the perceived traits of the target. In addition, behaviors that are triggered directly by the target's behaviors are labeled as *interactive*, a class that would presumably include both imitative acts and reciprocal or complementary acts, such as responding to a question. Those triggered primarily by visual or sensory cues are termed *conditioned* behaviors, those based on categorizations of the target are termed *discriminatory*, and those derived from one's orientation toward the target are termed *customary*. Finally, behavioral responses that are driven by representations internal to the action system, and not by any of the other forms of representation, are characterized as *compulsive*.

TABLE 1.3
Forms of Human Behavior Delineated by Associated Systems Theory

Form of Behavior	Representational Basis	Definition
Interactive	Behavioral observations	Behaviors, including both imitative and complementary behaviors, that are triggered by others' acts.
Conditioned	Sensory representations	Acts triggered by environmental or visual cues.
Discriminatory	Categorizations	Positive or negative responses to target's group membership.
Reasoned	Trait attributes	Acts shaped by the perceived attributes of the target.
Instrumental	Evaluations	Behaviors designed to produce desired consequences.
Consummatory	Affect	Acts engaged in for their own enjoyment.
Customary	Orientations	Habitual ways of acting toward a target individual.
Compulsive	Behavioral responses	Acts resulting from the internal operations of the action system, including some forms of spontaneous and habitual behavior, and behaviors stimulated by the actor's other ongoing activities (e.g., mannerisms used while speaking).

Note. Although it is assumed that most behaviors are stimulated by a whole complex of associations of various forms, some common types of behaviors may be principally stimulated by one or another form of cognitive representation. Such "pure" types are included here.

Predicting Behavior From Attitudes and Other Judgments

Now that the implications of AST for judgments and behaviors have been considered, it is possible to address issues concerning the relationship between the two. Such issues have long been important in the attitude area (Wicker, 1969), but have been neglected in social cognition both because research in this area has rarely used behavioral measures (Fiske & Taylor, 1991) and because social cognition theories have tended to be vague about their behavioral implications (Landman & Manis, 1983). Yet it is clearly important to understand the extent to which verbal judgments about people are predictive of behavioral responses, and the AST approach provides some tentative answers.

Verbal judgments are likely to predict behaviors when the judgments and the behaviors are based on the same underlying representations. For example, Millar and Tesser (1989) showed that affectively based attitudes predict affectively based (consummatory) behaviors, whereas cognitively based attitudes predict cognitively based (instrumental) behaviors.

One instance where judgment and behavior both depend on the same underlying representations is when past behavioral responses are used as a basis for both judgments (as in D. Bem's, 1972, self-perception theory) and subsequent behaviors (Chaiken & Baldwin, 1981). For example, Ross, McFarland, Conway, and Zanna (1983) demonstrated that priming subjects to think of past behaviors consistent with a particular attitude increases subsequent consistency between their attitudinal judgments and their actual behaviors. Another instance where judgment and behavior both depend on the same underlying representations is when attribute inferences or evaluations provide the basis for both reported judgments (Carlston, 1980b) and actual behavior (e.g., Fazio & Williams, 1986). Behaviors are especially likely to be based on attribute inferences when they are analytic in nature (such as voting for someone because of his or her perceived traits), or when the inferences or evaluations are particularly accessible (Fazio, Powell, & Herr, 1983).[9]

Even when judgment and behavior are based on different representations, the judgments may provide reasonable prediction of the behaviors, provided that the implications of the two underlying representations are consistent with each other. Thus, if a perceiver has both bad feelings and negative inferences about a target person, it may make little difference which representation contributes to reported judgments and which underlies other behaviors. This raises an important issue: To what extent are people's different representations likely to have equivalent implications? The AST approach makes some interesting suggestions.

Different representations are likely to be consistent with each other to the extent that they have "grown up together" and are products of similar events (see Fazio & Zanna, 1981). To summarize points made earlier, (a) different kinds of representations are hypothesized to derive from the operations of different functional systems, (b) the engagement of these systems logically depends on the nature of one's activities with a target person, and (c) the general nature of these activities should relate to the different kinds of involvement depicted in Fig. 1.8. Therefore, if one has been behaviorally and cognitively involved with a target at the same time, one is likely to develop behavioral and cognitive representations that are consistent with each other. Similarly, if one has been behaviorally

---

[9]According to Fazio et al. (1982), one way that evaluations (attitudes) become highly accessible is through repeated expression. From the AST perspective, repeated verbal expression of an evaluation would be expected to strengthen the associative link between the percept and the evaluation, thereby increasing the likelihood that the evaluation would be retrieved and used in either judgmental or behavioral responses. This characterization is quite similar to Fazio's accessibility interpretation.

and affectively involved with a target at the same time, one is likely to develop behavioral and affective representations that are consistent, and so on.

Of course, this assumes that the nature of these different involvements is consistent, which is probably ordinarily the case, but may not always be. Consider an employee forced to interact politely with a detested customer, colleague, or superior. In this case, the cognitive, affective, and action systems are all simultaneously engaged, but the representations that are being generated, linked, and reinforced are inconsistent with each other. These different representations will therefore have different implications, making the correspondence between the employee's judgments and behaviors uncertain. For example, evaluative judgments based on representations of negative thoughts and feelings may not predict "habitual" behaviors that are based on past behavioral interactions. Furthermore, the more frequently the employee has interacted with the detested individual, the more pronounced the inconsistencies among different forms of representation may have become.

Nonetheless, the simultaneous engagement of different systems ordinarily seems likely to result in greater inter-representational consistency (see, e.g., Rosenberg, 1960). When people are able to think and interact freely, different forms of representation are likely to become synchronized. In other words, we are likely to behave positively toward people we like, eliciting positive behaviors from them and reinforcing positive affective and trait components of our impressions (Miller & Turnbull, 1986). In contrast, we may not act so well toward people we dislike, and the unpleasant experiences that result may reinforce various negative forms of representation. Thus, as Fazio and his associates (e.g., Fazio et al., 1982, Fazio, Powell & Herr, 1983) have demonstrated in the attitude realm, greater direct experience with an object is likely to increase the correspondence between expressed judgments and behaviors.

In the Fazio et al. (1982) research, some subjects formed impressions of puzzles by playing with them directly, whereas others only learned and thought about the puzzles. Consequently, the direct-play group was cognitively and behaviorally involved with the puzzles, whereas the latter group was only cognitively involved. The former group should have developed consistent forms of evaluative and behavioral representation, whereas the latter group may not have. As expected, puzzle evaluations by the former group predicted their behaviors during a subsequent free-play period, whereas evaluations by the latter group did not. Similarly, AST predicts that impressions formed through personal interaction are likely to be characterized by greater inter-representational consistency than impressions formed on the basis of communications from others.

ADDITIONAL INFLUENCES ON THE USE OF REPRESENTATIONS

Up to this point, a variety of factors have been described that may affect the generation, accessibility, and use of different forms of impression-related representation. In these next sections, several additional factors are discussed that emerge specifically from consideration of the systemic roots of representations. The first section explores the possibility that the engagement of different mental systems by impression-irrelevant activities can affect the generation or use of impressional representations. The next section suggests that different people tend to rely more or less on different processing systems, and thus on different forms of representation.

These systemic concerns have direct analogues in work on the priming of individual concepts. For example, the activation of particular concepts during unrelated activities can influence the activation of impression-relevant representations (Higgins et al., 1985), and there are individual differences in the "chronic" accessibility of different impressional concepts (Bargh & Thein, 1985). Bargh et al. (1986) showed that these sources of activation can contribute additively to concept use, and Bargh, Lombardi, and Higgins (1988) demonstrated that individual chronicity effects become more pronounced as longer delays diminish the effects of situational priming. The possibility raised here is that the activation of entire functional systems, either by recent activities or by stable dispositions, may evidence similar "priming" phenomena.

Priming and Preoccupation of Mental Systems

Bryden and Ley (1983) primed subjects with words that varied in imagery and affective value. Their intention was to produce activity in the nondominant hemisphere, where emotional imagery is believed to be processed (see also Paivio, 1986). They then tested subjects on facial recognition and dichotic listening tasks using affective material, with the stimuli presented to either the dominant or nondominant side of the body. They found that priming with either positive or negative word lists resulted in improved performance on nondominant presentations of the affective performance tasks, and that this effect was greater for high-imagery words than for low-imagery words. Bryden and Ley concluded that:

> there is greater activity in the right [nondominant] hemisphere than in the left when either high imagery or highly emotional words have been presented. This increased right-hemisphere activity *makes the right hemisphere more*

receptive to incoming stimuli, and consequently, produces relatively better
performance in the left visual field, or at the left ear. . . . (p. 38, italics added)

Possibly, engagement of any one of the primary processing systems makes
that system "more receptive" to the processing of material and consequently, improves utilization of representations related to that system. In
other words, "warming up" a processing system might increase the efficiency with which the system operates and the likelihood that that system
will be employed. Consistent with this possibility, Klatzky, Pellegrino,
McCloskey, and Doherty (1989) showed that subjects were able to judge the
sensibility of action descriptions more quickly if they were first primed to
form their hands into suitable shapes. Additionally, Kroll and Potter (1984)
showed that subjects can determine the sensibility of pictures more quickly
when preceding trials involve pictures than when they involve text. Such
systems-priming effects may reflect either a global increase of excitation
within the system, or increased accessibility of particular procedures or
concepts at some hierarchical level within the system.

The specific implications of such a "warming up" effect are that a person
who has recently had an emotional experience may be more inclined to rely
on affective representations in constructing various responses (see Schwarz,
1990); one who has been engaged in verbal or analytic activities should be
more likely to access semantic representations; one who has been actively
engaged in motor activities or behavioral interaction might be more likely to
utilize behavioral representations; and one who has engaged in perceptual
or imagination tasks might be biased toward visual representations. If these
speculations are correct, the impressions that people report, the judgments
that they make, and even the actions they engage in may be influenced by
functional systems that have recently been most active.

However, it is also plausible that the activation of a functional system for
one purpose may interfere with its use for another, at least under some
circumstances. For example, Brooks (1968) showed that memory for verbal
information is most readily disrupted by concurrent vocal activity, and that
memory for visual (spatial) information is most readily disrupted by
concurrent visual activity. Englekamp (1991) found that unrelated physical
movements reduced the retrievability of action sentences (e.g., "hammering
a nail") that were originally learned while making related physical motions.
Similarly, Saltz and Nolan (1981) had subjects learn sentences with the aid
of motoric enactment, visual imagery, or verbal-only instructions, and then
attempted to interfere with recall for these sentences by using competing
motoric, visual, and verbal tasks. Recall was only impaired when the
competing task related to the same system (motoric, visual, or verbal) as the
learning procedure.

These interference results suggest that the visual, verbal, and action systems have capacity limitations, and that engagement in an unrelated activity may interfere with the effective utilization of the engaged system for other purposes. Such capacity limitations probably exist for the affective system as well. It is seemingly difficult to extract specific information from one's affective system when feeling a competing emotional response. Indeed, the evidence overwhelmingly suggests that one's current emotional responses may be mistaken for the affective information one is seeking (see Clore & Parrott, 1991).

The relationship between these kinds of system-specific capacity limitations, and the capacity of the cognitive system more generally, are unclear. For example, Gilbert (e.g., Gilbert & Osborne, 1989; Gilbert, Pelham, & Krull, 1988) demonstrated that cognitive busyness can affect the impressions that people form from behavioral information. The question that arises from the present formulation is whether some kinds of busyness (e.g., verbal) are more likely to interfere with some processes (e.g., trait inference) than others (e.g., visual recognition).

If the utilization of a functional system may either facilitate or interfere with the use of that system for an unrelated task, what determines when one kind of effect obtains rather than the other? Perhaps the essential consideration is the extent to which the system in question is still preoccupied by its prior use. If the prior task is completed so that there is no need to maintain the activation of specific representations within the system, some facilitation of subsequent activities that relate to the system may occur. However, if the prior task is not complete, so that a respondent needs to maintain the activation of those specific representations, interference may be more likely to occur. The practical implication of such interference is that it may sometimes be difficult for people to reliably access stored representations from functional systems that are preoccupied with other tasks.

Individual Differences in System Utilization

People's reliance on different forms of representation may be affected by stable, individual-difference characteristics, as well as by transitory activities. Some people may tend to rely more on verbal forms of representation, some on visual forms, some on affect, and some on action (cf. Anshel & Ortiz, 1986). Such differences could occur in any or all of the various stages of processing discussed earlier—that is, in the generation of representations, in their translation into other forms, or in their retrieval and use during memory, judgment, and behavior. Moreover, such differences could originate in either biological or experiential differences. Biologically speaking, there appear to be normal variations in the processing efficiency of different functional systems, and these can produce variations in the "abilities" underlying cognition (Kolb & Whishaw, 1990). Additionally, people's experience with different kinds of social involvements is likely to affect their development of relevant representations and procedures, and the strength of associative linkages between different kinds of higher order representations. For instance, a hermit would presumably have an action system that is underdeveloped in terms of goals, scripts, and actions relating to social interaction.

Individual differences may have important implications for impression processes. People engaged in essentially similar interactions may react differently, and emerge with rather different impressions, because they tune in to different representations of their own experience. One person might remember a hostess as being beautiful, another that she behaved formally, a third that she was Swedish, a fourth that she seemed likable, a fifth that she made him or her feel uncomfortable, and so on. In a sense, each person's impression reflects a different facet of the same proverbial elephant. As a consequence, each person's reactions, memories, descriptions, and emotions toward this person may differ considerably. In fact, research suggests that there are often considerably more similarities in one perceiver's description of two different target persons than in two perceivers' descriptions of the same target (Dornbusch et al., 1965; see also Park, 1986).

A variety of individual-difference measures have been developed that may relate to people's use of different mental systems. With regard to visual imagery, for example, such measures include the Vividness of Visual Imagery Questionnaire (Marks, 1973, 1989) and the Individual Difference Questionnaire (Paivio, 1971), which specifically assesses preferences for visual versus verbal processing. The Need for Cognition scale (Cacioppo & Petty, 1982) may relate to the more "cognitive" or analytic functions of the verbal system.[10] Different features of affective processing are captured by measures of affective intensity (Larsen & Diener, 1987), sensitivity (Katkin, 1985), and style (Ehrlich & Lipsey, 1969). Finally, the Self-Monitoring scale (Snyder, 1974) seems to relate to the action system.

Self-Monitoring. Self-monitoring provides a useful illustration of the manner in which such individual-difference measures may relate to the current systems approach. The connection between self-monitoring and the action system seems like an obvious one, given that self-monitoring deals

---

[10]There is some evidence that people high in need for cognition have better recall for others' behaviors, particularly when those behaviors are inconsistent with initial impressions (Srull, 1981). However these results appear to reflect the more extensive analytic processing that high need-for-cognition subjects engage in (Lassiter, Briggs, & Slaw, 1991), rather than greater facility with behavior observations in general.

with the manner in which people plan, carry out, and regulate their behavior in social situations (Snyder & Cantor, 1980). High self-monitors are generally characterized as sensitive and behaviorally responsive to social norms and situational factors, whereas low self-monitors are characterized as attentive to internal feelings and beliefs (Snyder, 1974). This suggests that high self-monitors may have relatively well-developed action systems, and tend to rely on representations associated with this system. For example, high self-monitors are more adept at altering their own behaviors (Lippa, 1976), as well as interpreting the meaning of others' behaviors (Snyder, 1979).

Additionally, Jamieson, Lydon, and Zanna (1987) found that high self-monitors were more strongly attracted to others with similar activity preferences, whereas low self-monitors were more attracted to people with similar attitudes. Low self-monitors may have relatively undeveloped action systems, and may tend to rely instead on representations associated with the verbal and affective systems. This characterization is consistent with studies showing that low self-monitors tend to have more accessible attitudes (Kardes, Sanbonmatsu, Voss, & Fazio, 1986), to act in a manner consistent with their attitudes (Snyder & Swann, 1976), to explain their own behavior in dispositional terms (Snyder, 1976), and to be more influenced by mood and fatigue (Snyder, 1979). Additionally, in an advertising setting, low self-monitors are more affected by perceived product attributes, whereas high self-monitors are more affected by product appearance (DeBono & Snyder, 1989; Snyder & DeBono, 1985).

Other research suggests that high self-monitors not only have elaborately developed action systems, but that they may also attend more closely to visual representations. For example, high self-monitors are more influenced by the physical attractiveness of others, whereas low self-monitors are more influenced by personality characteristics (Snyder, Berscheid, & Matwychuk, 1988; Snyder & Simpson, 1984). High self-monitors are also better at constructing mental images of particular kinds of prototypic individuals (although low self-monitors are better at constructing images of themselves; Snyder & Gangestad, 1981). Finally, Hosch and Platz (1984) found that high self-monitors have especially good episodic memories (*behavioral observations*, in AST terminology)—a form of representation closely related to both the action and visual systems. Thus, the most apt characterization of self-monitoring may be that high self-monitors tend to emphasize the concrete forms of representation (behavioral responses and visual appearance), whereas low self-monitors tend to emphasize the abstract forms (personality traits and affective responses).

If this characterization of self-monitoring is correct, then AST suggests several implications. First, it implies that self-monitoring should be related to other individual-difference measures, such as those assessing visual orientation. Second, in terms of the antecedents of impressional representations, the concrete (visual and action) orientation of the high self-monitors is consistent with histories involving considerable interpersonal experience, mostly of a relatively nonreflective and nonemotional nature. In contrast, the abstract (verbal and affective) orientation of the low self-monitors is more consistent with histories involving less interpersonal experience, but greater rumination and emotion. This is supported by past research in that, for example, high self-monitors tend to have more dating partners, but shallower relationships (Snyder & Simpson, 1984), and low self-monitors tend to be more emotional and reflective (Snyder, 1987). Third, in terms of the consequences of impressional representations, the concrete orientation of high self-monitors may imply less enduring, less stable, and less consistent general impressions than low self-monitors tend to have.

Self-Report Measures.   In general, it is unclear how well self-report measures, such as the Self-Monitoring Scale, relate to people's actual usage of different mental systems and representations. Such measures were not created with systemic distinctions in mind; as a consequence, they may correspond to systems use in complex ways. For example, some critics have suggested that the Self-Monitoring Scale is multifaceted and forces respondents to report on a variety of different characteristics of their social and cognitive styles (Briggs & Cheek, 1988). Additionally, people may have difficulty introspecting about their reliance on different forms of representation (see, e.g., Nisbett & Wilson, 1977; but see also Smith & Miller, 1978). Consequently, other ways of assessing representational preferences may be desirable.

One obvious alternative is to assess people's relative reliance on different forms of representation in open-ended descriptions (see, e.g., Fiske & Ruscher, 1989; McGuire & Padawer-Singer, 1976). By classifying the descriptors that people actually use, it may be possible to identify different "impressional styles" that tend to emphasize one form of representation (e.g., a *stereotypical* style emphasizing categorizations) or one dimension of representation (e.g., a *self-referent* style emphasizing action and affect representations) over others. Alternatively, people may differ in representational complexity, with some tending to rely primarily on one salient form of representation, and others tending to use a variety of different forms of representation. Whether people can accurately report on these inclinations is an unanswered empirical question.

A SYSTEMATIC SUMMARY AND CONCLUSION

This chapter argues for an approach to the study of impressions that is *systematic* in a variety of different senses:

systematic 1. Of, characterized by, based upon or constituting a system. 2. Carried on in a step by step procedure. 3. Characterized by purposeful regularity; methodical. 4. Of or pertaining to a classification or taxonomy. (*The American Heritage Dictionary*, 1980 p. 1306)

Mental Systems

First, this approach suggests that cognitive representations of the sort that social cognition researchers typically study may best be understood in terms of the mental (or "functional") systems that they serve. At a basic level, cognitive representations are merely traces of past "doings," which the brain stores in progressively higher order constructs until they become sufficiently abstract and general that they can interact appropriately with representations from other systems. It is at this general level—as trait concepts, behavioral scripts, stereotypical categories, or whatever—that they become most accessible to people, including social psychologists. But their origins and connections to the mental systems that employ them are also important, in ways outlined in this chapter.

Systematic Consideration of Multiple Representations

Second, this approach suggests that the study of social representation may benefit from the systematic consideration of all of the different forms of representation that people are likely to employ. As Medin (1988) noted, the "idea of multiple representation and processing types" stands in contrast to approaches that assume that "people are relentlessly doing the same thing (e.g., abstracting prototypes) more or less all of the time" (p. 121). As he also noted, multimodal models, such as Brewer's (1988) dual-process model, have been "gaining currency" in social cognition. Other multirepresentational models of impressions (usually dual-representational models) have been described by Andersen and Klatzky (1983), Carlston (1980a), Fiske and Pavelchak (1986), Klein and Loftus (1993), Lynn et al., (1985), Wyer and Martin (1986), and Wyer and Srull (1989).

Of these, perhaps the most relevant to issues raised here is Wyer and Srull's (1989) social information-processing model, which similarly focuses on the "impressions" generated of individuals (see Wyer & Carlston, 1994). This model is multimodal (i.e., it specifies several kinds of storage and processing units) and multirepresentational (i.e., it can accommodate a variety of different kinds of information, including behaviors, goals, traits, images, and general evaluations). However, this model differs from AST in ways that are fairly characteristic of other social cognition models as well. The key elements of the Wyer and Srull model derive principally from abstract, functional considerations, and reflect the theoretical requirements of an information-processing system (see also Hastie & Carlston, 1980) more than known characteristics of cognitive activity or representation. In contrast, AST takes a more "bottom–up" approach, beginning with the features of brain systems and the kinds of cognitive content that they characteristically implicate. Both models are probably metaphorical, but the AST metaphor is more closely linked to the metaphors commonly used to characterize basic mental systems.

Additionally, in the Wyer and Srull (1989) model, different kinds of informational content about a given individual stand in no necessary relationship to each other, except that they may be independently stored in the same "bin" when they relate to the same processing objective. In contrast, the presumed organization of different kinds of content is central to AST. Despite these differences, however, AST is not really intended to provide an alternative to Wyer and Srull's model, or to other multimodal models of impression. It is more intended to be integrative, supplementary, and sometimes even complementary to other theories.

The Organizational System

Third, the approach detailed in this chapter is systematic in that it specifies an organizational system, or structure, that links various forms of representation to each other and to important perceptual and response systems (see Fig. 1.2). The arrangement of representational forms in this structure is intended to reflect some basic theoretical assumptions, to convey important similarities among representational forms, and to suggest novel hypotheses about the origins and effects of different kinds of social relationships.

To appreciate the range of considerations represented in the structure, consider the arrangement of representations in the top row of the figure. A linear ordering is depicted, proceeding from visual representations (appearance) on the left, through categorizations in the middle, to verbal representations (personality traits) on the right. As already noted, the intermediate position of categorizations captures the fact that these tend to possess both visual and verbal features, and reflects the assumption that categorizations fall between visual appearance and personality traits in abstractness. The linear ordering is also consistent with the apparent sequence of visual processing along the polymodal pathway in the temporal cortex (from identification, to categorization, to naming), as well as with a variety of findings in cognitive psychology. For example, Potter and Faulconer (1975) found that pictures of objects, such as people's faces, can be categorized faster than they can be named, whereas words, such as written names, can be named more quickly than they can be categorized. These patterns are consistent with the argument that visual and categorization processes are more closely related than visual and verbal processes. The same linear sequence of processes was suggested by Young, Hay, and Ellis (1986), who found that subjects can classify faces as familiar (a visual process) faster than they can classify them by occupation (a categorization process), but they can classify them by occupation faster than they can name them (a verbal process).

The linear ordering of these representations from left to right is also hypothesized to reflect the sequence in which representations are typically formed as an interpersonal relationship evolves from purely observational to increasingly cerebral. On the other hand, representations based on verbal descriptions might proceed in the opposite direction—from personality traits, through categorizations, to imagined appearance. Often, however, the visual and verbal systems will be employed simultaneously so that the order in which representations are formed should simply reflect the relative strength of the cognitive procedures that operate on the particular stimulus features available.

Finally, the depicted linear ordering also implies that personality traits, categorizations, and visual appearance should be progressively less related to verbal outputs (judgments and communications), but progressively more related to visual outputs (imagination). Thus, for example, categorizations should generally influence trait ascriptions more than visual appearance does, and should generally be more involved in imagination than person-ality traits are. These implications are depicted in Fig. 1.9, along with those relating to other systems.

The kinds of considerations outlined here for the top row of Fig. 1.2 also come into play for other systems, and for the other linear orderings of representations captured in this figure. The supporting evidence may not always be as strong, but the same systematic logic pervades the full organizational structure.

Taxonomic Systems

The final sense in which I argue for systematic approaches to impression processes relates to the fourth and most specialized definition of the term: "pertaining to a classification or taxonomy." The desirability of taxonomic (or "free-response") approaches has been emphasized by several researchers (e.g., Fiske & Cox, 1979; McGuire & McGuire, 1991), especially because it allows subjects to frame their responses in terms of the kinds of represen-tations that are most meaningful to them. I have been skeptical of such approaches in the past (Carlston, 1991, 1992; see also Fiske & Ruscher, 1989), and remain convinced that they introduce special concerns, especially when they are used to assess underlying cognitive representation. A variety of such concerns were detailed earlier. Researchers may need to take special steps to encourage utilization of difficult-to-express representations, and to emphasize the value of expressing all forms of content associated with a target person. Additionally, researchers need to develop and exploit alternative methods for assessing the full range of different representations that people appear to use.

However, I am also increasingly enthusiastic about the potential of free-response methods when combined with proper precautions, a theory-based taxonomy, and specialized analytic methods such as multidimensional scaling. The AST taxonomy that I have developed with Sparks has evolved across a number of studies, and will undoubtedly continue to evolve as it is tested and refined. Yet it seems to offer considerable promise in allowing free descriptions to be related to basic forms of representation, and in permitting such descriptions to be scored in terms of such superordinate dimensions as abstractness and self-reference.[11] As detailed in Table 1.1, the AST taxonomy relates somewhat to prior taxonomic systems, especially the one described by Fiske and Cox (1979). Moreover, as detailed in Tables 1.2 and 1.3, AST suggests related taxonomies for characterizing interpersonal judgments and behaviors, allowing for a theoretically coherent linkage between people's representations and their responses.

Concluding Remarks

AST represents an attempt to introduce all of these kinds of systematicity into theorizing about impressional representations. In an attempt to show the heuristic value of doing so, I have climbed out onto a number of limbs, and it wouldn't surprise me too much if I fell off a few. I trust that the remaining chapters in this book can help readers determine where I am in danger and where I am suitably supported. In any case, the particular speculations advanced here are probably less important than the "systematicity" of the approach.

To summarize, this approach reflects the premise that most basic forms of cognitive representation relate to the mental systems involved in vision, language, affect, and action. The recorded experiences of these mental systems constitute all knowledge, as Carlyle noted in the epigraph. Moreover, this knowledge represents material that those systems need to execute their functions. As Fiske (1992) suggested, "thinking is for doing," and what the mind does involves these basic mental systems. In summary, then, cognitive representations are distillations from past activities and experiences that guide future activities and experiences. This suggests that there

---

[11]No, a copy of the system is not available in the lobby after the show. However, a booklet (Carlston & Sparks, 1992b) is available from the author that describes the current version of the taxonomy, its theoretical rationale, the category definitions, and some coding guidelines.

are a variety of different kinds of cognitive representations, that these are systematically related to each other, that they derive in logical ways from people's experiences, and that they contribute in systematic ways to the various activities in which people engage.

ACKNOWLEDGMENTS

I thank Scott Phillips, Terry Powley, Eliot Smith, Cheri Sparks, and Robert Wyer for their helpful comments on earlier drafts of this chapter. I also thank Cheri Sparks for her assistance in researching Table 1.1, and Scott Phillips for his proposal of Fig. 1.1

REFERENCES

Abelson, R. P. (1981). The psychological status of the script concept. *American Psychologist*, *36*, 715–729.

Alba, J. W., & Hasher, L. (1983). Is memory schematic? *Psychological Bulletin*, *93*, 203–231.

The American Heritage Dictionary of the English Language. (1980). Boston: Houghton Mifflin.

Andersen, S. M., & Klatzky, R. L. (1983). Traits and social stereotypes: Levels of categorization in person perception. *Journal of Personality and Social Psychology*, *53*, 235–246.

Anderson, J. R. (1978). Arguments concerning representations for mental imagery. *Psychological Review*, *85*, 249–277.

Anderson, J. R. (1982). Acquisition of cognitive skill. *Psychological Review*, *89*, 369–406.

Anderson, N. H. (1988). A functional approach to person cognition. In T. K. Srull & R. S. Wyer, Jr. (Eds.), *Advances in social cognition: A dual process model of impression formation* (Vol. 1, pp. 37–51). Hillsdale, NJ: Lawrence Erlbaum Associates.

Anderson, R. A., & Anderson, S. W. (1991, May). *The domain of social cognition: Findings from cognitive neuroscience.* Paper presented at the meeting of the Midwestern Psychological Association, Chicago, IL.

Anderson, R. C. (1971). Encoding processes in the storage and retrieval of sentences. *Journal of Experimental Psychology*, *91*, 338–340.

Anshel, M. H., & Ortiz, M. (1986). Effect of coding strategies on movement extent as a function of cognitive style. *Percepetual and Motor Skills*, *63*, 1311–1317.

Bargh, J. A. (1984). Automatic and conscious processing of social information. In R. S. Wyer & T. K. Srull (Eds.), *Handbook of social cognition* (Vol. 3, pp. 1–43). Hillsdale, NJ: Lawrence Erlbaum Associates.

Bargh, J. A. (1989). Conditional automaticity: Varieties of automatic influence in social perception and cognition. In J. S. Uleman & J. A. Bargh (Eds.), *Unintended thought* (pp. 3–51). New York: Guilford.

Bargh, J. A., Bond, R. N., Lombardi, W., & Tota, M. E. (1986). The additive nature of chronic and temporary sources of construct accessibility. *Journal of Personality and Social Psychology*, *50*, 869–878.

Bargh, J. A., Lombardi, W. J., & Higgins, E. T. (1988). Automaticity of chronically accessible constructs in person X situation effects on person perception: It's just a matter of time. *Journal of Personality and Social Psychology*, *55*, 599–605.

Bargh, J. A., & Thein, R. D. (1985). Individual construct accessibility, person memory, and the recall-judgment link: The case of information overload. *Journal of Personality and Social Psychology, 49*, 1129–1146.

Bassili, J. N. (1989). Traits as action categories versus traits as person attributes in social cognition. In J. N. Bassili (Ed.), *On-line cognition in person perception* (pp. 61–89). Hillsdale, NJ: Lawrence Erlbaum Associates.

Battistich, V. A., Assor, A., Messe, L. A., & Aronoff, J. (1985). Personality and person perception. In P. Shaver (Ed.), *Review of personality and social psychology: Vol. 6. Self, situations, and social behavior* (pp. 185–208). Beverly Hills, CA: Sage.

Beach, L., & Wertheimer, M. (1961). A free-response approach to the study of person cognition. *Journal of Abnormal and Social Psychology, 62*, 367–374.

Bem, D. J. (1972). Self-perception theory. In L. Berkowitz (Ed.), *Advances in experimental social psychology* (Vol. 6, pp. 1–62). San Diego, CA: Academic Press.

Boring, E. G. (1930). A new ambiguous figure. *American Journal of Psychology, 42*, 444–445.

Bower, G. H. (1981). Mood and memory. *American Psychologist, 36*, 129–148.

Breckler, S. J. (1984). Empirical validation of affect, behavior, and cognition as distinct components of attitude. *Journal of Personality and Social Psychology, 47*, 1191–1205.

Breckler, S. J., & Wiggins, E. C. (1989). On defining attitude and attitude theory: Once more with feeling. In A. R. Pratkanis, S. J. Breckler, & A. G. Greenwald (Eds.), *Attitudes structure and function* (pp. 407–428). Hillsdale, NJ: Lawrence Erlbaum Associates.

Brewer, M. (1988). A dual process model of impression formation. In T. K. Srull & R. S. Wyer (Eds.), *Advances in social cognition: A dual process model of impression formation* (Vol. 1, pp. 1–36). Hillsdale, NJ: Lawrence Erlbaum Associates.

Briggs, S. R., & Cheek, J. M. (1988). On the nature of self-monitoring: Problems with assessment, problems with validity. *Journal of Personality and Social Psychology, 54*, 663–678.

Brooks, L. R. (1968). Spatial and verbal components of the act of recall. *Canadian Journal of Psychology, 22*, 349–368.

Brown, R., & Kulik, J. (1977). Flashbulb memories. *Cognition, 5*, 73–99.

Bryden, M. P., & Ley, R. G. (1983). Right-hemispheric involvement in the perception and expression of emotion in normal humans. In K. M. Heilman & P. Satz (Eds.), *Neuropsychology of human emotion* (pp.6–44). New York: Guilford.

Cacioppo, J. T., & Petty, R. E. (1982). The need for cognition. *Journal of Personality and Social Psychology, 42*, 116–131.

Cantor, N., & Kihlstrom, J. F. (1985). Social intelligence: The cognitive basis of personality. In P. Shaver (Ed.), *Review of personality and social psychology: Vol. 6. Self, situations, and social behavior* (pp. 15–34). Beverly Hills, CA: Sage.

Cantor, N., & Kihlstrom, J. F. (1987). *Personality and social intelligence.* Englewood Cliffs, NJ: Prentice-Hall.

Cantor, N., & Mischel, W. (1977). Traits as prototypes: Effects on recognition memory. *Journal of Personality and Social Psychology, 35*, 38–48.

Carlston, D. E. (1980a). Events, inferences and impression formation. In R. Hastie, T. Ostrom, E. Ebbesen, R. Wyer, D. Hamilton, & D. Carlston (Eds.), *Person memory: The cognitive basis of social perception* (pp. 89–119). Hillsdale, NJ: Lawrence Erlbaum Associates.

Carlston, D. E. (1980b). The recall and use of traits and events in social inference processes. *Journal of Experimental Social Psychology, 16*, 303–328.

Carlston, D. E. (1991). Free association and the representation of complex cognitive structures. In T. K. Srull & R. S. Wyer, Jr. (Eds.), *Advances in social cognition* (Vol. 4, pp. 87–96). Hillsdale, NJ: Lawrence Erlbaum Associates.

Carlston, D. E. (1992). Impression formation and the modular mind: The associated systems theory. In L. L. Martin & A. Tesser (Eds.), *The construction of social judgments* (pp. 301–341). Hillsdale, NJ: Lawrence Erlbaum Associates.

Carlston, D. E., & Skowronski, J. J. (1986). Trait memory and behavior memory: The effects of alternative pathways on impression judgment response times. *Journal of Personality and Social Psychology, 50,* 5–13.

Carlston, D. E., & Skowronski, J. J. (1988). *Trait memory and behavior memory: II. The effects of conceptual social knowledge on impression judgment response times.* Unpublished manuscript, University of Iowa, Iowa City, IA.

Carlston, D. E., & Sparks, C. (1992a, May). *A theory-based approach to the analysis of free descriptions of people.* Paper presented at the meetings of the Midwestern Psychological Association, Chicago, IL.

Carlyle, T. (1907). *Critical and miscellaneous essays* (Vol. II). London: Chapman & Hall.

Carlston, D. E., & Sparks, C. (1992b). *Person representation classification scheme.* Unpublished manuscript, Purdue University, West Lafayette, IN.

Chaiken, S., & Baldwin, M. W. (1981). Affective-cognitive consistency and the effect of salient behavioral information on the self-perception of attitudes. *Journal of Personality and Social Psychology, 41,* 1–12.

Clark, M. S., & Isen, A. M. (1982). Toward understanding the relationship between feeling states and social behavior. In A. Hastorf & A. Isen (Eds.), *Cognitive social psychology* (pp. 73–108). New York: Elsevier.

Clark, M. S., Milberg, S., & Erber, R. (1988). Arousal-state-dependent memory: Evidence and implications for understanding social judgments and social behavior. In K. Fiedler & J. Forgas (Eds.), *Affect, cognition, and social behavior* (pp. 63–83). Toronto, Canada: Hogrefe.

Clore, G. L., & Parrott, W. G. (1991). Moods and their vicissitudes: Thoughts and feelings as information. In J. Forgas (Ed.), *Emotion and social judgment* (pp. 107–123). Oxford: Pergamon.

Cohen, A. R. (1961). Cognitive tuning as a factor affecting impression formation. *Journal of Personality, 29,* 235–245.

Cohen, D., March, J. G., & Olsen, J. P. (1972). A garbage can model of organizational choice. *Administrative Science Quarterly, 17,* 1–25.

Collins, A., & Loftus, E. F. (1975). A spreading activation theory of semantic memory. *Journal of Verbal Learning and Verbal Behavior, 8,* 240–247.

Conway, M. A. (1990). Associations between autobiographical memories and concepts. *Journal of Experimental Psychology: Learning, Memory and Cognition, 16*(5), 799–812.

Cook, S. W. (1978). Interpersonal and attitudinal outcomes in cooperating interracial groups. *Journal of Research and Development in Education, 12,* 97–113.

Cotton, J. L. (1985). Cognitive dissonance in selective exposure. In D. Zillman & J. Bryant (Eds.), *Selective exposure to communication* (pp. 11–33). Hillsdale, NJ: Lawrence Erlbaum Associates.

Damasio, A. R. (1989a). The brain binds entities and events by multiregional activation from convergence zones. *Neural Computation, 1,* 123–132.

Damasio, A. R. (1989b). Multiregional retroactivation: A systems level model for some neural substrates of cognition. *Cognition, 33,* 25–62.

DeBono, K. G., & Snyder, M. (1989). Understanding consumer decision-making processes: The role of form and function in product evaluation. *Journal of Applied Social Psychology, 19,* 416–424.

Devine, P. G., Sedikides, C., & Fuhrman, R. W. (1989). Goals in social information processing: The case of anticipated interaction. *Journal of Personality and Social Psychology, 56*(5), 680–690.

Dodd, D. H., & Bradshaw, J. M. (1980). Leading questions and memory: Pragmatic constraints. *Journal of Verbal Learning and Verbal Behavior, 19,* 695–704.

Dornbusch, S. M., Hastorf, A. H., Richardson, S. A., Muzzy, R. E., & Vreeland, R. S. (1965). The perceiver and the perceived: Their relative influence on the categories of interpersonal cognition. *Journal of Personality and Social Psychology, 1,* 434–440.

Eagly, A. H., & Chaiken, S. (1993). *The psychology of attitudes.* Fort Worth, TX: Harcourt Brace Jovanovich.

Ebbesen, E. B., & Allen, R. B. (1979). Cognitive processes in implicit personality trait inferences. *Journal of Personality and Social Psychology, 37,* 471–488.

Ehrlich, H. J., & Lipsey, C. (1969). Affective style as a variable in person perception. *Journal of Personality, 37,* 522–540.

Englekamp, J. (1991). Memory of action events: Some implications for memory theory and for imagery. In C. Cornoldi & M. A. McDaniel (Eds.), *Imagery and cognition* (pp. 183–219). New York: Springer-Verlag.

Farah, M. J. (1988). Is visual imagery really visual? Overlooked evidence from neuropsychology. *Psychological Review, 95,* 307–317.

Farah, M. J. (1989). The neural basis of mental imagery. *Trends in Neurosciences, 12,* 395–399.

Fazio, R. H. (1986). How do attitudes guide behavior? In R. M. Sorrentino & E. T. Higgins (Eds.), *The handbook of motivation and cognition: Foundations of social behavior* (pp. 204–243). New York: Guilford.

Fazio, R. H. (1987). Self-perception theory: A current perspective. In M. P. Zanna, J. M. Olson, & C. P. Herman (Eds.), *Social influence: The Ontario Symposium* (Vol. 5, pp. 129–149). Hillsdale, NJ: Lawrence Erlbaum Associates.

Fazio, R. H. (1989). On the power and functionality of attitudes: The role of attitude accessibility. In A. R. Pratkanis, S. J. Breckler, & A. G. Greenwald (Eds.), *Attitude structure and function* (pp. 153–179). Hillsdale, NJ: Lawrence Erlbaum Associates.

Fazio, R. H., Chen, J., McDonel, E. C., & Sherman, S. J. (1982). Attitude accessibility, attitude-behavior consistency, and the strength of the object-evaluation association. *Journal of Experimental Social Psychology, 18,* 339–357.

Fazio, R. H., & Cooper, J. (1983). Arousal in the dissonance process. In J. T. Cacioppo & R. E. Petty (Eds.), *Social psychophysiology* (pp. 122–152). New York: Guilford.

Fazio, R. H., Powell, M. C., & Herr, P. M. (1983). Toward a process model of the attitude-behavior relation: Accessing one's attitude upon more observation of the attitude object. *Journal of Personality Social Psychology, 44,* 723–735.

Fazio, R. H., & Williams, C. J. (1986). Attitude accessibility as a moderator of the attitude-perception and attitude-behavior relations: An investigation of the 1984 presidential election. *Journal of Personality and Social Psychology, 51,* 505–514.

Fazio R. H., & Zanna, M. P. (1981). Direct experience and attitude-behavior consistency. In L. Berkowitz (Ed.), *Advances in experimental social psychology,* (Vol. 14, pp. 162–203). New York: Academic Press.

Fishbein, M. (1963). An investigation of the relationship between belief about an object and the attitude toward that object. *Human Relations, 16,* 233–240.

Fiske, A. P. (1991). *Structure of social life.* New York: The Free Press.

Fiske, A. P., Haslam, N., & Fiske, S. T. (1991). Confusing one person with another: What errors reveal about the elemenary forms of social relations. *Journal of Personality and Social Psychology, 60,* 656–674.

Fiske, S. T. (1980). Attention and weight in person perception: The impact of negative and extreme behavior. *Journal of Personality and Social Psychology, 38,* 889–906.

Fiske, S. T. (1982). Schema-triggered affect: Applications to social perception. In M. S. Clark & S. T. Fiske (Eds.), *Affect and cognition: The 17th annual Carnegie symposium on cognition* (pp. 55–78). Hillsdale, NJ: Lawrence Erlbaum Associates.

Fiske, S. T. (1992). Thinking is for doing: Portraits of social cognition from daguerreotype to laserphoto. *Journal of Personality and Social Psychology, 63,* 877–889.

Fiske, S. T., & Cox, M. G. (1979). Person concepts: The effect of target familiarity and descriptive purpose on the process of describing others. *Journal of Personality, 47,* 136–161.

Fiske, S. T., & Pavelchak, M. A. (1986). Category-based vs. piecemeal-based affective responses: Developments in schema-triggered affect. In R. M. Sorrentino & E. T. Higgins (Eds.), *Handbook of motivation and cognition* (pp. 167–203). New York: Guilford.

Fiske, S. T., & Ruscher, J. B. (1989). On-line processes in category-based and individuating impressions: Some basic principles and methodological reflections. In J. N. Bassili (Ed.), *On-line cognition in person perception* (pp. 61–89). Hillsdale, NJ: Lawrence Erlbaum Associates.

Fiske, S. T., & Taylor, S. E. (1991). *Social cognition* (2nd ed.). New York: McGraw-Hill.

Frable, D. E. S., & Bem, S. L. (1985). If you are gender schematic, all members of the opposite sex look alike. *Journal of Personality and Social Psychology, 49,* 459–468.

Frey, D. (1986). Recent research on selective exposure to information. *Advances in Social Psychology, 19,* 41–80.

Fussell, S. R., & Krauss, R. M. (1992). Coordination of knowledge in communication: Effects of speakers' assumptions about what others know. *Journal of Personality and Social Psychology, 62,* 378–391.

Gardner, H. (1985). *Frames of mind: The theory of multiple intelligences.* New York: Harper Collins.

Gilbert, D. T. (1989). Thinking lightly about others: Automatic components of the social inference process. In J. S., Uleman, & J. A., Bargh, (Eds.), *Unintended thought* (pp. 189–211). New York: Guilford.

Gilbert, D. T., & Hixon, J. G. (1991). The trouble of thinking: Activation and application of stereotypic beliefs. *Journal of Personality and Social Psychology, 60,* 509–517.

Gilbert, D. T., & Osborne, R. E. (1989). Thinking backward: Some curable and incurable consequences of cognitive busyness. *Journal of Personality and Social Psychology, 57,* 940–949.

Gilbert, D. T., Pelham, B. W., & Krull, D. S. (1988). On cognitive busyness: When person perceivers meet persons perceived. *Journal of Personality and Social Psychology, 54(5),* 733–740.

Goethals, G. R., & Reckman, R. F. (1973). The perception of consistencey in attitudes. *Journal of Experimental Social Psychology, 9,* 491–501.

Gordon, C. (1968). Self conceptions: Configurations of content. In C. Gordon & K. J. Gergen (Eds.), *The self in social interaction: Classic and contemporary perspectives* (Vol. 1, pp. 115–136). New York: Wiley.

Gorelick, P. B., & Ross, E. D. (1987). The aprosodias: Further functional-anatomical evidence for the organisation of affective language in the right hemisphere. *Journal of Neurology, Neurosurgery and Psychiatry, 50,* 553–560.

Grice, H. (1975). Logic and conversation. In P. Cole & J. Morgan (Eds.), *Syntax and semantics: Vol. 3. Speech acts* (pp. 68–134). New York: Academic Press.

Griffin, D. W., Dunning, D., & Ross, L. (1990). The role of construal processes in overconfident predictions about the self and others. *Journal of Personality and Social Psychology, 59,* 1128–1139.

Grossberg, S. (1988). Nonlinear neural networks: Principles, mechanisms, and architectures. *Neural Networks, 1,* 17–62.

Hamilton, D. L. (Ed.). (1981). *Cognitive processes in stereotyping and intergroup behavior.* Hillsdale, NJ: Lawrence Erlbaum Associates.

Hamilton, D. L., & Trolier, T. K. (1986). Stereotypes and stereotyping: An overview of the cognitive approach. In J. F. Dovidio & S. L. Gaertner (Eds.), *Prejudice, discrimination, and racism* (pp. 127–163). Orlando, FL: Academic Press.

Hartwick, J. (1979). Memory of trait information: A signal detection analysis. *Journal of Experimental Social Psychology, 15,* 533–552.

Harvey, J. H., Ickes, W. J., & Kidd, R. F. (1976). *New directions in attribution research* (Vol. 1). Hillsdale, NJ: Lawrence Erlbaum Associates.

Harvey, J. H., Yarkin, K. L., Lightner, J. M., & Town, J. P. (1980). Unsolicited interpretation and recall of interpersonal events. *Journal of Personality and Social Psychology, 38,* 551–568.

Hastie, R., & Carlston, D. E. (1980). Theoretical issues in person memory. In R. Hastie, T. Ostrom, E. Ebbesen, R. Wyer, D. Hamilton, & D. Carlston (Eds.), *Person memory: The cognitive basis of social perception* (pp. 1–53). Hillsdale, NJ: Lawrence Erlbaum Associates.

Hastie, R., & Kumar, P. A. (1979). Person memory: Personality traits as organizing principles in memory for behaviors. *Journal of Personality and Social Psychology, 37,* 25–38.

Hastie, R., Park, B., & Weber, R. (1984). Social memory. In R. S. Wyer, Jr., & T. K. Srull (Eds.), *Handbook of social cognition* (Vol. 2, pp. 151–212). Hillsdale, NJ: Lawrence Erlbaum Associates.

Hebb, D. O. (1949). *The organization of behavior: A neuropsychological theory.* New York: Wiley.

Hebb, D. O. (1980). *Essay on mind.* Hillsdale, NJ: Lawrence Erlbaum Associates.

Higgins, E. T., Bargh, J. A., & Lombardi, W. (1985). The nature of priming effects on categorization. *Journal of Experimental Psychology: Learning, Memory, and Cognition, 11,* 59–69.

Higgins, E. T., McCann, C. D., & Fondacaro, R. (1982). The "communication game": Goal-directed encoding and cognitive consequences. *Social Cognition, 1,* 21–37.

Hoffman, C., Mischel, W., & Baer, J. S. (1984). Language and person cognition: Effects of communicative set on trait attribution. *Journal of Personality and Social Psychology, 46,* 1029–1043.

Hoffman, H. S., & Ison, J. R. (1980). Reflex modification in the domain of startle: I. Some empirical findings and their implications for how the nervous system processes sensory input. *Psychological Review, 87,* 175–189.

Holyoak, K. J., & Gordon, P. C. (1984). Information processing and social cognition. In R. S. Wyer & T. K. Srull (Eds.), *Handbook of social cognition* (Vol. 1, pp. 39–70). Hillsdale, NJ: Lawrence Erlbaum Associates.

Hosch, H. M., & Platz, S. J. (1984). Self-monitoring and eyewitness accuracy. *Personality and Social Psychology Bulletin, 10,* 289–292.

Ickes, W., Stinson, L., Bissonnette, V., Garcia, S. (1990). Naturalistic social cognition: Empathetic accuracy in mixed-sex dyads. *Journal of Personality and Social Psychology, 59,* 730–742.

Jacome, D. E. (1991). Kluver, Cucy, and the Kluver–Bucy syndrome. *American Journal of EEG Technology, 31,* 267–278.

Jamieson, D. W., Lydon, J. E.,, & Zanna, M. P. (1987). Attitude and activity preference similarity: Differential bases of interpersonal attraction for low and high self-monitors. *Journal of Personality and Social Psychology, 53,* 1052–1060.

Johnson, M. K., & Raye, C. L. (1981). Reality monitoring. *Psychological Review, 88,* 67–85.

Johnson. M. K., Raye, C. L., Foley, H. J., & Foley, M. A. (1981). Cognitive operations and decision bias in reality monitoring. *American Journal of Psychology, 94,* 37–64.

Jones, E. E. (1986). Interpreting interpersonal behavior: The effects of expectancies. *Science, 234,* 41–46.

Jones, E. E., & Davis, K. E. (1965). From acts to dispositions: The attributional process in person perception. In L. Berkowitz (Ed.), *Advances in experimental social psychology* (Vol. 2, pp. 220–266). New York: Academic Press.

Kardes, F. R., Sanbonmatsu, D. M., Voss, R. T., & Fazio, R. H. (1986). Self-monitoring and attitude accessibility. *Personality and Social Psychology Bulletin, 12,* 468–474.

Katkin, E. S. (1985). Blood, sweat, and tears: Individual differences in autonomic self-perception. *Psychophysiology, 18,* 252–267.

Katz, P. A., Silvern, L., & Coulter, D. K. (1990). Gender processing and person perception. *Social Cognition, 8*(2), 186–202.

Katz, D., & Stotland, E. (1959). A preliminary statement to a theory of attitude structure and change. In S. Koch (Ed.), *Psychology: A study of a science* (Vol. 3, pp. 423–475). New York: McGraw-Hill.

Kenny, D. A. (1991). A general model of consensus and accuracy in interpersonal perception. *Psychological Review, 98*, 155–162.

Kihlstrom, J. F., & Cantor, N. (1984). Mental representations of the self. In L. Berkowitz (Ed.), *Advances in experimental social psychology* (Vol. 17, pp. 1–47). New York: Academic Press.

Klatzky, R. L. (1984). Visual memory: Definitions and functions. In R. S. Wyer, Jr., & T. K. Srull (Eds.), *Handbook of social cognition* (Vol. 2, pp. 233–270). Hilldsale, NJ: Lawrence Erlbaum Associates.

Klatzky, R. L., & Andersen, S. M. (1988). Category-specificity effects in social typing and personalization. In T. K. Srull & R. S. Wyer (Eds.), *Advances in social cognition: A dual process model of impression formation* (Vol. 1, pp. 91–102). Hillsdale, NJ: Lawrence Erlbaum Associates.

Klatzky, R. L., Pellegrino, J. W., McCloskey, B. P., & Doherty, S. (1989). *Journal of Memory and Language, 28*, 56–77.

Klein, S. B., & Loftus, J. (1993). The mental representation of trait and autobiographical knowledge about the self. In T. K. Srull & R. S. Wyer (Eds.), *Advances in social cognition* (Vol. 5, pp. 1–49). Hillsdale, NJ: Lawrence Erlbaum Associates.

Klein, S. B., Loftus, J., Trafton, J. G., & Fuhrman, R. W. (1992). Use of exemplars and abstractions in trait judgments: A model of trait knowledge about the self and others. *Journal of Personality and Social Psychology, 63*, 739–753.

Kolb, B., & Whishaw, I. Q. (1990). *Fundamentals of human neuropsychology* (3rd ed.). San Francisco: Freeman.

Konorski, J. (1967). *Integrative activity of the brain*. Chicago: University of Chicago Press.

Kosslyn, S. M. (1981). The medium and the message in mental imagery: A theory. *Psychological Review, 88*, 46–66.

Kosslyn, S. M., & Pomerantz, J. R. (1977). Imagery, propositions and the form of internal representations. *Cognitive Psychology, 9*, 52–76.

Kroll, J. F., & Potter, M. C. (1984). Recognizing words, pictures and concepts: A comparison of lexical, object and reality decisions. *Journal of Verbal Learning and Verbal Behavior, 23* 39–66.

Kruskal, J. B., & Wish, M. (1978). *Multidimensional scaling*. Beverly Hills, CA: Sage.

Laird, J. D., Wagener, J. J., Halal, M., & Szegda, M. (1982). Remembering what you feel: The effects of emotion on memory. *Journal of Personality and Social Psychology, 42*, 646–657.

Landman, J., & Manis, M. (1983). Social cognition: Some historical and theoretical perspectives. In L. Berkowitz (Ed.), *Advances in experimental social psychology* (Vol. 16, pp. 40–125). Orlando, FL: Academic Press.

Langer, E., Blank, A., & Chanowitz, B. (1978). The mindlessness of ostensibly thoughtful action: The role of "placibic" information in interpersonal interaction. *Journal of Personality and Social Psychology, 36*, 635–642.

Larsen, R. J., & Diener, E. (1987). Affect intensity as an individual difference characteristic: A review. *Journal of Research in Personality, 21*, 1–39.

Lassiter, G. D., Briggs, M. A., & Slaw, R. D. (1991). Need for cognition, causal processing, and memory for behavior. *Personality and Social Psychology Bulletin, 17*, 694–700.

Lazarus, R. S. (1982). Thoughts on the relations between emotion and cognition. *American Psychologist, 37*, 1019–1024.

Linton, M. (1982). Transformations of memory in everyday life. In U. Neisser (Ed.), *Memory observed: Remembering in natural contexts* (pp. 77–91). San Francisco: Freeman.

Linville, P., & Carlston, D. E. (1994). Social cognition perspective on self. In P. G. Devine,

D. L. Hamilton, & T. M. Ostrom (Eds.), *Social cognition: Contributions to classic issues in social psychology* (pp. 143–193). New York: Springer-Verlag.

Lippa, R. (1976). Expressive control and the leakage of dispositional introversion–extraversion during role-playing teaching. *Journal of Personality, 44*, 541–559.

Livesley, W. J., & Bromley, D. B. (1973). *Person perception in childhood and adolescence.* London: Wiley.

Lombardi, W. J., Higgins, E. T., & Bargh, J. A. (1987). The role of consciousness in priming effects on categorization: Assimilation versus contrast as a function of awareness of the priming task. *Personality and Social Psychology Bulletin, 13*, 411–429.

Lynn, M., Shavitt, S., & Ostrom, T. (1985). Effects of pictures on the organization and recall of social information. *Journal of Personality and Social Psychology, 49*, 1160–1168.

Malpass, R. S., & Kravitz, J. (1969). Recognition for faces of own and other race. *Journal of Personality and Social Psychology, 13*, 330–334.

Marcel, A. J. (1983). Conscious and unconscious perception: An approach to the relations between phenomenal experience and perceptual process. *Cognitive Psychology, 15*, 238–300.

Marks, D. F. (1973) Imagery differences and eye movements in the recall of pictures. *Perception and Psychophysics, 14*, 407–412.

Marks, D. F. (1989). Bibliography of research utilizing the Vividness of Visual Imagery Questionnaire. *Perceptual and Motor Skills, 69*, 707–718.

Martin, L. L. (1986). Set/reset: Use and disuse of concepts in impression formation. *Journal of Personality and Social Psychology, 51*, 493–504.

Martindale, C. (1991). *Cognitive psychology: A neural-network approach.* Pacific Grove, CA: Brooks/Cole.

McArthur, L. Z. (1982). Judging a book by its cover: A cognitive analysis of the relationship between physical appearance and stereotyping. In A. Hastorf & A. Isen (Eds.), *Cognitive social psychology* (pp. 149–211). New York: Elsevier.

McGuire, W. J., & McGuire, C. V. (1991). The content, structure and operation of thought systems. In R. S. Wyer, Jr., & T. Srull (Eds.), *Advances in social cognition: A dual process model of impression formation* (Vol. 4, pp. 1–78). Hillsdale, NJ: Lawrence Erlbaum Associates.

McGuire, W. J., & Padawer-Singer, A. (1976). Trait salience in the spontaneous self-concept. *Journal of Personality and Social Psychology, 33*, 743–754.

Medin, D. L. (1988). Social categorization: Structures, processes, and purposes. In T. K. Srull & R. S. Wyer, Jr. (Eds.), *Advances in social cognition: A dual process model of impression formation* (Vol. 1, pp. 119–126). Hillsdale, NJ: Lawrence Erlbaum Associates.

Millar, M. G., & Tesser, A. (1986). Effects of affective and cognitive focus on the attitude-behavior relation. *Journal of Personality and Social Psychology, 51*(2), 270–276.

Millar, M. G., & Tesser, A. (1989). The effects of affective-cognitive consistency and thought on the attitude-behavior relationship. *Journal of Experimental Social Psychology, 25*, 189–202.

Millar, M. G., & Tesser, A. (1992). The role of beliefs and feelings in guiding behavior: The mismatch model. In L. L. Martin & A. Tesser (Eds.), *The construction of social judgments* (pp. 301–341). Hillsdale, NJ: Lawrence Erlbaum Associates.

Miller, C. T. (1988). Categorization and the physical attractiveness stereotype. *Social Cognition, 6*, 231–251.

Miller, D. T., & Turnbull, W. (1986). Expectancies and interpersonal processes. In M. R. Rosenzweig & L. W. Porter (Eds.), *Annual review of psychology* (Vol. 37, pp. 233–256). Palo Alto, CA: Annual Review.

Neely, J. H. (1976). Semantic priming and retrieval from lexical memory: Evidence for facilitatory and inhibitory processes. *Memory and Cognition, 4*, 648–654.

Newman, L. S., & Uleman, J. S. (1989). Spontaneous trait inference. In J. S. Uleman & J. A. Bargh (Eds.), *Unintended thought* (pp. 155–188). New York: Guilford.

Niedenthal, P. M. (1990). Implicit perception of affective information. *Journal of Experimental Social Psychology, 26,* 505–527.

Nisbett, R. E., & Ross, L. (1980). *Human inference: Strategies and shortcomings of social judgment.* Englewood Cliffs, NJ: Prentice-Hall.

Nisbett, R. E., & Wilson, T. D. (1977). Telling more than we can know: Verbal reports on mental processes. *Psychological Review, 84,* 231–259.

Ostrom, T. M. (1975, August). *Cognitive representation of impressions.* Paper presented at the meeting of the American Psychological Association, Chicago, IL.

Paivio, A. (1971). *Imagery and verbal processes.* New York: Holt, Rinehart & Winston.

Paivio, A. (1986). *Mental representations: A dual coding approach.* New York: Oxford University Press.

Park, B. (1986). A method for studying the development of impressions of real people. *Journal of Personality and Social Psychology, 51,* 907–917.

Park, B., & Flink, C. (1989). A social relations analysis of agreement in liking judgments. *Journal of Personality and Social Psychology, 56,* 506–518.

Potter, M. C., & Faulconer, B. A. (1975). Time to understand pictures and words. *Nature, 253,* 437–438.

Pratto, F. (1991). Control, emotions, and laws of human behavior. *Psychological Inquiry, 2,* 202–203.

Pylyshyn, Z. W. (1981). The imagery debate: Analogue media versus tacit knowledge. *Psychological Review, 88,* 16–45.

Ray, G. B. (1986). Vocally cued personality prototypes: An implicit personality theory approach. *Communication Monographs, 53,* 266–276.

Rodin, M. J. (1987). Who is memorable to whom: A study of cognitive disregard. *Social Cognition, 5,* 144–165.

Roediger, H. L III, & Neely, J. H. (1982). Retrieval blocks in episodic and semantic memory. *Canadian Journal of Psychology, 36,* 213–242.

Rosenberg, M. J. (1960). A structural theory attitude dynamics. *Public Opinion Quarterly, 24,* 319–341.

Rosenberg, S., & Sedlak, A. (1972). Structural representations of implicit personality theory. In L. Berkowitz (Ed.), *Advances in experimental social psychology* (Vol. 10, pp. 235–297). New York: Academic Press.

Ross, M., McFarland, C., Conway, M., & Zanna, M. P. (1983). Reciprocal relation between attitudes and behavior recall: Committing people to newly formed attitudes. *Journal of Personality and Social Psychology, 45,* 257–267.

Rothbart, M. (1988). Categorization and impression formation: Capturing the mind's flexibility. In T. K. Srull & R. S. Wyer (Eds.), *Advances in social cognition: A dual process model of impression formation* (Vol. 1, pp. 139–144). Hillsdale, NJ: Lawrence Erlbaum Associates.

Rumelhart, D. E., & McClelland, J. L. (Eds.). (1986). *Parallel distributed processing* (Vol. 1). Cambridge, MA: MIT Press.

Sagar, H. A., & Schofield, J. W. (1980). Racial and behavioral cues in black and white children's perceptions of ambiguously aggressive acts. *Journal of Personality and Social Psychology, 39,* 590–598.

Saltz, E., & Nolan, S. D. (1981). Does motoric imagery facilitate memory for sentences? A selective interference test. *Journal of Verbal Learning and Verbal Behavior, 20,* 322–332.

Schneider, D. J. (1973). Implicit personality theory: A review. *Psychological Bulletin, 79,* 294–309.

Schneider, D. J. (1991). Social cognition. *Annual Review of Psychology, 42,* 527–561.

Schneider, W., & Shiffrin, R. M. (1977). Controlled and automatic human information processing: I. Detection, research and attention. *Psychological Review, 84,* 1–66.

Schooler, J. W., & Engstler-Schooler, T. Y. (1990). Verbal overshadowing of visual memories:

Some things are better left unsaid. *Cognitive Psychology, 22,* 36–71.

Schooler, J. W., & Tanaka, J. W. (1991). Composites, compromises and CHARM: What is the evidence for blend memory representations? *Journal of Experimental Psychology: General, 120,* 96–100.

Schwarz, N. (1990). Feelings as information: Informational and motivational functions of affective states. In R. Sorrentino & E. T. Higgins (Eds.), *Handbook of motivation and cognition: Foundations of social behavior* (Vol. 2, pp. 527–561). New York: Guilford.

Sedikides, C. (1990). Effects of fortuitously activated constructs versus activated communication goals on person impression. *Journal of Personality and Social Psychology, 58,* 397–408.

Shallice, T. (1978). The dominant action system: An information-processing approach to consciousness. In K. S. Pope & J. L. Singer (Eds.), *The stream of consciousness: Scientific investigations into the flow of human experience* (pp. 117–157). New York: Plenum.

Shepard, R. N., & Podgorny, P. (1978). Cognitive processes that resemble perceptual processes. In W. K. Estes (Ed.), *Handbook of learning and cognitive processes.* (pp. 189–237). Hillsdale, NJ: Lawrence Erlbaum Associates.

Sherman, S. J., Judd, C. M., & Park, B. (1989). Social cognition. *Annual Review of Psychology, 40,* 281–326.

Skowronski, J. J., & Carlston, D. E. (1989). Negativity and extremity biases in social inference: A review of explanations. *Psychological Bulletin, 105,* 131–142.

Skowronski, J. J., Carlston, D. E., & Isham, J. T. (1993). Implicit versus explicit impression formation: The differing effects of overt labeling and covert priming on memory and impressions. *Journal of Experimental Social Psychology, 29,* 17–41.

Smith, E. R. (1989). Procedural efficiency: General and specific components and effects on social judgment. *Journal of Experimental Social Psychology, 25,* 500–523.

Smith, E. R., Branscombe, N. R., & Bormann, C. (1988). Generality of the effects of practice on social judgment tasks. *Journal of Personality and Social Psychology, 54,* 385–395.

Smith, E. R., & Miller, F. D. (1978). Theoretical note. Limits on perception of cognitive processes: A reply to Nisbett and Wilson. *Psychological Review, 85*(4), 355–362.

Snyder, M. (1974). The self-monitoring of expressive behavior. *Journal of Personality and Social Psychology, 30,* 526–537.

Snyder, M. (1976). Attribution and behavior: Social perception and social causation. In J. H. Harvey, W. J. Ickes, & R. F. Kidd (Eds.), *New directions in attribution research* (Vol. 1, pp. 53–72). Hillsdale, NJ: Lawrence Erlbaum Associates.

Snyder, M. (1979). Self-monitoring processes. In L. Berkowitz (Ed.), *Advances in experimental social psychology* (Vol. 12, pp. 86–131). New York: Academic Press.

Snyder, M. (1987). *Public appearances: Private realities.* New York: Freeman.

Snyder, M., Berscheid, E., & Matwychuk, A. (1988). Orientations toward personnel selection: Differential reliance on appearance and personality. *Journal of Personality and Social Psychology, 54,* 972–979.

Snyder, M., & Cantor, N. (1980). Thinking about ourselves and others: Self-monitoring and social knowledge. *Journal of Personality and Social Psychology, 39,* 222–234.

Snyder, M., & DeBono, K. G. (1985). Appeals to image and claims about quality: Understanding the psychology of advertising. *Journal of Personality and Social Psychology, 49,* 586–597.

Snyder, M., & Gangestad, S. (1981). Hypothesis-testing processes. In J. H. Harvey, W. J. Ickes, & R. F. Kidd, (1976). *New directions in attribution research* (Vol. 1, pp. 171–198). Hillsdale, NJ: Lawrence Erlbaum Associates.

Snyder, M., & Simpson, J. A. (1984). Self-monitoring and dating relationships. *Journal of Personality and Social Psychology, 47,* 1281–1291.

Snyder, M., & Swann, W. B. (1976). When actions reflect attitudes: The politics of impression management. *Journal of Personality and Social Psychology, 34,* 1034–1042.

Snyder, M., & Swann, W. B. (1978). Hypothesis-testing processes in social interaction. *Journal of Personality and Social Psychology, 36*, 1202–1212.

Srull, T. K. (1981). Person memory: Some tests of associative storage and retrieval models. *Journal of Experimental Psychology: Human Learning and Memory, 7*, 440–463.

Swann, W. B., & Miller, L. C. (1982). Why never forgetting a face matters: Visual imagery and social memory. *Journal of Personality and Social Psychology, 43*, 475–480.

Tesser, A., & Leone, C. (1977). Cognitive schemas and thought as determinants of attitude change. *Journal of Experimental Social Psychology, 13*, 340–356.

Thompson, S. C., & Kelley, J. J. (1981). Judgments of responsibility for activities in close relationships. *Journal of Personality and Social Psychology, 41*, 469–477.

Thorndike, E. L. (1920). A constant error in psychological ratings. *Journal of Applied Psychology, 4*, 25–29.

Tourangeau, R., & Rasinski, K. A. (1988). Cognitive processes underlying context effects in attitude measurement. *Psychological Bulletin, 103*, 299–314.

Tulving, E. (1972). Episodic and semantic memory. In E. Tulving & W. Donaldson (Eds.), *Organization and memory* (pp. 381–403).New York: Academic Press.

Tulving, E. (1983). *Elements of episodic memory*. Oxford, England: Clarendon.

Tulving, E. (1993). Self-knowledge of an amnesic individual is represented abstractly. In T. K. Srull & R. S. Wyer (Eds.), *The mental representation of trait and autobiographical knowledge about the self: Advances in social cognition* (Vol. 5, pp. 147–156). Hillsdale, NJ: Lawrence Erlbaum Associates.

Uleman, J. S., & Bargh, J. A. (1989). *Unintended thought*. New York: Guilford.

Vallacher, R. R., & Wegner, D. M. (1987). What do people think they are doing? Action identification and human behavior. *Psychological Review, 94*, 3–15.

Walsh, K. W. (1978). *Neuropsychology*. London: Churchill.

White, J. D., & Carlston, D. E. (1983). The consequences of schemata for attention impressions and recognition in complex social interactions. *Journal of Personality and Social Psychology, 45*, 538–549.

Wicker, A. W. (1969). Attitudes vs. actions: The relationship of verbal and overt behavioral responses to attitude objects. *Journal of Social Issues, 41*, 41–78.

Williams, M. (1979). *Brain damage, behavior and the mind*. New York: Wiley.

Wilson, H. R., & Cowan, J. D. (1972). Excitatory and inhibitory interactions in localized populations of model neurons. *Biophysical Journal, 12*, 1–24.

Wilson, P. R. (1968). Perceptual distortion of height as a function of ascribed academic status. *Journal of Social Psychology, 74*, 97–102.

Wilson, T. D., Dunn, D. S., Bybee, J. A., Hyman, D. B., & Rotondo, J. A. (1984). Effects of analyzing reasons on attitude-behavior consistency. *Journal of Personality Social Psychology, 47*, 5–16.

Wilson, T. D., & Schooler, J. W. (1991). Thinking too much: Introspection can reduce the quality of preferences and decisions. *Journal of Personality and Social Psychology, 60*, 181–192.

Winter, L., & Uleman, J. S. (1984). When are social judgments made? Evidence for the spontaneousness of trait inferences. *Journal of Personality and Social Psychology, 47*, 237–252.

Wyer, R. S., Jr., Budesheim, T. L., & Lambert, A. J. (1990). Cognitive representations of conversations about persons. *Journal of Personality and Social Psychology, 58*, 218–238.

Wyer, R. S., Jr., & Carlston, D. E. (1979). *Social cognition, inference and attribution*. Hillsdale, NJ: Lawrence Erlbaum Associates.

Wyer, R. S., Jr., & Carlston, D. E. (1994). The cognitive representation of persons and events. In R. S. Wyer & T. K. Srull (Eds.), *Handbook of social cognition* (2nd ed., Vol. 1, pp. 41–98). Hillsdale, NJ: Lawrence Erlbaum Associates.

Wyer, R. S., Jr., & Martin, L. L. (1986). Person memory: The role of traits, group stereotypes and specific behaviors in the cognitive representation of persons. *Journal of Personality and Social Psychology, 50,* 661–675.

Wyer, R. S., Jr., & Srull, T. K. (1989). *Memory and cognition in its social context.* Hillsdale, NJ: Lawrence Erlbaum Associates.

Young, A. W., Hay, D. C., & Ellis, A. W. (1986). Getting semantic information from familiar faces. In H. D. Ellis, M. A. Jeeves, F. Newcombe, & A. Young (Eds.), *Aspects of face processing* (pp. 123–135). Dordrecht, Netherlands: Martinus Nijhoff.

Zajonc, R. B. (1980). Feeling and thinking: Preferences need no inferences. *American Psychologist, 35,* 151–175.

Zajonc, R. B., & Markus, H. (1984). Affect and cognition: The hard interface. In C. E. Izard, J. Kagan, & R. B. Zajonc (Eds.), *Emotions, cognition, and behavior* (pp. 73–102). Cambridge, England: Cambridge University Press.

Zanna, M. P., & Rempel, J. K. (1988). Attitudes: A new look at an old concept. In D. Bar-Tal & A. Kruglanski (Eds.), *The social psychology of knowledge* (pp. 315–334). New York: Cambridge University Press.

Zarate, M. A., & Smith, E. R. (1990). Person categorization and stereotyping. *Social Cognition, 8*(2), 161–185.

2 Thinking About Things and People

Colin Martindale
University of Maine

I have elsewhere (Martindale, 1981, 1991) presented a model of general cognition similar to the one described by Carlston (chap. 1, this volume). Although most theories of person perception are based on the assumption that our knowledge about other people is stored in semantic memory, Carlston argues that it is distributed among several mental modules. This is a novel and useful idea. I have always thought of the action system solely as an output module. It makes perfect sense that it could do double duty and also serve as a memory system. It also makes sense that perceptual systems are not solely input modules. The massive amount of evidence concerning the influence of knowledge on perception is consistent with Carlston's use of perceptual systems as memory systems.

ASSOCIATIVE SYSTEMS THEORY

Carlston postulates four basic mental systems: the perceptual system, the verbal–semantic system, the affective system, and the action system. Each of these accounts for different aspects of the impression we have of another person. Because these systems are interconnected in specific ways, four secondary aspects of representation arise. For example, behavioral observations arise from an integration of perceptual appearances and behavioral responses. The interaction is shown in a metaphorical way in Carlston's Fig. 1.1.

Let us regard Fig. 1.1, for a moment, not as a metaphor, but as a picture of columns of cortex with degree of overlap indicating amount of interconnection. Note that there is no overlap between the perceptual system and the affective system, nor between the action system and the verbal system. This strikes me as unlikely. Visual appearance can certainly evoke strong affective responses ranging from love at first sight to revulsion. A touch can lead to anything from affection to anger, depending on whether it was desired. Note that, in this case, we also have to bring in the verbal–semantic module. It is in this module that a person would have stored the information as to whether he or she wanted to be touched by the person in question.

The lack of overlap between the action system and the verbal–semantic system seems unlikely as well. Personality traits (in the verbal–semantic system) are surely inferred from behavioral responses and behavioral observations (in the action system, and the overlap between the action system and the visual system). It would seem that Fig. 1.1 should be redrawn so that all four circles overlap. This would add five new areas of overlap. The central area, where all four modules overlap, can be ignored because it defeats the notion of modularity. This leaves us with four areas in which three of the four modules overlap. These could be regarded as modules in their own right, or as all three modules acting in concert. If we keep things symmetrical, there is no way to get the simple two-way overlaps that I wanted (verbal system–action system and perceptual system–affective system). Thus, the metaphor breaks down because it cannot represent connections that must certainly exist. Let us retain it for a moment, nonetheless, to see if it gives us any new insights. At first glance, it might seem that *Confusing Systems Theory* might be a good name for such a revised model. However, the mind operates in confusing ways.

At present, there is no consensus among cognitive psychologists as to the relationships among semantic memory, episodic memory, and procedural memory (what Carlston and I call the *action system*). At one extreme, some argue that these are three discrete memory stores. At the other extreme, some argue that they are one memory store accessed in three different ways. It is clear that episodic and semantic memories are intimately related. Much of our general or semantic knowledge is inferred from episodic memories. If we see a person repeatedly exhibiting certain behaviors, we infer – usually automatically – that he or she is, say, an extrovert. However, episodic memory for events that we do not understand is extremely poor.

I was initially surprised that Carlston did not include episodic memory as one of his basic mental systems. However, it emerges at the intersection of the perceptual and action systems as what he calls *behavioral observations* (see, e.g., Carlston's Fig. 1.5). This cannot be right, however. To form an episodic memory, we certainly have to perceive it. We may interpret it in terms of our own actions. Most importantly, however, we must understand it. This involves semantic memory. Thus, if we revised Fig. 1.1 so that the circles overlapped, behavioral observations should be places in the region where the perceptual, semantic, and action systems overlap—not, as in Carlston's model, in the region where only the perceptual and action systems overlap. The latter region would correspond to interpreting a set of perceived actions, but having no understanding at all of the point or meaning of the actions. This is something we seldom do.

By the same token, orientations clearly involve semantic knowledge (see the examples in Fig. 1.5). Thus, they should be moved to the area where semantic, action, and affective systems overlap. As for the overlap between only affective and action systems—where Carlston places orientations—I cannot think what, if anything, would belong there in the case of person perception. In terms of behavior, this overlap might correspond to reflex actions (e.g., screaming "gracious me" when a hammer hits one's finger rather than the nail). However, even in this case, perception, affect, and action are involved.

As for Carlston's other secondary impressional representations—categories and evaluations—it seems reasonable to leave evaluations where they are. One might consider portioning categories into several of the overlapping regions. Carlston's multidimensional scaling results indicate that categories are a mixed bag. Some (e.g., sex, race) do involve both perceptual and semantic systems. Others (e.g., introvert) are seen as personality traits. One certainly thinks of categories (e.g., Nazi) that involve the affective system. It is easy to think of categories (e.g., mugger approaching one with a knife) that involve all four of the systems: One sees him, understands the situation, feels fear, and knows the appropriate action to take.

In arguing for more interconnections among systems, I have not perturbed Carlston's system, but merely suggested that he slightly relocate some of his impressional representations. Some of the new interconnections are probably of no relevance to person perception. For example, there must be massive direct connections between semantic memory and the action system: We know the meaning or purpose of our own actions. This is of no relevance to person perception. What is relevant there—behavioral observations—is the triple interconnection among perceptual, semantic, and action systems. Furthermore, I have suggested that two overlaps—action systems-perceptual systems and action systems-affective systems—that Carlston emphasized are also irrelevant for impression formation.

When dealing with the brain, our safest assumption is that everything is connected with everything else. However, experimentation and common sense allow us to ignore, at least for the sake of simplicity, some of these connections. Consider the case of a dead cat. Depending on its state of decomposition, it will elicit affective responses in you such as sadness or revulsion: The connections from the perceptual systems to the affective system are very strong. Now consider the opposite case. If of sound mind, no matter how sad you are, you will not hallucinate a dead cat. Animistic or physiognomic perception will "color" your perceptions a bit. Thus, perception can cause affect, but affect can only influence perception: The connections from the affective to the perceptual systems are rather weak. For a first approximation, we can ignore them. By the same token, the semantic system can influence the affective system, but not vice versa. It is easy to make someone happy or sad by providing semantic information about him or herself. No degree of joy or sorrow will make a person believe that a dog has five legs, however. Thus, we can get rid of a lot of the extra overlaps among systems that I felt compelled to bring in.

THINGS AND PEOPLE

Carlston argues that Associative Systems Theory (AST) should be just as applicable to our impressions of things in general as to our impressions of people. Asch (1958) pointed out that the majority of terms used to describe psychological traits are, or were in the past, used to describe properties of natural objects. Some words have become specialized to refer only to psychological traits. Asch pointed out that the original physical referent can often be found in the etymology of such words. In other cases, one must resort to a good dictionary. To give but one example, *sad* was formerly used to describe densely packed soil and heavy metal.

Some of my own research is relevant to the question of whether we think about people and objects in similar or isomorphic ways. Martindale and Martindale (1988) tested the ancient Greek theory that there is a correspondence between the four elements and the four temperaments (i.e., melancholic–earth, sanguinic–air, choleric–fire, and phlegmatic–water). Before describing what we found, I should perhaps explain what possessed us to undertake such an experiment. It is a well-guarded secret, but the four temperaments correspond perfectly to the quadrants formed by the two most important axes—extraversion–introversion and neuroticism–stability—found in general tests of personality (Eysenck, 1967). Why should there be any relationship between elements and temperaments? Bachelard (1942/1983) made a compelling case that such a relationship exists, at least in poetry.

We selected 80 words—10 descriptive of each temperament and 10 descriptive of each element. Examples are *active*, *ambitious*, and *bossy* for choleric; and *burn*, *fire*, and *flame* for fire. Each word was printed on a card, and 36 undergraduates were asked to sort the cards into piles so that similar words were in the same pile. Element words were printed in a different color ink than temperament words. The only constraint on subjects was that each pile of cards had to contain at least one word printed in red and one word printed in black.

After testing whether subjects agreed — they did — a similarity matrix was derived from the sortings, and multidimensional scaling was done on it. The first two axes accounted for about 97% of the variance. Not only did subjects combine element and temperament words in the predicted manner at $p < .001$, but they did so in the correct way. On one axis, air–sanguinic words were opposed to earth–melancholic words; on the second axis, fire–choleric words were opposed to water–phlegmatic words. None of the subjects had the slightest idea what the experiment was about, and many said the task was difficult because they could not see much of any relationship between the element words and the temperament words. Nonetheless, their performance was close to perfect. For example, discriminant analysis of the points in multidimensional space showed 100% correct classification of air and sanguinic words.

Allport (1937) found personality trait descriptors to be organized in a circumplex surrounding two axes. He explicitly noted that the quadrants corresponded to the four temperaments. The words in Russell's (1980) circumplex model of affect seem to correspond with the four temperaments, as do the words in Wiggin's (1980) circumplex model of interpersonal behavior. To find out, we had subjects sort words from these models, as well as element and temperament words. In one experiment, we used different colors of ink with the constraint to put at least one of each of the types of words in each pile. In a second experiment, all of the words were printed in black, and there were no constraints. In both cases, results were as predicted. Surprisingly, results were much more significant when there were no constraints.

It would seem that elements, personality traits, affects, and interpersonal behaviors are all mapped on the same grid. This is at least indirectly supportive of Carlston's contention that AST may be as applicable to "rocks and stereos" (p. 29) as it is to people.

PEOPLE VERSUS THINGS

If people and things share the same memory space, one wonders if there is any trade-off. That is, the more space consumed by representations of people, the less space left for knowledge of nonsocial objects. I am reminded of the no doubt apocryphal story of the ornithologist who became headmaster of a large school. He decided that it would be polite to learn each student's name, but had to desist when he found that, for each name learned, he forgot the name of a bird.

It would seem that someone who devotes a lot of semantic memory to social representations might have less room for nonsocial concepts and vice versa. Of course, there is the confounding variable of interest. Someone who is extremely interested in socializing may be uninterested in, say, scientific concepts. Perhaps the trade-off comes at the level of interest, rather than the level of memory. Given that degree of interest in social versus other topics could be controlled, it would be interesting to see if the impressional representations of those with a lot of nonsocial knowledge are relatively impoverished.

If there is anything at all to this speculation, one would expect the impressional representations of highly creative people to be quite sketchy or impoverished. Such people feel genuine affection toward abstract concepts. Probably the most extreme example is the mathematician, Ramanujan, who had a genuine love for certain "beautiful" numbers. However, they are often cold or even cruel toward people. Recall Lord Byron expressing to his wife his heartfelt desire that she would die during childbirth. In a biographical study of a number of creative geniuses, H. Gardner (personal communication, December 13, 1991) planned to assign scores ranging from −10 to +10 as to interpersonal warmth. He found that he did not need the top half of the scale. Einstein got the highest score: zero, or completely neutral. Eysenck (1993) cited several studies reporting high correlations between creativity and psychoticism (which subsumes traits such as cold, aloof, and antisocial).

Creative people certainly tend to be less interested in other people than the average person. They are certainly more interested in nonsocial concepts than the ordinary person. Thus, they must devote more of semantic memory to nonsocial material. I know of no studies on the topic, but I would expect that the impressional representations of highly creative people are relatively undifferentiated—not because of capacity limitations, but simply because people tend to be uninteresting to them.

Carlston's model also allows us to make some predictions as to which aspects of creative people's impressional representations should be weak and strong. Given the coldness of creativity mentioned previously, we would expect affective responses to be weak. By the same token, we would expect orientations (how can I use this person?) to be well developed.

There seems to be a trade-off between semantic and episodic memory: The better one is, the worse the other is. This is the absent-minded professor syndrome. One can certainly find it in the biographies of highly creative people (Martindale, 1989). An extreme example is Sir Isaac Newton, who would occasionally leave his house in the morning having forgotten to dress. He was attending so much to concepts (semantic memory) that he did not store in episodic memory whether he had shaved, gotten dressed, and so on. Accordingly, we would expect the impressional representations of creative people to be biased toward personality traits (semantic) and away from behavioral observations (episodic).

CONCLUSION

Carlston has presented an interesting theory about person perception. In the first section, I quibbled a bit about technical details. In the second section, I offered a bit of evidence that indirectly supports his contention that AST is relevant not just to people, but to everything. The third section of my commentary may seem tangential, but it is included as indirect praise of Carlston's theory. One of the best things a good theory can do is generate new and testable hypotheses in the least expectable places.

REFERENCES

Allport, G. W. (1937). *Personality: A psychological interpretation*. New York: Holt, Rhinehart & Winston.

Asch, S. E. (1958). The metaphor: A psychological inquiry. In R. Tagiuri & L. Petrullo (Eds.), *Person perception and interpersonal behavior* (pp. 86–94). Stanford, CA: Stanford University Press.

Bachelard, G. (1983). *Water and dreams* (E. R. Farrell, Trans.). Dallas, TX: Pegasus Foundation. (Original work published 1942)

Eysenck, H. J. (1967). *The biological basis of personality*. Springfield, IL: Charles C. Thomas.

Eysenck, H. J. (1993). Creativity and personality: Suggestions for a theory. *Psychological Inquiry, 4*, 147–178.

Martindale, A. E., & Martindale, C. (1988). Metaphorical equivalence of elements and temperaments: Empirical studies of Bachelard's theory of imagination. *Journal of Personality and Social Psychology, 55*, 836–848.

Martindale, C. (1981). *Cognition and consciousness*. Homewood, IL: Dorsey.

Martindale, C. (1989). Personality, situation, and creativity. In J. A. Glover, R. R. Ronning, & C. R. Reynolds (Eds.), *Handbook of creativity* (pp. 211–232). New York: Plenum.

Martindale, C. (1991). *Cognitive psychology: A neural-network approach*. Pacific Grove, CA: Brooks/Cole.

Russell, J. A. (1980). A circumplex model of affect. *Journal of Personality and Social Psychology, 39*, 1161–1176.

Wiggins, J. S. (1980). Circumplex models of interpersonal behavior. *Review of Personality and Social Psychology, 1*, 265–294.

3

Fishing With the Right Associative Net: Appreciation and Apprehension Regarding Associated Systems Theory

Scott Van Manen
Susan T. Fiske
University of Massachusetts at Amherst

The history of science might be described as a quest for ever more inclusive theories. In this view, a theory as comprehensive as Associated Systems Theory (AST) brings the field of social cognition one step farther in its evolution. The integration of such vital and diverse fields as neuropsychology, parallel distributed processing, and social perception is an impressive achievement. The fact that AST continues past this point—to show applications in such disparate areas as self-monitoring and attitude–behavior consistency—is all the more striking.

Yet one might also think that a less abstract level is the appropriate territory of social psychology. For example, as Taylor (1981) noted, in the late 1960s, social psychology turned from the more macrotheoretical focus, such as all grander versions of consistency theory, to a more minitheoretical focus.

A third possibility is that, to some extent, the level of abstraction of a theory is determined by the phenomena it addresses. For example, we would expect a theory that addresses the antecedents of divorce to be less abstract than a general theory of cognition. Although it is doubtful that the divorce theory will explain general cognition as well as the general cognition theory, it is also doubtful that the general theory of cognition will explain divorce as well as the divorce theory.

In this sense, theories are like fishing nets: They are designed to catch, or account for, phenomena. Some nets—those loosely knit with large holes— are better for catching bigger, more complicated phenomena, but they may let the little ones get away. Conversely, the tightly knit nets catch the little phenomena, but the big ones often avoid the net completely.

Therefore, we approach AST with a mixture of appreciation and apprehension. On the one hand, we are impressed with the cathedral-like grandeur of AST, and we are excited about some of its important implications. Specifically, AST implies that target impressions need not be defined as a person node, but may instead be represented as activation across various hierarchical levels. In addition, AST implies that the range of the activation of these hierarchical levels reflects how the impression is being used. Both of these ideas have interesting applications for the field of social cognition, which we address later.

On the other hand, we suspect that, by its very comprehensiveness, AST may draw attention away from its handling of simpler psychological processes. In this sense, we may liken AST to a fishing net with large holes, perfect for catching the big, complicated phenomena, but letting some of the smaller, simpler ones get away. Therefore, we focus on such processes that may not require—and may escape—the AST net; our examples are observational learning and affective response.

We begin by briefly reviewing the tenets of AST that are most important to this discussion. AST proposes four systems: the visual (perceptual) system, the verbal system, the affective system, and the behavioral system. Each system is fully hierarchical, encompassing representations from the most concrete to the most abstract. As can be seen in Carlston's Fig. 1.1, the four overlapping cones representing the four systems resemble the four legs of a table. Each "leg" is grounded in its own basic characteristic input–output processes. For example, the basic input mechanism for the visual system may be the visual cortex. This basic mechanism, in turn, supports higher levels of representation specific to the system. Near the "surface" of the table, where the abstract levels of the systems converge, is the work space, in some ways resembling working memory, where information may pass between systems. As the figure indicates, activation on the visual cortex must be translated to a more abstract form before it can be translated to the verbal system.

In addition, the four systems differ in overall level of abstraction, so that the affective and verbal systems are more abstract than the behavioral and visual systems. Therefore, two of the legs on this table may be shorter than the other two—a point we address more fully later. The four systems also differ in the degree to which they are self-referent, so that the affective and behavioral systems are more self-referent, and the visual and verbal systems are more target referent. Finally, although AST is primarily a model of impression formation of individual targets, Carlston also shows its application to diverse areas of the field of psychology.

LEVELS AND INTENSITIES OF ACTIVATION

We propose that two concepts implied by AST potentially clarify the topics of level of representation and cognitive effort. We term these concepts *cross-level activation* and *range of activation*.

As with many other psychological theories (Cantor & Mischel, 1979; Carver & Scheier, 1981; Emmons, 1989; Epstein, 1980; Martindale, 1991; Rosch, 1978; Vallacher & Wegner, 1987), AST assumes a hierarchical structure in which representations that are more specific (and thus concrete) are organized under representations that are more general (and thus abstract). These abstract representations are organized under representations that are even more abstract. Thus, in Carlston's Fig. 1.5, we note that *somewhat helpful* and *positive affect* are subsumed under *likable*, which is subsumed, in turn, by the label *friend*. *Friend* is then subsumed under the *person node*, labeled *Ed*, which organizes all the impression information.

Although in some ways AST assumes a traditional information structure, it assumes a nontraditional *use* of this structure. As we elaborate next, social cognitive theory often uses the concept of *motion* within the schematic structure, whereas AST assumes that the individual may simultaneously spread information processing across various levels of the schematic structure. This theoretical difference in schema use has interesting implications for the understanding of cognitive effort and the action-identification theory, which is addressed in the next two sections.

Cross-Level Activation

In many social cognitive perspectives, the person node *is* the person impression. According to this view, the person node represents a summary of the information contained in the various connected feature nodes, and therefore generally enhances the efficiency of impression-formation processes. In contrast, Carlston uses the person node as a kind of shorthand in describing AST. Consistent with parallel distributed processing, in Carlston's view, "concepts are not represented by simple nodes, but rather by patterns of activation across feature nodes" (p. 23).

AST implies that this pattern of activation may involve several levels within the hierarchy—a process one might term *cross-level activation*. For example, Carlston cites literature (e.g., Damasio, 1989; Farah, 1989) indicating that, when retrieving information, people "may actually reactivate structures within the primary system that was involved in the initial perception or production of this material" (p. 5). Therefore, this kind of impression retrieval is not merely a matter of retrieving a summarized version of information about the person, but also may involve retrieval of basic information through reactivation of the actual input mechanisms. For example, when we recall what someone said on a particular occasion, we may recall the sound of the person's voice using auditory areas of the brain and envision the person's appearance by reactivating patterns in the visual cortex. Cross-level activation seems a likely part of this process. Presumably, the activation of the primary system (input mechanism) occurs in concert with activation at higher levels; otherwise, it would seem a useless exercise.

Further evidence that AST assumes cross-level activation is found in Carlston's discussion of spreading inhibition. An interesting problem is how the individual eventually settles on one member of a group of competing mental representations. For example, suppose you are trying to remember an episode in which your friend, Jean, was helpful. Presumably, you have many instances you could call into memory that fulfill your requirements, and for a moment you may review them, causing them all to be momentarily activated. Having selected one episode, perhaps the time she jump started your car, how do you manage to keep the activated, but nonselected, no-longer-needed representations from flooding into consciousness?

The concept of spreading inhibition explains this phenomenon by proposing that, once a representation is identified, alternative representations are inhibited. As Carlston notes, "Martindale (1991) suggested that concepts at one level of a system hierarchy tend to inhibit other concepts at the same level" (p. 23). If representations on the same level are inhibited, activation between levels is relatively more likely. Therefore, we may assume that, under some circumstances, activation spreads "vertically" across representations at *different* levels, and inhibition spreads "horizontally" across representations on the *same* level.

Social cognition theories often propose a different mechanism for focusing on one of many representations. Instead of cross-level activation, these theories often imply that the individual somehow moves about within the information structure, much as someone might move around a house (e.g., Vallacher & Wegner, 1987; cf. Pennebaker, 1989). As in a house, the most salient area is in the same room, and the most accessible areas are connected and close. Accordingly, the individual is at any moment at only one location in the information hierarchy, and competing representations are not a problem, being in different "rooms." However, if, we assume cross-level activation, the individual's cognitive processing need not be limited to one level at a time, so that general impressions can be activated along with specific, concrete representations.

Although the motion metaphor has been adequate in most cases, we feel that simultaneous cross-level activation more accurately represents some cognitive processes. For example, action identification theory (Vallacher & Wegner, 1987) enlists the motion metaphor when it proposes that the individual moves to a more specific level of representation in response to difficulty. In action identification, subjects' "location" (their level of representation) is indicated by their description (or identification) of their actions. Thus, someone having difficulty getting a job might report more concern with a specific aspect of the process, such as the line spacing on the resume. Attention to the more specific level may be adaptive, if in fact a problem exists on the more specific level. In contrast, someone having no difficulty might never attend to such details and thus remain focused at a more abstract level.

Clearly, focusing on more specific processes might be an adaptive response to difficulty in many situations. However, we can also imagine situations when such a shift might be counterproductive, such as when the difficulty is caused by faulty general assumptions. To return to our previous example, difficulty finding a job might indicate a poor choice of vocation (e.g., haberdasher to the Amazon basin), instead of difficulty with lower level mechanisms (e.g., line spacing on the resume). In such cases, it would be more adaptive, even intuitively predictable, for the individual to go to a higher level representation (e.g., self-doubt) in response to difficulty.

Perhaps the most adaptive response of all would be simultaneously attending to both abstract and concrete levels, thus allowing the individual to evaluate the concrete in terms of the abstract and vice versa. In our example, we can imagine the harried job applicant worrying about the specifics of the resume while simultaneously questioning the whole job-search enterprise. Under the motion metaphor, it seems odd that the individual could cognitively bilocate (i.e., move to a more concrete level and a more general level simultaneously). Vallacher (1993) explained the phenomenon of concurrent concrete-level attention and self-doubt by stating that any mismatch between level of ability and level of control causes self-consciousness. We would add that if, instead of a motion metaphor, we assume cross-level activation, we have a parsimonious explanation of how the individual may simultaneously increase attention to higher and lower levels of representation.

Range of Activation

Instances in which the individual plumbs the basic level of mental representation should provide the representation with increased detail and accuracy. Although impression retrieval may involve such thorough processes at times, it need not always do so. For example, when discussing "caricaturization," Carlston mentions "mental base touching" (p. 43), meaning that people at times retrieve incomplete representations of the target comprised of only the most salient information. Thus, according to Carlston, instances of impression processing may differ in the extent to which concrete levels of the impression are activated. We suggest that these processes differ in what we would call *range of activation*. On one occasion, a simple, caricature-like version of the impression may be retrieved; we would call this *lazy activation*. On another occasion, a more complex version, including both concrete and abstract representations, may be retrieved; we would call this *effortful activation*.

As a construct, range of activation may shed light on effortful versus noneffortful information processing. Several cognitive-motivational theories (e.g., Brewer, 1988; Chaiken, Liberman, & Eagly, 1989; Fiske & Neuberg, 1990; Petty & Cacioppo, 1986) assume that, when motivated, individuals can apply more effortful information processing, and thus increase the amount of information attended to at a given instance. For example, Fiske and Neuberg's impression-formation continuum model contains an initial step in which the target is perceived in a stereotyped form. If perceivers are motivated to expend more effort, they may then individuate the target (i.e., flesh out the impression with concrete details that accurately represent the target). Similarly, the Chaiken et al. heuristic-systematic model assumes that "systematic processing is more effortful than heuristic processing" (p. 218), and allows the individual to scrutinize a wider domain of knowledge.

Motion metaphor theories are not designed to address the problem of how information at various levels of representation can be combined and compared. Therefore, if we rely on the traditional assumption that information processing consists of cognitively moving about in hierarchical information structures, it is difficult to imagine how increased effort (more moving about) would lead to more detailed representations. Focusing on concrete details would seem to cause us to lose access to more abstract representations and vice versa.

Range of activation explains how effortful and less effortful, lazy processing may differ. Specifically, in addition to those representational levels activated in less effortful processing, effortful processes should include a broader range of representational levels. Thus, effortful thought processes tend to include more specific details by activating basic areas of the structure, as well as more abstract levels of representation. One implication of this increased range is that information that is effortfully retrieved may be remembered more accurately. Less effortful, lazy processing should use a narrower range of representational levels, with fewer concrete levels and fewer accurate details. It is specifically this effect of effort that is proposed by cognitive-motivational theorists.

AST AND SIMPLE PSYCHOLOGICAL PROCESSES

One striking feature of AST is the range of psychological phenomena it addresses. Thus far, we have focused on two useful concepts that can be deduced from AST cross-level activation and range of activation. Now we step back from this global view and focus on the implications of AST in some simple psychological processes.

As noted earlier, according to AST, all four systems are fully hierarchical and associated only at abstract levels. Therefore, information must be translated to an abstract level in order to pass from one system to another, and thus abstract representations travel shorter routes of translation into other systems than do concrete representations. These conditions of AST raise some interesting questions about simple, seemingly unmediated psychological processes. For example, how would observational learning occur in the AST model? According to AST, the first step in learning by observation would be input to the visual system. The visual information is then translated vertically into an abstract representation, eventually entering an area where the visual and action systems overlap. This overlap allows the information to be translated over to the action system. While being translated, the information becomes hybrid, taking on properties of the new (behavioral) system and retaining some of the properties of the old (visual) system. The hybrid abstract action information is then respecified (i.e., reendowed) with all the specific information needed to perform the behavior.

This seems a rather circuitous route to learning, say, how to thread a needle or throw a ball. We wonder whether AST can be applied to the phenomenon of direct imitation. For example, it is difficult to imagine what abstract information would necessarily be inferred from such simple processes. According to AST, with no abstracted information, the information cannot pass between systems. A much simpler path would be to assume a direct link between the concrete levels of the visual and action systems, with no abstract-level mediation.

We might also wonder about affective responses to visual stimuli, such as when a photograph brings us to tears. In the AST model, the visual and affective systems are distant, suggesting that such responses are largely mediated by a lengthy route of either behavioral observations to orientation to affective response, or by way of categorizations and evaluations. Either of these routes seems rather complicated for such a seemingly basic phenomenon as an emotional response. By way of explanation, AST proposes that such seemingly complicated responses may become automated (proceduralized). However, this explanation seems inadequate, given the notion that emotional responses may be easily habituated (e.g., Bersheid, 1982). For example, it is difficult to imagine how automation (proceduralization) could explain why one might cry when first rediscovering a photograph of a loved one, but not on subsequent discoveries. In fact, the automated association explanation would seem to predict that tears are more likely upon the later discovery.

The Action System as Redundant With the Self-System

We have noted that AST provides rather complicated explanations for what would seem to be basic processes. In its defense, it could be said that AST was not intended to address issues such as affective response and observational learning. Rather, it is intended to be a model of impression formation of individual targets. However, this defense seems disingenuous in context of Carlston's application of AST to a vast expanse of phenomena (e.g., the classification of nonsocial objects). Yet even if we ignore questions about these related psychological processes, AST raises difficult questions in the more central social cognitive area of the self, partially because of how the four systems are defined.

The AST action system resembles what might be termed a *self-system*. We feel that this aspect of the action system, when combined with the assumption that each system has its own output mechanism, complicates AST's taxonomy with respect to basic emotional responses to others.

AST's action system resembles a self-system at several points. First, rather than assuming that behaviors of self and others fall into the same cognitive category, AST's action system deals exclusively with *self*-behavior. Carlston states that, in AST, behaviors of others are treated as "a secondary form of representation" (p. 6). Second, the action system resembles a self-system in its various levels of abstraction. At the lowest level, the action system controls basic motor units of the individual; at the highest level, it is linked to self-concept. Third, the action system is described as being the most self-oriented and concrete of the four systems, further securing its status as a self-system.

As just mentioned, AST presents a circuitous route for the processes of observational learning and affective response. The close identification of the action system with the self-system, when combined with AST's assumption that each system has its own output mechanisms, raises even more puzzles. For example, if we believe that behaviors and emotional responses belong to two different systems, to what system do certain "covert" responses to others (e.g., increased heart rate) belong? Our intuition is that this response may be a combination of affective and behavioral responses, yet this is impossible in AST because a response can be output from only one system. Alternatively, to say that this response is part of the action system would seem to contradict its status as an emotional response at the most basic level. However, to classify it as an emotional response would seem to defy AST's premise that self-behavior is under the control of the action system.

A problem for AST seems to be one of determining where to draw the line between action output and affective output. It is difficult to classify unintentional behavioral responses, such as fidgeting when nervous, spontaneous facial expressions, and increased heart rate. Would crying in sympathy with another person's troubles be an action-system response (and thus self-referent) or an affective (and thus nonbehavioral) response?

AST's assumption that each system has its own characteristic input mechanisms (see Carlston's Fig. 1.9) is similarly troublesome. For example, "perceptual input" to the perceptual system must be distinct from "self-perception" input to the action system. This leads to the unlikely conclusion that a different system is involved in watching one's own foot step than in watching someone else's foot step.

Full Hierarchy in AST

As is by now familiar, AST indicates that each system is fully hierarchical from concrete to abstract, containing lower, middle, and upper level processes. This structure is represented in Carlston's Fig. 1.1. In addition, AST is later described as having four systems that differ in their level of abstraction.

A full hierarchy in each system is difficult to reconcile because each system differs in level of abstraction. To return to our table metaphor, AST proposes that each leg of the table spans the same distance from concrete to abstract, while at the same time proposing that the legs differ in length. None of the possible resolutions to the apparent contradiction seems plausible. For example, suppose we assume that, despite the appearance of parallel levels of abstraction depicted in Carlston's Fig. 1.1, the verbal system represents a complete hierarchy that is, overall, more abstract than the perceptual system. This implies that the most basic level of the verbal system is more abstract than the most basic level of the perceptual system. Similarly, the most abstract level of the verbal system would be more abstract than the most abstract level of the perceptual system. From this reasoning, it would seem that the verbal system lacks the most basic-level mechanisms, and the perceptual system lacks the most abstract-level mechanisms. In what sense, then, can they be fully hierarchical?

The same issue can be raised when comparing the action system to the affective system. It would seem that the action system, being less overall abstract, might lack a most abstract level. Yet elsewhere, the most abstract level of the action system is described as linked to the self-concept. In what sense does this lack a most abstract level?

We might also note that neurological evidence for a basic verbal system is scant. A major problem here is that all verbal areas of the brain are association areas that function to combine information from other regions of the brain. This would seem to indicate that the verbal system does not possess its own specialized input mechanisms, and therefore is not fully hierarchical.

Translation of Representations Between Systems

The AST model proposes that all systems may interact by overlapping at abstract levels. As mentioned previously, some translations between systems are easier to imagine than others. For example, the translation from the abstract area of the verbal system to the concrete level of the visual system seems counterintuitive. In support of the claim that this translation can occur, Carlston cites Wilson's (1968) research showing that persons of high academic status are perceived as being taller. We would expect that the relatively concrete verbal representation, shown by the word *tall*, might more readily activate a specific visual representation than would the more abstract verbal representation shown by the words *high academic status*. Interestingly, AST makes the opposite prediction.

To understand why AST makes this prediction, we must recall that, according to AST, abstract representations travel shorter routes of translation into other systems than do concrete representations. Therefore, the verbal representation *high academic status*, being more abstract than the verbal representation *tall*, should be more easily translated into a concrete visual representation. To be translated into a concrete visual representation, *high academic status* would be first translated into abstract visual information, and then vertically down the visual system into more concrete visual representations. In comparison, a relatively concrete verbal representation such as *tall* must first be translated upward in the verbal system into more abstract representations. Only then can it be translated into an abstract visual representation, and continue down the visual system to the concrete level.

Other issues arise when we consider AST from a neuropsychological perspective. Overall, the evidence from neuropsychology supporting AST is impressive. Carlston describes neural pathways from the visual to verbal systems, visual to action systems, and verbal to action systems, and he suggests a pathway from the affect to action systems. Unfortunately, the pathways in the opposite direction have yet to be described, although according to AST they exist. We cannot assume that simply because a pathway leads in one direction, the same path also flows in the opposite direction. For example, neurological evidence of a pathway from the action to the visual system would lend further credence to AST's proposal that information translates between all adjacent systems at the abstract level.

To summarize, four arguments mitigate against the model that all four systems are fully hierarchical and associated only at abstract levels. First, contradictions arise from the close association of the action system with the self-system. Second, certain predictions made by AST for translations between systems seem unlikely. Third, proposing that all four systems are fully hierarchical apparently contradicts the proposal that they differ in their level of abstraction. Fourth, there is a lack of neuropsychological evidence for all but the intuitively likely neurological pathways proposed by AST.

CONCLUSION

AST makes an unarguably important contribution to social cognition theory. It provides a much needed example of how parallel distributed processing and neuropsychology have implications that we ignore to our own detriment. We have focused on two interesting implications of AST — cross-level activation and range of activation — and have mentioned areas where these concepts might apply. In addition, we have noted that, although impressive, AST raises some difficult questions and predicts some seemingly unlikely cognitive processes. Even so, AST illuminates a truly promising and exciting direction for the development of social cognition. We hope that pointing out some of these questions serves to further psychology's development in this direction.

We have likened psychological theories to fishing nets designed to "catch" phenomena. Fishing in the stream of thoughts and their processes, we psychologists often design our nets to catch the phenomena that interest us most. When our goal is to catch the large, complicated phenomena, we may risk letting the small ones get away. In our view, AST runs this risk.

ACKNOWLEDGMENTS

This work was partially supported by NIMH grant 41801 to Susan Fiske. Thanks to Karen-Jo Van Manen and Eric Coats for reviewing earlier versions of this manuscript.

REFERENCES

Bersheid, E. (1982). Attraction and emotion in interpersonal relationships. In M. S. Clark & S. T. Fiske (Eds.), *Affect and cognition: The 17th annual Carnegie Symposium on Cognition* (pp. 37–54). Hillsdale, NJ: Lawrence Erlbaum Associates.

Brewer, M. B. (1988). A dual process model of impression formation. *Advances in Social Cognition, 1,* 988–1001.

Cantor, N., & Mischel, W. (1979). Prototypes in person perception. In L. Berkowitz (Ed.), *Advances in experimental social psychology* (Vol. 12, pp. 3–52). New York: Academic Press.

Carver, C. S., & Scheier, M. F. (1981). *Attention and self-regulation: A control theory approach to human behavior.* New York: Springer-Verlag.

Chaiken, S., Liberman, A., & Eagly, A. H. (1989). Heuristic and systematic information processing within and beyond the persuasion context. In J. S. Uleman & J. A. Bargh (Eds.), *Unintended thought* (pp. 212–252). New York: Guilford.

Damasio, A. R. (1989). The brain binds entities and events by multiregional activation from convergence zones. *Neural Computation, 1,* 123–132.

Emmons, R. A. (1989). The personal striving approach to personality. In L. A. Pervin (Ed.), *Goal concepts in personality and social psychology* (pp. 87–126). Hillsdale, NJ: Lawrence Erlbaum Associates.

Epstein, S. (1980). The self-concept: A review and the proposal of an integrated theory of personality. In E. Staub (Ed.), *Personality: Basic issues and current research* (pp. 220–247). Englewood Cliffs, NJ: Prentice-Hall.

Farah, M. J. (1989). Is visual imagery really visual? Overlooked evidence from neuropsychology. *Psychological Review, 95*, 307–317.

Fiske S. T., & Neuberg, S. L. (1990). A continuum of impression formation, from category-based to individuating processes: Influences of information and motivation on attention and interpretation. In M. P. Zanna (Ed.), *Advances in experimental social psychology* (Vol. 23, pp. 1–74). New York: Academic Press.

Martindale, C. (1991). *Cognitive psychology: A neural-network approach*. Pacific Grove, CA: Brooks/Cole.

Pennebaker, J. W. (1989). Stream of consciousness and stress: Levels of thinking. In J. S. Uleman & J. A. Bargh (Eds.), *Unintended thought* (pp. 327–350). New York: Guilford.

Petty, R. E., & Cacioppo, J. T. (1986). The elaboration likelihood model of persuasion. *Advances in Experimental Social Psychology, 19*, 123–205.

Rosch, E. (1978). Principles of categorization. In E. Rosch & B. B. Lloyd (Eds.), *Cognition and categorization* (pp. 27–48). Hillsdale, NJ: Lawrence Erlbaum Associates.

Taylor, S. E. (1981). The interface of cognitive and social psychology. In J. Harvey (Ed.), *Cognition, social behavior, and the environment* (pp. 189–211). Hillsdale, NJ: Lawrence Erlbaum Associates.

Vallacher, R. R. (1993). Mental calibration: Forging a working relationship between mind and action. In D. M. Wegner & J. W. Pennebaker (Eds.), *Handbook of mental control* (pp. 443–472). Englewood Cliffs, NJ: Prentice-Hall.

Vallacher, R. R., & Wegner, D. M. (1987). What do people think they are doing? Action identification and human behavior. *Psychological Review, 94*, 3–15.

Wilson, T. D. (1968). Perceptual distortion of height as a function of ascribed academic status. *Journal of Social Psychology, 74*, 97–102.

4 Some Ruminations About Associated Systems

Robert S. Wyer, Jr.
University of Illinois at Urbana-Champaign

The understanding of person-impression formation that has evolved from research in social cognition has generally been limited to the processing of verbal information, largely consisting of trait descriptions, social categorizations, or general characteristics of behavior (cf. Asch, 1946; Fiske & Neuberg, 1990; Higgins & Bargh, 1987; Srull & Wyer, 1989). For this reason alone, the Associated Systems Theory (AST) proposed by Carlston (chap. 1, this volume), which explicitly takes into account the role of visually coded information, affective reactions, and even one's own behavior toward the target of an impression, is an important advance. As one of Carlston's long-time collaborators and associates (cf. Hastie et al., 1980; Wyer & Carlston, 1979, 1994), I have never ceased to admire his willingness to cross traditional conceptual and empirical boundaries in the pursuit of new and fruitful ways to examine social phenomena, and this admiration is clearly maintained by the formulation presented in chapter 1. The development of this formulation is obviously an ambitious undertaking, and his success to date is impressive.

In this regard, Carlston readily acknowledges that the conceptualization outlined in his chapter does not purport to be a complete account of social information processing in general, or, for that matter, person-impression formation in particular. Rather, it must be viewed as preliminary to a rigorous and extensive treatment of impression-directed information processing. Even in its present form, however, Carlston views his model as an "explanatory and heuristic theory rather than as simply an integrative scheme" (p. 3). The model appears to attain this objective. On the one hand, the theory is unique in its potential to touch bases with the physiology of the

99

human system, and to address a number of much more general social-judgment phenomena that are not usually conceptualized within a single theoretical framework. On the other hand, several intriguing implications of the formulation are identified that are well worth examining empirically. To criticize the present theory simply because it does not fulfill all of the requirements of a full-blown theoretical model, therefore, seems unfair. Rather, to the extent that criticisms are warranted at all, they should be viewed as constructive efforts to identify avenues in which future conceptual work might profitably be done in order to permit the formulation to realize its potential.

To this end, I have attempted to look more closely at the present model's attainment of three objectives that most general theories should fulfill. First, does the theory in its present form have explanatory power and predictive utility? Second, does the theory provide an a priori account of already established phenomena that have been identified in research in the domain to which it is directly applied (i.e., the mental representation of person impressions), and does it subsume the existing theoretical models that have been applied to these phenomena? Third, do existing models account for the phenomena postulated by the theory in perhaps more parsimonious and intuitively plausible ways?

EXPLANATORY POWER AND PREDICTIVE UTILITY

The two primary objectives of a theory of social information processing, like any theory, are explanation and prediction. These objectives are obviously interrelated. However, the criteria for evaluating a theory's attainment of each objective can differ. The explanatory power of a theory lies in its ability to account for empirically observed phenomena (not necessarily predicted) in terms of specifiable a priori assumptions and, at the same time, to exclude other possible explanations of the phenomena. The theory of memory developed by Raaijmakers and Shiffrin (1981) provides a good example of such a theory. This model permits numerous empirical phenomena to be localized in specific parameters of the model, each of which is tied to a specific processing assumption. Thus, the model can differentiate among a number of alternative psychological explanations of the phenomena that might be considered viable on a priori grounds.

A theory can often be conveyed in terms of a set of premises from which, in various combinations, a number of empirically verifiable conclusions can be logically derived. To the extent that these premises can be specified, empirical observations that are consistent with their implications demonstrate the model's predictive utility. More important, observations that are inconsistent with a logically derived conclusion imply that at least one of the premises that were used to derive the conclusion is invalid. Consequently, such observations typically stimulate a revision of the premises to account for the observed phenomenon while retaining the model's ability to address other, previously identified phenomena. This revision often permits new empirically testable conclusions to be generated. Thus, theory development is an ongoing process in which, at any given stage, the theory cannot only account for all of the observed phenomena that fall within its range of applicability, but can generate a priori hypotheses about new phenomena that have not yet been discovered.

For this theory building to occur, however, the theory must be sufficiently well specified that hypotheses can be logically derived on the basis of clearly stated a priori assumptions. Unless this is done, the theory may be unfalsifiable. Moreover, as Harris (1976) pointed out several years ago, in an analysis of several well-known theories of social psychology, the failure to specify precisely a theory's assumptions can create the illusion that the theory can account for phenomena that actually cannot be derived from it at all.

Although it is premature at the present stage of AST's development to expect this level of precision, this is obviously a goal that it must ultimately attain. In an effort to establish its logical coherence, I attempted to identify a set of premises that would permit the generation of predictions outlined in the chapter. However, I found myself unable to do so. This failure could reflect my own inadequacies and not the model's. Be that as it may, the exercise called my attention to two general problems that may be worth mentioning.

Definitions of the Representational Forms

Carlston postulates four different mental systems, which he denotes as visual/sensory, verbal, action, and affective. Each system presumably operates on a different type of stimulus input, and these operations generate different representational forms (visual appearance, traits and categories, observed behaviors, evaluations, affective reactions, etc.). These forms, in combination, provide the ingredients of a person impression. More than one system can be involved in the production of a given form or representation (see Carlston's Fig. 1.2), and the theory specifies the systems that are implicated in each case.

It is certainly reasonable to postulate different mental codes for representing visual information, verbal information, affective reactions, and the behavior that one personally generates in response to a stimulus. Nevertheless, the distinction between these codes, and the nature of the mental systems that theoretically give rise to them, are not as clear as they appear to be on first consideration. Although ambiguities surround all four mental systems and the forms they generate, the action and affective systems provide examples.

Action System. This system is implicated both in "behavior responses" and "behavioral observations" (see Carlston's Fig. 1.2). Behavioral responses are apparently mental representations of one's *own* actions toward the target of one's impression, whereas behavioral observations are representations of the target's actions. The nature of the action system that might be involved in the construction of these two representational forms is not clear to me. On the one hand, the action system appears to function as a behavior-generating device. However, such a device would be irrelevant to the coding of *another's* observed behavior. On the other hand, the action system could be viewed as an interpretative device that codes both observations of the target's behavior and one's own behavior toward the target in a common mental "language." The nature of this language, however, is not specified. If the language is proprioceptive, it would apply to one's own behavior but not to another's. Another possibility is that the language is sensory. Thus, the representation formed of an interaction with a student might consist, in part, of a visually and auditorially coded observation of his telling me that he passed his qualifying examinations and, in part, of the "observation" of my own behavior of patting him on the back. If this is so, however, the action system is not clearly different from the sensory system, which presumably encodes sensory information independently of whether it pertains to behavior or to other types of stimulus input (e.g., physical appearance).

A third possibility is that the action system makes use of several different visual, auditory, and proprioceptive codes in representing behavior, depending on which type of input is involved (e.g., visual input from a behavioral observation, auditory input from another's verbal utterance or one's own, proprioceptive feedback from one's own behavior, etc.). However, this assumption leads to confusion as to how one's interaction with a target person might be represented. Such an interaction presumably consists of a series of behaviors between the target and oneself. It seems unlikely that the different aspects of the interaction are independently coded by the sensory and action systems, with those aspects that fall within the purview of each system being stored independently in areas of the sort depicted in Carlston's Fig. 1.2. (If this were the case, the way in which temporal sequences of actions that occur in the interaction are reconstructed would be hard to conceptualize.) It makes more sense to assume that sequences of interactive behaviors are coded in similar terms, and in a way that permits the sequence of actions performed by both parties to be preserved. But if so, what type of mental code is used, and which system is responsible for it?

This ambiguity might be resolved by conceptualizing the action system as composed of a number of different systems, each of which operates on a different type of stimulus information, but as having the capacity to assign a common mental code of the information that is independent of the modality in which it received. This assumption, however, would seem to compromise the postulate that the action system, or the type of representation generated by it, is distinct from the verbal or sensory systems. There would clearly not be much correspondence between these mental systems and the type of stimulus material on which they operate. If this is so, the value of postulating the systems seems limited.

The recognition by AST that one's representation of another's behavior can also include a coding of one's own behavior as either a determinant, consequence, or correlate is nonetheless an attractive feature. The inclusion of one's own behavior in the representation of an interaction with another is consistent with Tulving's (1993) conception of episodic memory, and also permits the model to touch bases with self-perception theory (Bem, 1972). It is important to recognize that the construal of the implications of one's behavior toward a person for one's impression of this person (e.g., the inference that one likes a person, based on awareness that one has complimented the person during an interaction with him or her) requires a higher order inference that is likely to implicate the verbal system. Of course, this inference might not be made unless it is necessary to make a judgment or attain other specific processing objectives. Nonetheless, the potential of the theory to take these possibilities into account is noteworthy.

Affective System. People obviously have affective reactions to a person, and these reactions are undoubtedly used as information in conceptualizing one's liking for the person (Clore, Schwarz, & Conway, 1994; Griffitt & Veitch, 1971; Schwarz & Clore, 1988). However, as in the case of the action system, it is unclear whether this system is conceptualized as an affect-generating device, as an encoding mechanism that transforms the affective reactions one experiences into a mental representation of the target, or both. For related reasons, it is unclear whether the "affective response" that is contained in a person representation is a mental coding of a previous affective reaction that was elicited by a target person at some earlier time, or a coding of a new reaction to previously acquired knowledge about the person that occurs at the time the knowledge is retrieved from memory. This distinction seems important. At this writing, I personally experience only a weak negative reaction to the name *Ronald Reagan*. However, I distinctly recall having had a very strong reaction to the name when I encountered it during the early 1980s. The initial physical reaction has dissipated over time, but the memory of its intensity is retained. In terms of Carlston's formulation, it is not clear to me how this is conceptualized. That is, which constitutes the affective response that composes my impression of Reagan: the encoding of my earlier affective reaction to him, the encoding of my present reaction, or both?

An additional ambiguity is related. That is, it seems likely that affective reactions are often conditioned responses to features of any or all of the other seven representational forms that compose the target impression (vision images, traits, behavioral observations, etc.). To this extent, the reactions are likely to be elicited spontaneously in the course of retrieving them from memory. (For evidence that affective reactions can be activated by virtually all previously formed concepts, see Bargh, Chaiken, Govender, & Pratto, 1992.) Thus, these affective responses, if not the mental representations of them, are likely to be associated with any or all other representational forms. Carlston acknowledges this possibility in discussing the associative linkages among representations (see Fig. 1.5). However, he nevertheless hypothesizes (p. 24) that associations are relatively stronger between representational forms that are physically proximate in the system (see Carlston's Fig. 1.2). To the extent that affective reactions are conditioned responses to visual images, categories, or observed behaviors, this seems unlikely to be true.

Interrelatedness of Representational Forms

The identification of the eight representational forms that underlie person-impression formation, and the assumption that different systems govern the processing of information in these forms, seems quite reasonable. Certainly these representational forms exist. Moreover, an experience with a target person is likely to implicate several of these systems simultaneously. That is, we interact with a target person in a social situation in which we obtain information about the person's visual appearance, his or her verbal statements and nonverbal behavior, one's affective reactions to this behavior, and one's own behavioral responses to those of the target. If we have several different experiences with the target person at different points in time, these systems are presumably implicated each time. This possibility raises a further consideration, however. Assuming that the representational forms exist, the features that compose any given experience with a target person could be stored in memory in two general ways.

First, Carlston assumes that the eight representational forms that are generated by the mental systems he postulates are stored in memory at different general locations that are reserved for these particular forms. Thus, the features of any given experience might be represented at different locations, along with associative pathways that connect the features encoded in one form to those encoded in a second (p. 24 and Fig. 1.5). As each additional experience with a target person occurs, this process is repeated, and so the representations of each form accumulate. As noted earlier,

Carlston postulates that representations of a particular form are, on the average, more closely associated with one another than with representations of a different form (p. 24). Thus, for example, the representation of a woman's visual appearance at one point in time would, in general, be more closely associated with a representation of her appearance at a different time than with an encoding of one's affective responses to the person, or of one's overt behavior toward her, at the time the information was obtained. In other words, knowledge is organized in memory according to representational form, rather than according to the situation or experience in which the knowledge was acquired.

The second, alternative possibility, of course, is that the four different mental systems performed by Carlston operate simultaneously on the array of stimulus information that composes a given encounter with the target person, and that the product of these operations is a single representation of the experience in which all forms are meaningfully integrated. This representation is then stored in memory as a configural unit of knowledge independently of the representations that have been formed of other experiences. Thus, I may have a visually and verbally coded memory of Carlston discussing attribution phenomena with me in my office one afternoon during his graduate school years at Illinois, along with my feelings of awe and my spontaneous categorization of him as "brilliant." This memory, which includes all representational forms in a spatially and temporally organized fashion, may be stored in memory as a unit, independently of a representation that was formed several years later that describes his interactions with my children in the park on a sunny day in Germany. It seems intuitively clear that the features that compose each recalled experience, although in different forms, are all much more closely associated with one another than they are with the similar forms that compose the other experience.

Of course, a representation that has been stored in one form can be retrieved from memory later in the course of pursuing a particular objective, and can be operated on in a way that generates additional representational forms (e.g., trait encoding, evaluations, categorization, etc.). These new forms, separately or in combination, might be stored in memory independently of the representations that were used to generate them. To this extent, the more recently formed representations come to be retrieved and used in the future without the need to access the earlier ones. These observations are consistent with Carlston's assumption that the forms of representation generated by the verbal system can be stored separately from other forms. However, this independence is the consequence of particular information-processing goals that require the construction of such verbally coded representations, and is not inherent in the relationships among the mental systems themselves.

The relative merits of these two alternative conceptualizations are not fully explored by Carlston in chapter 1, and the empirical evidence bearing on them is not known to me. If such evidence is in fact unavailable, it may be worth obtaining in future research on the theory.

THE NEED FOR PROCESSING ASSUMPTIONS

The second question I address here concerns the ability of AST to account for memory phenomena that have already been identified in impression-formation research. Before embarking on this discussion, a few more general observations are in order.

At the present early stage of his theorizing, Carlston chose to focus on the content and structure of person representations, rather than the processes whereby these representations are constructed. It seems unlikely that all representational forms of the sort that Carlston postulates are constructed automatically, simply as a result of exposure to the stimulus material on which the four primary mental systems operate. Nor are these forms automatically retrieved at the time one wishes to make an impression-relevant judgment or behavioral decision. However, without specifying the cognitive processes that govern the encoding, organization, storage, and retrieval of stimulus information, and without circumscribing the conditions in which these operations are performed, a conceptualization of the mental representation of the information is of limited utility.

The distinction between structure and process is of course sometimes illusory. As Anderson (1978) pointed out several years ago, a model that assumes the formation of different situation-specific mental representations and a single retrieval process can often be translated into a mathematically equivalent model that assumes a single mental representation, but different situation-specific retrieval mechanisms. Be that as it may, a model of mental representation that does not make some explicit processing assumptions is limited in the predictions it can generate.

In presenting his formulation, Carlston employs an associative-network metaphor and postulates that both spreading-activation and spreading-inhibition mechanisms govern the accessibility of the various representational forms he postulates. As some of his own research (e.g., Carlston & Skowronski, 1986) testifies, this metaphor is very useful in accounting for several of the phenomena that AST addresses. However, the metaphor seems unlikely to be sufficient to account for a wide range of other impression-formation phenomena. To provide such an account, the cognitive operations that are involved at different stages of processing (encoding, organization, storage, retrieval, inference, etc.) must be explicated.

In this regard, impression formation is often a conscious, goal-directed cognitive activity, and the representations that are formed are likely to differ when subjects have this goal than when they have other objectives in mind (Hamilton, Katz, & Leirer, 1980; Hastie & Kumar, 1979; Srull, 1981; Wyer & Gordon, 1982). The cognitive operations that are involved in impression formation are likely to require the coding of some representational forms in terms of others. For example, one may need to construe the implications of one's affective reactions to a target for one's evaluation of the target, or to identify the implications of either one's own behavior toward the target, or the target's own behavior, for the target's traits. These processes are unlikely to occur automatically in the absence of an impression-formation goal, and may sometimes not even occur when such a goal exists. The conditions in which the processes occur, and the factors that govern them, must ultimately be specified.

In AST, this is apparently done by postulating a set of productions or procedures (cf. Anderson, 1983; Smith, 1990) that are used to transform one representational form into another, and presumably to generate additional cognitions or overt responses. The ability of AST to account for the wide range of phenomena to which Carlston has applied it requires an a priori specification of these procedures. It is undoubtedly premature to demand this of the theory at its present stage of development. However, it seems reasonable to expect a new theory of person impression formation either to incorporate the processes postulated by previous models or to explain for the same phenomena implied by these models in different ways. This is particularly true with respect to the construction and use of the mental representational forms to which the model directly applies.

It is unclear to me, however, that the present conceptualization fulfills this expectation. That is, a number of memory phenomena observed in previous impression-formation research, and implied by more circumscribed theories of person memory and judgment, appear to be outside the range of those for which the present model has clear implications. It is conceivable that, with additional assumptions about the representational processes involved, this shortcoming can be eliminated. However, given that the model purports to be a theory of mental representation, I found this deficiency a bit disconcerting. Some of our recent work provides examples of the phenomena that need to be explained.

In much laboratory research on person impression formation, subjects receive trait and behavioral information about a target person (e.g., Hastie & Kumar, 1979; Srull & Wyer, 1989). In these conditions, subjects often have better recall of behaviors that are inconsistent with an initial evaluative concept they have formed of the person. However, when subjects are given adequate time to think about the information they have received (either as it is presented or subsequently), they have relatively better recall of behaviors that are consistent with their initial concept (Wyer & Martin,

1986; see also Srull & Wyer, 1989). The person memory model postulated by Srull and Wyer (1989) accounts for these effects in terms of cognitive processes similar to those postulated by Abelson (1959) to underlie the resolution of belief dilemmas. Specifically, subjects first attempt to understand why the inconsistent behaviors occurred, and the cognitive activity involved in this *inconsistentency resolution* gives these behaviors an initial recall advantage. Given more time, however, subjects engage in *bolstering* (i.e., they review behaviors that are consistent with their concept of the person in an attempt to confirm its validity). When this activity is performed, it can increase the recall of the consistent behaviors to a level that exceeds the recall of inconsistent ones.

However, different results occur when behavioral information about a target person is of a different type or is conveyed in a different context. For example, the inconsistency resolution and bolstering processes assumed by the Srull and Wyer model predominate only when the behaviors performed by the target are of little personal or social relevance (e.g., "read bedtime stories to neighbors' children," "failed a driver's license examination three times," etc.). Different cognitive processes are elicited by behaviors that have implications for social issues and whose desirability is controversial (e.g., "picketed an abortion clinic"). Wänke and Wyer (1994) found that when a target person is described as having performed the latter type of behaviors, subjects have better recall of those they personally consider to be undesirable, or reflect opinions with which they personally disagree, independently of the behaviors' consistency with subjects' initial trait-based concept of the actor. Apparently, subjects think about socially relevant behaviors with reference to their general world knowledge about the issues to which the behaviors pertain, rather than their specific knowledge about the target person.

As Wyer and Gruenfeld (1994, in press) noted, behavioral information that is conveyed in a conversational context may be thought about in terms of its pragmatic implications (i.e., why the speaker conveyed the information), rather than its literal implications for the traits of the behaver. Thus, as reported by Wyer, Budesheim, Lambert, and Swan (1994), a speaker's descriptions of a person's behavior in the presence of this person are thought about more extensively (and, therefore, are better recalled later) if the behaviors described are undesirable and, therefore, mentioning them violates a conversational norm to be polite. In contrast, a person's descriptions of his or her own behavior are thought about more extensively (and thus are better recalled) if they are favorable, and consequently violate a norm to appear modest.

More generally, subjects who listen to a conversation about a person typically focus their attention on the speakers, forming impressions of them on the basis of what they say about the person they are discussing (e.g., a speaker who describes the target in favorable terms is inferred to be likable, whereas a speaker who disparages the target is judged to be dislikable). The behaviors the speakers mention are then thought about with reference to these speaker-based concepts in an attempt to confirm the concepts' validity (Wyer, Budesheim, & Lambert, 1990). These findings provide further support for the conclusion that people who receive information about a person in a conversational context are inclined to construe the pragmatic implications of the information rather than its literal implications for the person to whom it refers.

The findings summarized previously have typically been conceptualized in terms of the model of person memory and judgment proposed by Srull and Wyer (1989). This model makes explicit assumptions about the cognitive activities that occur in the course of forming a person impression on the basis of verbal information, and the effects of these activities on the content and structure of the representation that is formed. It makes equally explicit assumptions about the processes of extracting information from the representations at the time of recall. Based on these latter assumptions, the amount, type, and order of the recalled information can be used to infer the structure of the representation that was actually formed from the information and the cognitive processes that were likely to have produced it. Thus, although the results reported by Wänke and Wyer (1994) and obtained when information was conveyed in a conversational context were not predicted by the encoding assumptions of the original model (Srull & Wyer, 1989; Wyer & Srull, 1989), their implications for the representations that were actually formed and the processes that governed their construction could nevertheless be conceptualized by applying the model's retrieval assumptions (for more detailed discussion of these representations, see Wyer, Lambert, Budesheim, & Gruenfeld, 1992).

The research summarized earlier does not invalidate any of the assumptions that underlie AST. Carlston's theory makes salient the fact that this research was conducted in a limited paradigm. Impression formation in natural situations is often based, in part, on visual and affective information, as well as verbal information, and it is likely to produce mental representations that differ radically from any of those to which existing models of person-impression formation pertain (for further discussion of these differences, see Wyer, Swan, & Gruenfeld, in press). However, the examples serve to point out that in order to provide a conceptual understanding of the content and structure of the representations that underlie person-impression formation, AST must ultimately state much more precisely the mental processes that govern the construction and use of these representations than it does at its present stage of development.

ALTERNATIVE CONCEPTUALIZATIONS

AST calls attention to numerous theoretical and empirical issues that have not been identified previously in impression-formation research. Nevertheless, it seems appropriate to consider its conceptual value in relation to that of other formations that have been proposed. Some of these conceptualizations, notably by Brewer, Fiske, and others, are discussed elsewhere in this volume. An additional model of social information processing, with which I am more familiar, is the "bin" conceptualization proposed by Wyer and Srull (1986, 1989). In its most recent version, this conceptualization purports to specify not only the general structure of social memory, but also the cognitive principles that govern the storage of information in memory and its later retrieval and use in making judgments and decisions. The model provides for the processing of different types of information, and for the construction of different types of representations from this information, depending on the processing objectives that exist. Thus, it would seem to account, in principle, for many of the phenomena identified by Carlston while avoiding some of the ambiguities noted earlier.

Although the "bin" model is noted by Carlston in chapter 1, certain aspects of the formulation may be worth reiterating in the present context. According to the model, permanent memory consists of a number of different "storage bins." Each bin contains units of knowledge (representations) that pertain to a given referent (e.g., a particular person or event). The bin is identified by a "header," which is composed of a set of verbal or nonverbal features that define the referent and circumscribe the bin's contents. These features can include name of the referent, trait or social categories that have been frequently associated with the referent, and a nonverbal representation of the referent's physical appearance. The bin contains a number of different mental representations, the content and structure of which depend on the type of information on which they are based and the processing goals that gave rise to their construction. In the case of a person, for example, one representation might include a verbal or nonverbal encoding of the person's usual behavior in a given type of situation. Another might consist of a sequence of temporally related events depicting one's own interaction with the individual in a specific situation. The latter representation could contain both verbal and nonverbal features, thoughts one had in the course of the interaction, affective reactions that occurred, and so on. Still other representations might consist of simply a verbal coding of a single trait or evaluative judgment, or a configuration of traits and behaviors that was formed in the course of pursuing a particular objective that required its construction.

The particular content and structure of any given representation, which is formed in the pursuit of a particular processing goal, is determined by encoding and organizational operations that are specific to this goal. Thus, the verbally coded trait and behavioral representations postulated by Srull and Wyer's (1989) person memory model are presumably a result of such operations. However, other operations are likely to be applied when different types of stimulus information are presented, or when other goals exist. One implication of this conceptualization is that a given representation can potentially consist of a variety of different verbally and nonverbally coded features that are spatially, temporally, or otherwise organized in relation to one another. Thus, it could include several different representational forms of the sort postulated by Carlston. However, each representation is stored independently of others in the bin, where it can be retrieved and used to attain a particular objective that exists at some later time (e.g., making a judgment, a behavioral decision, communicating a specific experience, etc.). The retrieval processes are further specified by the model, and generally imply that the accessibility of a given representation is a function of the frequency and recency of its acquisition and use.

The Wyer and Srull model, as applied to impression formation, is also incomplete. For example, not all sequences of cognitive operations that might occur in the course of forming a person impression, and that govern the use of a representation as a basis for judgments and decisions, are clearly articulated. This is particularly true in the case of representations formed from nonverbally coded information. It appears on the surface to have many of the advantages of AST without the accompanying disadvantages. For example, it allows for the construction of representations consisting of features that are coded in different modalities, based on different types of stimulus information. However, it allows for a clearer articulation of the cognitive processes that underlie the construction of these representations, and the contingency of these processes on the type of information provided (as does Carlston's formulation) as well as the processing objectives that underlie information acquisition. In addition, it postulates the rules that guide how additional representations are constructed from earlier ones in the course of pursuing objectives that come into play subsequently. Finally, it specifies the processes that govern the relative accessibility of different representations and, therefore, the likelihood of using them to make a judgment. Thus, it can account for phenomena similar to that obtained by Carlston and Skowronski (1986).

As Carlston points out, AST is not intended to be an alternative to the Wyer and Srull model, but rather is complementary to this as well as other theories. However, the question arises as to what AST in its present form accomplishes that the Wyer and Srull model does not, and what empirical phenomena it can explain that the latter model cannot address. My guess is that several such phenomena exist, but I have not been able to identify them.

Recognition of this fact does not diminish the ultimate importance of AST as a powerful conceptual tool. The many phenomena that Carlston has already been able to conceptualize within the framework of the theory testify to its potential value. Moreover, there is little doubt that once the theory becomes more fully developed, many of the questions I have raised in this commentary will be answered and the ambiguities identified will be eliminated. Once this is done, the model will be a major conceptual advance in our understanding of impression-formation phenomena that can be applied effectively both in and out of the laboratory. I look forward eagerly to the attainment of this objective.

REFERENCES

Abelson, R. P. (1959). Models of resolution of belief dilemmas. *Journal of Conflict Resolution, 3*, 343–352.

Anderson, J. R. (1978). Arguments concerning representations for mental imagery. *Psychological Review, 85*, 249–277.

Anderson, J. R. (1983). *The architecture of cognition.* Cambridge, MA: Harvard University Press.

Asch, S. E. (1946). Forming impressions of personality. *Journal of Abnormal and Social Psychology, 46*, 1230–1240.

Bargh, J. A., Chaiken, S., Govender, R., & Pratto, F. (1992). The generality of the automatic attitude activation effect. *Journal of Personality and Social Psychology, 62*, 893–912.

Bem, D. J. (1972). Self-perception theory. In L. Berkowitz (Ed.), *Advances in experimental social psychology* (Vol. 6, pp. 1–62). New York: Academic Press.

Carlston, D. E., & Skowronski, J. J. (1986). Trait memory and behavior memory: The effects of alternative pathways on impression judgment response times. *Journal of Personality and Social Psychology, 50*, 5–13.

Clore, G. L., Schwarz, N., & Conway, M. (1994). Affective causes and consequences of social information processing. In R. S. Wyer & T. K. Srull (Eds.), *Handbook of social cognition* (2nd ed., Vol. 1, pp. 324–417). Hillsdale, NJ: Lawrence Erlbaum Associates.

Fiske, S. T., & Neuberg, S. L. (1990). A continuum model of impression formation: From category-based to individuating processes. In M. Zanna (Ed.), *Advances in experimental social psychology* (Vol. 23, pp. 1–74). San Diego, CA: Academic Press.

Griffitt, W., & Veitch, R. (1971). Hot and crowded: Influences of population density and temperature on interpersonal affective behavior. *Journal of Personality and Social Psychology, 17*, 92–98.

Hamilton, D. L., Katz, L. B., & Leirer, V. O. (1980). Cognitive representation of personality impressions: Organizational processes in first impression formation. *Journal of Personality and Social Psychology, 39*, 1050–1063.

Harris, R. J. (1976). The uncertain connection between verbal theories and research hypotheses in social psychology. *Journal of Experimental Social Psychology, 12*, 210–219.

Hastie, R., & Kumar, P. A. (1979). Person memory: Personality traits as organizing principles in memory for behavior. *Journal of Personality and Social Psychology, 37*, 25–38.

Hastie, R., Ostrom, T. M., Ebbesen, E. B., Wyer, R. S., Hamilton, D. L., & Carlston, D. E. (1980). *Person memory: The cognitive basis of social perception.* Hillsdale, NJ: Lawrence Erlbaum Associates.

Higgins, E. T., & Bargh, J. A. (1987). Social cognition and social perception. In M. R.

Rosenzweig & L. W. Porter (Eds.), *Annual review of psychology* (Vol. 38, pp. 369–425). Palo Alto, CA: Annual Reviews.

Raaijmakers, J. G. W., & Shiffrin, R. M. (1981). Search of associative memory. *Psychological Review, 88*, 93–134.

Schwarz, N., & Clore, G. L. (1988). How do I feel about it? The information function of affective states. In K. Fiedler & J. Forgas (Eds.), *Affect, cognition, and social behavior* (pp. 44–62). Toronto: Hagrefe International.

Smith, E. R. (1990). Content and process specificity in the effects of prior experiences. In T. K. Srull & R. S. Wyer (Eds.), *Advances in social cognition* (Vol. 3, pp. 1–59). Hillsdale, NJ: Lawrence Erlbaum Associates.

Srull, T. K. (1981). Person memory: Some tests of associative storage and retrieval models. *Journal of Experimental Psychology: Human Learning and Memory, 7*, 440–462.

Srull, T. K., & Wyer, R. S. (1989). Person memory and judgment. *Psychological Review, 96*, 58–83.

Tulving, E. (1983). *Elements of episodic memory.* Oxford, England: Clarendon.

Wänke, M., & Wyer, R. S. (1994). *Individual differences in person memory and impression formation: The effects of socio-political ideology and ingroup vs. outgroup membership on responses to socially relevant behavior.* Unpublished manuscript, University of Illinois, Champaign, IL.

Wyer, R. S., Budesheim, T. L., & Lambert, A. J. (1990). Person memory and judgment: The cognitive representation of informal conversations. *Journal of Personality and Social Psychology, 58*, 218–238.

Wyer, R. S., Budesheim, T. L., Lambert, A. J., & Swan, S. (1994). Person memory and judgment: Pragmatic influences on impressions formed in a social context. *Journal of Personality and Social Psychology, 66*, 254–267.

Wyer, R. S., & Carlston, D. E. (1979). *Social cognition, inference and attribution.* Hillsdale, NJ: Lawrence Erlbaum Associates.

Wyer, R. S., & Carlston, D. E. (1994). The cognitive representation of persons and events. In R. S. Wyer & T. K. Srull (Eds.), *Handbook of social cognition* (2nd ed., Vol. 1, pp. 41–98). Hillsdale, NJ: Lawrence Erlbaum Associates.

Wyer, R. S., & Gordon, S. E. (1982). The recall of information about persons and groups. *Journal of Experimental Social Psychology, 18*, 128–164.

Wyer, R. S., & Gruenfeld, D. H. (1994). Information processing in interpersonal communication. In D. E. Hewes (Ed.), *The cognitive bases of interpersonal communication* (pp. 5–47). Hillsdale, NJ: Lawrence Erlbaum Associates.

Wyer, R. S., & Gruenfeld, D. H. (in press). Information processing in social contexts. In M. P. Zanna (Ed.), *Advances in experimental social psychology.* San Diego, CA: Academic Press.

Wyer, R. S., Lambert, A. J., Budesheim, T. L., & Gruenfeld, D. H. (1992). Theory and research on person impression formation: A look to the future. In L. Martin & A. Tesser (Eds.), *The construction of social judgments* (pp. 3–36). Hillsdale, NJ: Lawrence Erlbaum Associates.

Wyer, R. S., & Martin, L. L. (1986). Person memory: The role of traits, group stereotypes and specific behaviors in the cognitive representation of persons. *Journal of Personality and Social Psychology, 50*, 661–675.

Wyer, R. S., & Srull, T. K. (1986). Human cognition in its social context. *Psychological Review, 93*, 322–359.

Wyer, R. S., & Srull, T. K. (1989). *Memory and cognition in its social context.* Hillsdale, NJ: Lawrence Erlbaum Associates.

Wyer, R. S., Swan, S., & Gruenfeld, D. H. (in press). Information processing in informal conversations. *Social Cognition.*

5 Some Metasystematic Thoughts on a Systematic Approach to Social Cognition

Klaus Fiedler
University of Heidelberg, Germany

The aim of a systems approach to social cognition is to overcome a stage of theory formation that is characterized by a number of well-established microtheories built around rather specific experimental paradigms, but a lack of an overarching macrotheory that allocates a taxonomic place and a functional role to specific models. This is an ambitious aim and, I should add, a timely one, given the current state of affairs in cognitive social psychology. Donal Carlston is among the few theorists (see also Fiske & Pavelchak, 1986; Forgas, 1992; Wyer & Srull, 1989) who have tackled this important and complex problem, and no doubt the degree of sophistication he has reached in his Associated Systems Theory (AST) approach is impressive. Expanding the original distinction of four basic systems (visual, verbal, affective, and action system), Carlston arrives at a 3 × 3 classification of the modes in which person-related information can be represented. Although AST is introduced as a bottom–up approach that starts from given phenomena and features of brain systems rather than axiomatic or normative considerations, the classifications are neatly ordered in terms of two underlying dimensions: concreteness versus abstractness and target versus self-reference. The elegance and inner consistency of AST is due to the fact that the same 3 × 3 scheme within the same two generic dimensions can be discovered at various levels of assessment: at the conceptual level of mental subsystems (Fig. 1.2), in a neurological and anatomical inquiry of brain systems and associated clinical disorder (Fig. 1.3), a corresponding taxonomy of human behaviors (Table 1.3), or the empirical level in an INDSCAL analysis of format-free verbalizations of person-related information (Carlston & Sparks, 1992). Such convergence creates a feeling of validity and an intuitive conviction that the AST taxonomy must be at the heart of system organization.

Like most readers of Carlston's chapter, I am impressed by its conceptual elegance, but I am even more stimulated to think about it seriously and critically. I believe the purpose of the *Advances* series is to invite open criticism and debate, and raising controversial issues is perhaps the best service one can do to Carlston's approach. Having appreciated the assets and heuristical value of AST, I use the remainder of this chapter to figure out the approach's problems and to delineate some debatable arguments. I first raise the question of why a systems approach is so important for theory and research. The answer to this question is then applied to an evaluation of the AST approach — to work out some problematic and neglected aspects of AST. The final and greatest part of this chapter is devoted to examples and illustrations of phenomena I believe should be covered by a future extension and refinement of the AST approach.

WHY DO WE NEED A SYSTEMS APPROACH AT THE MACROTHEORETICAL LEVEL?

Among the numerous good reasons for systematic, as opposed to piece-meal, theorizing, I want to emphasize three related points that seem to be particularly relevant to research in social cognition. The first point pertains to the incompleteness and restrictedness of traditional work within the confines of specific paradigms. What makes the specific priming, person memory, or attribution theories so unsatisfactory, despite so much supporting evidence, that we need to look for a new systems approach? One sensible answer is that causal explanations based on these theories (much like intuitive causal explanations; see Einhorn & Hogarth, 1986) specify only sufficient but not necessary conditions. This holds for virtually any theory developed in the context of psychological experimentation. There is good evidence that trait priming has the potential to produce a judgment bias (Higgins, Rholes, & Jones, 1977). Although trait priming is sufficient, it is by no means necessary. Other treatments may also suffice to produce a similar bias. Likewise, enhanced salience of a stimulus may be sufficient for enhanced memory, but it is of course not the only factor to influence memory. Thus, the notion of a "cause" that has developed in experimental psychology is one of a sufficient set of conditions; it does not exclude that alternative causes have the same effect. As a consequence, there is always uncertainty about the contribution of various alternative "causes" under natural conditions, outside the specific paradigms. For instance, trait priming can be reliably demonstrated under controlled conditions, but we never know whether trait priming is overridden by, say, factors of visual appearance when stimuli are not presented in the verbal representation mode. Therefore, a main purpose of a systems approach is to overcome this uncertainty, and to replace the multiple sufficient causes with a system that allocates each cause its place within a holistic framework.

The second part of the answer is related to the first. In order to achieve a holistic framework for multiple sufficient conditions, the systematization needs to have systemic or emergent properties that exceed the properties of its building blocks. In chemistry, for instance, the periodic system is more than a listing of all chemical elements: It has generic properties that allow for the description and explanation of chemical differences between substances. In fact, the principles underlying the periodic system could be used, historically, to predict the existence of elements that were not yet known at that time. This analogy shows that a system has to go beyond its constituents. In other words, the system should be anchored in dimensions or variables that introduce new principles and insights, as well as result from abstraction or factor analysis of the phenomena to be systematized. This important lesson was learned from MacCorquodale and Meehl's (1948) distinction of theoretical constructs and intervening variables. In this respect, it is highly unlikely that a bottom–up approach can really provide a good systematization. Instead, a theoretically useful system should be based on variables or constructs that widen the theoretical perspective and link the constituents to independent or external factors.

The third and final part of my answer is that the number of insights and innovations to be gained from a systematic model depends on the number of constraints the model introduces. If the model does not commit itself to specific restrictions to be tested and falsified, its impact will remain rather modest. A fertile systematization should not only link to external variables that create new relationships, but it should place restrictions on the empirical world.

A CRITICAL APPRAISAL OF AST AS A FERTILE METATHEORY

A major source of criticism is the AST's almost exclusive reliance on the verbal–semantic relationships between the terms used to denote the 3 × 3 subsystems. Just as the use of semantic differentials was criticized because it imposes a semantic structure on the empirical work, or just as personality research was criticized as confusing valid trait relations with semantic similarities between trait labels (Shweder, 1977), the present approach runs the danger of confusing the semantic and empirical worlds, and reifying semantic concepts as cognitive systems or brain systems. If we consider the semantic concepts used to denote the 3 × 3 modes of representation, there can be no doubt that the meanings of *visual appearance, categories,* and *personality traits* refer to some target person, whereas the meanings of *behavioral responses, orientations,* and *affective responses* refer to states or processes within the subject. Likewise, *visual appearance, behavioral observations,* and *behavioral responses* refer to concrete behaviors, whereas *personality traits, evaluations,* and *affective responses* refer to more abstract states or traits.

What evidence is available to support the claim that the conceptual elegance underlying the two-dimensional classification of these concepts is not completely reducible to a nice pattern in the semantic space? At first glance, the mapping of representational systems on a corresponding classification of brain systems and clinical disorders would appear to provide cogent evidence. But how strong and independent is this evidence? Is it not possible, and even highly plausible, that the number and multitude of brain systems only reflect the number and multitude of conceptual hypotheses guiding neuropsychological research? For any verbal label denoting a psychological system, a center or pathway can be localized in the brain. Given the existence of a concept for long- and short-term memory, visual and verbal memory, and analytical or wholistic thinking, a corresponding brain system can be identified. Indeed, I cannot think of a single concept for a subsystem that cannot be projected onto the human brain. Thus, as long as there is no compelling independent evidence from brain research and cognitive psychology, and as long as brain research is not shown to disconfirm competing systems approaches, the brain systems can be suspected to reflect the very semantic concepts that have guided brain research.

A similar point can be made with reference to the empirical analyses of format-free verbalizations that seem to support the 3 × 3 taxonomy. If the semantic relationships of the taxonomy are imposed on the coding of verbal utterances because the coders actually utilize the taxonomy to classify the verbal materials, it is no surprise that the same verbal–semantic structure will be rediscovered in multivariate analyses of the coded data. To the extent that this major criticism is justified—and AST reflects a semantic meaning structure rather than a valid structure of subsystems to be distinguished functionally and empirically—the AST approach would not fulfill the previously mentioned criteria. Such a system approach would not be anchored in extrinsic variables or constructs, would place little restrictions on the phenomena, and would not clarify the causal structure of the various subsystems. Moreover, the interpretation of AST as a bottom–up approach would not be upheld if it merely reflected the researchers' semantic structure.

It would be cynical to deny the obvious distinctions among concepts such as *visual appearance, affective responses,* and *personality traits,* and to pretend that the uncontestable contents of the taxonomy are nothing but a play with words. Of course, this is not the point I want to make here. Vision, affect, language, and the other subsystems are real and clearly distinguishable; presumably the intuitive insight into these realities gave rise to the semantic concepts. Identifying the subsystems' referentiality is one thing, but their qualification as different subsystems is a completely different thing. There is a phenomenological difference between visual and verbal representations, but the crucial question is whether vision and language constitute different subsystems governed by different rules and principles. Differentiating subsystems raises at least two problems: (a) the validity of the variables supposed to underly the systematization, and (b) the assumption of discontinuities that justify the distinction of subsystems along the underlying variables. Closer inspection of both problems leads to many obvious difficulties.

For instance, take the basic assumption of the concrete–abstract dimension, which is central to AST. *Visual appearance* and *personality traits* are modes of representation located at opposite poles of this dimension. As already mentioned, our *language feeling* justifies the assumption that traits are abstract and visual appearance is concrete. However, is there any independent evidence or meaningful scientific basis for claiming that visual perception is less abstract than personality traits? I must confess I have tremendous difficulty following this and similar assumptions. The visual perception in reading or face recognition involves a high degree of abstraction from thousands of different manifestations of the same letter or face on the retina. Surely the vertical organization of vision is often much more sophisticated than the rather simple abstraction hierarchy that characterizes the relationship between traits and behaviors. A trait like *arrogant* abstracts from a few behavioral symptoms (e.g., a spiteful sneer, a mannerism in nonverbal conduct). By comparison, the visual perception of a word in skillful adult reading may involve a more sophisticated hierarchy of graphemic, orthographic, phonemic, and semantic categories. In any case, I see no sound basis for comparing intrinsically different things such as vision and traits in terms of abstraction.

In a similar vein, it is not immediately clear why *affective responses* and *behavioral responses* should differ extremely in terms of abstractness, or in what respect *personality traits* are located in the target, whereas *affective responses* reside within the subject. At the semantic level, again, I can cooperate with this language use, but as a scientist socialized in a Popperian context I also advocate the opposite: A trait may be conceived as a projection stemming from the subject, rather than something within the target, and an affective response may be nothing but a reflection of an external affordance.

There is an implicit but obvious assumption in AST that adjacent subsystems tend to resemble each other, and interact with each other, more than distant subsystems. At the same time, it is repeatedly mentioned that subsystems merge and combine in various ways, and that every subsystem may in principle interact with every other. Although the notion of interaction and blending subsystems does not necessarily weaken the theory, it should be apparent that the need to diagnose the operation or contribution of any one subsystem is crucial. All the interesting implications developed by Carlston are contingent on the ability to assess the operation of subsystems. For instance, his speculation that incomplete tasks in one subsystem may inhibit subsequent operations can only be pursued if the status of the system can be diagnosed. More generally, diagnostic tools are essential to any test of the AST model, with its central assumption that subsystems obey different laws and the magnitude of the differences should reflect the distance relationships.

A truly Popperian treatment of the AST framework that attempts to confront the theory with uncomfortable questions would lead to many other problematic issues, of which I mention only a few. For instance, one may wonder if there is no place for an auditory code in social perception and person representation (Scherer, 1986). Or one may ask whether there is a different AST model for blind people who lack the visual subsystem. If not, the question arises whether subsystems are necessary at all for complete functioning, or whether the function of one subsystem can be compensated by another subsystem. To anticipate the presumable outcome of such an inquiry, it may turn out that individual subsystems are neither sufficient nor necessary to explain certain phenomena.

The rather serious criticism expressed herein may actually be because AST does not fully meet the requirements we have specified for a fertile systems approach. That is, the theory does not provide a cogent framework for clarifying causal relationships, it is not anchored in external principles that open new perspectives, and it does not place strong constraints on the empirical world. However, the overly skeptical picture offered in the last few paragraphs exaggerates my actual reaction toward Carlston's chapter. In fact, I did recognize some intriguing facets of the AST that may eventually constitute what I would consider a fertile approach. For example, the section on generation and transformation has considerable theoretical potential: It highlights constructive processes in person memory that are detached from the world of empirical facts. Even more important, in my opinion, is the discussion of social processes affecting impressional representations, which links the various modes of internal representation to external variables that characterize the social ecology outside the individual. A systems approach that brings cognitive variables together with an analysis of ecological conditions may lead to completely new insights and theoretical innovations.

COGNITION AND ECOLOGY: SUGGESTIONS FOR
ELABORATION

Carlston argues that ". . . people's personal and social experiences are major determinants of the *forms* of representations that compose their impressions" (p. 40). That is, the relevance and prevalence of representation modes should depend on the frequency with which individuals are exposed to different kinds of information, engage in different kinds of interactions and communications, and make different kinds of inferences. To illustrate the ecological determinants of AST, he refers to differences in information-seeking behavior (e.g., a preference for seeking abstract and self-relevant information), communication styles (e.g., a preference for communicating abstract and affective information to close acquaintances and concrete visual information to strangers), and the higher frequency of positive than negative stimuli in everyday social behavior (Skowronski & Carlston, 1989). All this is neither new nor surprising, but leads to extremely important and innovative implications about the interface of cognition and ecology: Before we can understand the nature of cognitive representations and processes, we first have to understand the texture of the social ecology. Although the same insight was already anticipated in Brunswik's (1956) and Lewin's (1951) early writings, it was largely neglected in the last 20 years of intensive social cognition research. A comprehensive and systematic approach to understanding social cognition in context must inevitably reserve a prime position for ecological factors. In my view, this point is not made explicitly and radically enough in Carlston's AST. It only suggests that the likelihood of representation modes is a function of the frequency of encountering different kinds of information. However, a genuinely ecological perspective on social cognition will reveal that the meaning and explanation of many well-known phenomena will have to be revised once the "texture of the environment" is taken into account. Once the limits of the central nervous system are exceeded, and the systems approach is no longer confined to modalities within the individual's mind, a new class of cognitive–ecological interactions is made accessible. I try now to illustrate this central point with reference to several topics from my own recent research.

Language Ecology

In a language approach to social cognition based on the coding of format-free verbalizations, Semin and I (Fiedler & Semin, 1988; Fiedler, Semin, & Koppetsch, 1991; Semin & Fiedler, 1988, 1991) developed a taxonomy and coding scheme similar to those proposed by Carlston and Sparks (1992) or Fiske and Cox (1979). The notable difference is that we started from a linguistic taxonomy of different verb and adjective classes, rather than an empirical project of content analysis. It is interesting to note that canonical analyses of our language system fit nicely into the model of Carlston's Fig. 1.3. We also found two underlying dimensions for abstractness of descriptors and their locus of reference (to subject vs. object; see Semin & Fiedler, 1991). However, in our approach, language is not only an extraneous variable affecting the likelihood of (purely internal) modes of representation, but the linguistic ecology is considered an integral part of cognitive modeling (Fiedler & Semin, 1992). Language as a system is conceived as an extraindividual store of social knowledge and mode of representation that comes to interact with internal modes of representations. On the one side of this dialectic relationship, the lexical classes and rules of language use reflect the nature of cognitive processes striving for being communicated. On the other side, however, the rules of language use and communication determine the kind of information that is likely to be conveyed in the process of social learning and exchange.

Consider, for instance, the well-known actor–observer bias in attribution (Jones & Nisbett, 1972). The tendency to attribute others' behavior to dispositional factors within the person, and to attribute one's own behavior to external situational factors, has been traditionally explained in terms of differences in cognitive perspective (i.e., perceptual perspective or knowledge differences; see Watson, 1982). The role of language was hardly ever mentioned, and I guess it would have never been mentioned in a purely intraindividual systems approach. However, an analysis of the language used to describe others' and one's own behavior reveals that other-related descriptions involve more adjectives and abstract terms, but fewer concrete predicates (descriptive action verbs, interpretive action verbs) and adverbial details than self-related descriptions. This tendency toward higher abstractness in other-related language is not confined to explanations, but generalizes to descriptions of all kinds, suggesting that the language bias is independent of and more general than the attribution bias. The language bias also generalizes to different styles of describing ingroups and outgroups (Fiedler, Semin, & Finkenauer, 1993). However, if the language used to convey information about the self and others "mimics" an actor–observer bias (i.e., more dispositional terms assigned to others than the self), then the actor–observer effect is, to an unknown degree, contaminated with properties of the (linguistic) environment.

The intention here is to illustrate that opening a cognitive systems approach to ecological factors not only explains the frequency or likelihood of certain intracognitive phenomena, but also sheds a completely new light on the explanation of the cognitive phenomena. The widened scope of such a cognitive-ecological approach might also help to explain theoretical inconsistencies and puzzles. For instance, there is an obvious incongruency between the actor–observer bias and the prediction of an egocentric bias in close relationships (Ross & Sicoly, 1979), which states that people tend to attribute more responsibility to themselves than to their partners. The cognitive process theories underlying the traditional explanations of the two biases lead to opposite predictions: The advantage of self-related memories implies self-attributions, whereas a perceptual-perspective difference predicts partner attributions. However, if language is taken into account, the inconsistency is easily resolved. A partnership study by Fiedler et al. (1991) shows that both biases are simultaneously present in free descriptions of partners and the self, albeit at different language levels. Whereas the actor–observer bias appears at the adjective level, the egocentric bias prevails at the level of interpretive action verbs. Both findings fit the general notion that self-related language is more concrete and contextualized than other-related language.

Ecological Frequency Distributions and Cognitive Inferences

The language–cognition interface constitutes but one aspect of a comprehensive systems approach that takes the ecological context of social cognition into account. Using another example from a different area of research, I show finally that many findings of biased social representations can be explained without recourse to biased or selective processing, just by considering the density and distribution of stimuli in the environment. For this purpose, I refer to a fascinating paradigm developed by Hamilton and Gifford (1976) to demonstrate illusory correlations in the intergroup context. Social ecology is often characterized by skewed distributions. Observations about majorities are, by definition, more frequent than minority-related observations. Likewise, positive information is more usual and frequent than information about negative, norm-violating behaviors. Carrying such a skewed distribution into the experimental laboratory, Hamilton and Gifford presented their subjects with a stimulus series including 18 positive behaviors of Group A, 8 negative A behaviors, 9 positive behaviors of Group B and 4 negative B behaviors. Note that Groups A and B are the majority group and minority group, respectively, and the relative proportion of positive behaviors is constant for both groups. Despite the null correlation, however, the resulting impression of the minority is less positive than the impression of the majority, as evident from frequency judgments, cued-recall memory, and evaluative group ratings.

Within a purely cognitive approach, this phenomenon was traditionally explained in terms of the enhanced distinctiveness and salience of the absolutely rarest event category (i.e., negative minority behaviors were assumed to dominate the biased representation). However, recent research (Fiedler, 1991; Smith, 1991) has shown that the same illusory correlation phenomenon can be explained without any biased processing or selective memory. Speaking loosely, the bias against the minority reflects the fact that, although both groups manifest the same proportion of positive and negative behavior, there are twice as many observations for the majority to capture this regularity than minority-related observations. Just as probability learning is a function of the number of trials, the majority affords a longer sequence of trials for learning the prevalence of positive behaviors than the minority. In other words, the "informational tension" underlying the biased cognitive representation is already inherent in the skewed distribution of information in the environment.

In a recent article (Fiedler & Armbruster, 1994), we tried to explain the informational processes at the cognitive–ecological interface. Given some minimal assumptions about human information processing (e.g., that noise or error variance prevents perfect processing), it can be shown that an increasing sample of observations tends to accentuate the cognitive representation of whatever tendency prevails in the universe. Thus, if positive behavior is relatively frequent, it will be revealed in the majority more than in the minority (provided some noise or information loss in the system). Conversely, if negativity prevails, the majority will appear more negative. Using the same principle, a number of other biases can alternatively be explained as a reflection of skewed distributions in the environment (e.g., the effect of group discussions to enhance the prevailing attitude, or the tendency to discover more discriminable aspects in ingroups than outgroups). The assumption here is that group discussions increase the sample of observations, and more observations are available on the ingroup than the outgroup (see also the computer simulations by Linville, Fisher, & Salovey, 1989).

The point may not be plausible on intuitive grounds because we know from statistics that small samples have the same expected value as larger samples drawn from the same population. Therefore, if the degree of positivity is actually the same in the minority and the majority, differential sample sizes do not appear to account for biased outcomes. However, computer simulations, as well as formal reasoning, can be employed to demonstrate the manner in which a skewed environment generates biases and illusions. The principle is best explained in terms of distributed representations. Most socially meaningful variables (e.g., *honesty*, *attraction*, or *attitudes*) are not accessible to direct perception, but constitute "distal" entities (Brunswik, 1956) that have to be inferred from distributed patterns of more "proximal" cues (e.g., disguised smiling, pitch of the voice, or gaze to infer honesty or veracity). Thus, the information that passes the cognitive–ecological interface is a distributed pattern, or vector, of proximal elements or cues that are only probabilistically related to the distal entities. The elements of the distributed representation can be conceived as the features that constitute the meaning and interpretation of a stimulus event. Now imagine that several observations are drawn pertaining to the same distal entity. This amounts to generating several vectors of elements that bear a constant relation of, say, $r = 0.40$ to an original vector representing the distal entity and computing an aggregate over all vectors (e.g., the sum). It is easy to demonstrate that, as the number of sampled vectors increases, the aggregate pattern will more and more resemble the pattern defining the distal entity. That is, although the the expected value of each individual element is independent of sample size, the distributed pattern of the vector aggregate is sensitive to the number of observations. Although this may appear rather complicated and academic at first sight, it is actually a rather robust theory with few problematic assumptions and numerous implications to account for many kinds of cognitive biases.

In a way, the two examples given here for a cognitive–ecological systems approach are in contrast with Carlston's AST. AST is an intrapersonal approach resulting from a subdivision of the central nervous system (CNS) basis of cognition and relying heavily on linguistic intuition. By contrast, the ecological approach depicted here is more open: It allows for representations outside the individual, and links the cognitive system to an external world obeying completely different laws and requiring a new class of theoretical concepts. It is my personal conviction that even a sophisticated approach like AST could be further improved if it were opened to take the "conversation" between cognition and ecology into account, with all its emergent qualities.

CONCLUSION

My intention in this chapter was first to highlight the importance and conceptual elegance of Carlston's AST approach, and to appreciate the pioneering work. Then I provided a serious criticism of several aspects of the model, arguing that the present form of AST is too dependent on the researcher's semantics, and only attempts to place a semantic order on different kinds of representations within the individual's CNS. To qualify as a truly fertile systems approach, I argued that the model should be opened and linked to external variables that cannot be reduced to a taxonomy of internal subsystems. Then I revealed my own preference for ecological variables as a prime candidate for such an opened systems approach. The cognitive–ecological approach that I have tried to illustrate with two examples of my own research has all the properties of a fertile systematization: It has emergent qualities and leads to completely new perspectives on old phenomena, such that the familiar "causes" from the restricted paradigmatic research have to be revised accordingly. It creates new links between internal and external variables, and it places sufficient constraints on the empirical world that strong theory tests are possible. Although I could have made a similar point for other research strategies (e.g., a systems approach to the affective–cognitive regulation of behavior), it is my personal conviction that the current research and theorizing in social cognition could profit most, and achieve the greatest progress, from a systematic modeling of the interplay between cognitive processes and their ecological context.

REFERENCES

Brunswik, E. (1956). *Perception and the representative design of psychological experiments.* Berkeley, CA: University of California Press.

Carlston, D. E., & Sparks, C. (1992). *A theory-based approach to the analysis of free descriptions of people.* Paper presented at the meetings of the Midwestern Psychological Association, Chicago, IL.

Einhorn, H. J., & Hogarth, R. M. (1986). Judging probable cause. *Psychological Bulletin, 99,* 3–19.

Fiedler, K. (1991). The tricky nature of skewed frequency tables: An information loss approach to distinctiveness-based illusory correlations. *Journal of Personality and Social Psychology, 60,* 24–36.

Fiedler, K., & Armbruster, T. (1994). *Judgment biases and the distribution of information in the environment: Illustrations and simplistic computer simulations.* Manuscript submitted for publication.

Fiedler, K., & Semin, G. R. (1988). On the causal information conveyed by different interpersonal verbs: The role of implicit sentence context. *Social Cognition, 6,* 21–39.

Fiedler, K., & Semin, G. R. (1992). Attribution and language as a socio-cognitive environment. In G. R. Semin & K. Fiedler (Eds.), *Language, interaction and social cognition* (pp. 79–101). London: Sage.

Fiedler, K., Semin, G. R., & Finkenauer, C. (1993). The battle of words between gender groups. A language-based approach to intergroup processes. *Human Communication Research, 19,* 409–441.

Fiedler, F., Semin, G. R., & Koppetsch, C. (1991). Language use and attributional biases in close personal relationships. *Personality and Social Psychology Bulletin, 17,* 147–155.

Fiske, S. T., & Cox, M. G. (1979). Person concepts: The effects of target familiarity and descriptive purpose on the process of describing others. *Journal of Personality, 47,* 136–161.

Fiske, S. T., & Pavelchak, M. A. (1986). Category-based vs. piecemeal-based affective responses: Developments in schema-triggered affect. In R. M. Sorrentino & E. T. Higgins (Eds.), *Handbook of motivation and cognition* (pp. 167–203). New York: Guilford.

Forgas, J. P. (1992). Affect in social judgments and decisions: A multi-process model. In M. Zanna (Ed.), *Advances in experimental social psychology* (pp. 227–275). New York: Academic Press.

Hamilton, D. L., & Gifford, R. K. (1976). Illusory correlation in interpersonal perception: A cognitive basis of stereotypic judgment. *Journal of Experimental Social Psychology, 12,* 392–407.

Higgins, E. T., Rholes, W. S., & Jones, C. R. (1977). Category accessibility and impression formation. *Journal of Experimental Social Psychology, 13*, 141–154.

Jones, E. E., & Nisbett, R. E. (1972). The actor and the observer: Divergent perceptions of the causes of behavior. In E. E. Jones, D. Kanouse, H. H. Kelley, R. E. Nisbett, S. Valins, & B. Weiner (Eds.), *Attribution: Perceiving the causes of behavior* (pp. 79–94). Morristown, NJ: General Learning Press.

Lewin, K. (1951). *Field theory in social science: Selected theoretical papers.* New York: Harper & Row.

Linville, P. W., Fisher, G. W., & Salovey, P. (1989). Perceived distributions of the characteristics of in-group and out-group members: Empirical evidence and a computer simulation. *Journal of Personality and Social Psychology, 57*, 165–188.

MacCorquodale, K., & Meehl, P. E. (1948). On a distinction between hypothetical constructs and intervening variables. *Psychological Review, 55*, 95–107.

Ross, M., & Sicoly, F. (1979). Egocentric biases in availability and attribution. *Journal of Personality and Social Psychology, 37*, 322–336.

Scherer, K. R. (1986). Vocal affect expression: A review and a model for future research. *Psychological Bulletin, 99*, 143–165.

Semin, G. R., & Fiedler, K. (1988). The cognitive functions of linguistic categories in describing persons: Social cognition and language. *Journal of Personality and Social Psychology, 54*, 558–568.

Semin, G. R., & Fiedler, K. (1991). The linguistic category model, its bases, applications, and range. *European Review of Social Psychology, 2*, 1–30.

Shweder, R. A. (1977). Likeness and likelihood in everyday thought: Magical thinking in judgment about personality. *Current Anthropologist, 18*, 637–648.

Skowronski, N. J., & Carlston, D. E. (1989). Negativity and extremity biases in impression formation: A review of explanations. *Psychological Bulletin, 105*, 131–142.

Smith, E. R. (1991). Illusory correlation in a simulated exemplar-based memory. *Journal of Experimental Social Psychology, 27*, 107–123.

Watson, D. (1982). The actor and the observer: How are their perceptions of causality divergent? *Psychological Bulletin, 92*, 682–700.

Wyer, R. S., Jr., & Srull, T. K. (1989). *Memory and cognition in its social context.* Hillsdale, NJ: Lawrence Erlbaum Associates.

6 Mental Systems, Representation, and Process

Gabriel A. Radvansky
University of Notre Dame

In the target chapter (chap. 1, this volume), Donal Carlston presents his Associated System Theory (AST). The goal of this theory is to provide a framework for identifying the relevant dimensions of information that are used in deriving impressions of other people as individuals, although this framework could be extended to nonhuman animals and inanimate objects as well. His chapter can be roughly divided into two sections. In the first section, the different types of representational systems that are employed in deriving impressions of other people, as well as how those systems interact, are described. In the second section, the types of processes and conditions involved in the creation, organization, and use of these representations are described. The current chapter focuses on the issues raised in the first section—that of the representational systems—because this is where the AST model, as it is outlined here, has its greatest problems as a theory of associated mental systems.

According to Carlston, the AST model is concerned with the form of the mental representations used in the formation of impressions of other people, not with their content, and with how these different forms are employed in different situations where people gain impressions of other people. Each *system* in the AST framework is presented as relying on a unique representational form, as well as a set of processes that operate on those forms. These unique representations and procedures are tailor-made for each system to satisfy the system's particular needs. Carlston identifies four primary systems that compose the model, as well as four secondary systems. The secondary systems are hybrid combinations of the activities from two primary systems. The representational forms and processes of the secondary systems are emergent properties arising out of the combination of two of the primary systems. Carlston also implies that up to 25 different systems may be identified if a more fine-grained approach is taken. This increases the degrees of freedom for the model, allowing it to explain a larger dataset. However, because the more elaborate scheme is not considered a fundamental aspect of the model, only the eight central systems are considered here.

The representational forms that are used by the AST model are abstract, although their features correspond to the input and output needs of each particular system. Each of the four primary representational systems operates independently from the other systems at lower levels of processing, with no exchange of information. However, at higher levels of processing, some degree of overlap and interaction among the systems is assumed to occur. At these higher levels, each of the representational systems is assumed to retain its representational form, although the systems may share common processes and organizations. It is also at these higher levels of processing that the interaction of the primary systems gives rise to the secondary systems. This interaction and creation of the secondary systems provides a bridge across which the information from the separate systems can be shared during the formation of impressions of other people.

The following sections of this chapter describe three aspects of the representation and organization of information, as presented in the AST model, that need to be considered more fully. First, I discuss some of the problems the AST model has in the identification and organization of the different representational–processing systems. Second, I detail some problems with how the AST model presents the representational forms of the different systems. Third, I cover some notions concerning the differentiation between representation and process in building a theoretical model.

MULTIPLE MENTAL SYSTEMS

The purpose of delineating multiple memory systems is to identify sets of representations or processes that handle different types of information, are independent of one another, and that serve different functions. Different mental systems are often identified through some dissociation in their functioning, where a given manipulation affects one system but not another. Some of the most convincing evidence of system dissociation comes from neurological evidence, particularly when a particular neural structure is damaged or destroyed. In such case, the particular functions of a certain system may become compromised, or even disappear entirely, whereas the functions of other systems remain undisturbed. By identifying the different mental systems involved in a given processing task, such as forming an impression of a person, one can better understand the nature of the information being used, how it is represented, and how it is processed by the system.

In general, when researchers identify different mental systems, they make a distinction between the different types of representation and/or the different types of mental processes that are involved within each system. For example, in the most simple conception of the human information-processing system, the so-called standard or modal model of Atkinson and Shiffrin (1968), information was thought to pass through several different processing stages—a sensory register, a short-term store, and a long-term store. Information was represented in the sensory register in terms of a code corresponding to the initial input mode (visual, auditory, etc.), whereas information in the short-term store was represented in a verbal–linguistic code. Like the modal model of cognition, a theory that supposes different mental systems should relate the different representational and processing mechanisms unique to each system. A brief overview is given of some of the more successful theories of multiple systems in terms of how they satisfy these criteria.

Theories of Multiple Mental Systems

Some theories assume that information stored in different mental systems has different representational forms. There is a fundamental difference in the way that information is mentally coded, such as in the distinction between the procedural and declarative systems (e.g., Zola-Morgan & Squire, 1988). In general, the procedural system handles information pertaining to nonverbal actions or activities, such as knowing how to ride a bicycle or how to shift while driving a car. In contrast, the declarative system handles knowledge that can be readily articulated, such as the name of a favorite movie or where a friend was first met. This distinction is supported by neurological evidence that shows that some amnesic patients suffer from a loss in their declarative system, while the production system remains largely intact.

One of the major distinctions between declarative and procedural systems is the form in which information is represented in each of them. For example, in the ACT* model of human memory (Anderson, 1983), declarative knowledge is stored in the form of a complex of propositional structures, whereas procedural information is stored in a collection of if–then procedures that "fire" when needed.

Another example of a theory of separate memory systems that relies largely on a difference in representational forms is Paivio's (1971) dual-code theory. In that model, verbal and imagery information are stored and processed in two separate systems, each possessing a unique representa-

tional code. Verbal information is thought to be represented by a propositional code, whereas imagery information is represented by more analogical
mental images. Regardless of the theory supposing the different mental
systems, they all agree that the information represented in each system
should have a unique structure in order to best take advantage of the
information's content.

In addition to the specification of different representational codes,
theories of multiple mental systems specify that each mental system relies on
a different set of processing mechanisms, although a few processing
mechanisms may be common across systems. According to these theories, it
is *how* information is processed that separates one system from another.
One currently popular distinction is between implicit and explicit memory
systems (Graf & Schacter, 1985, 1987). The implicit memory system is
conceived of as being composed of the set of processes that influence the
current stream of processing or task without any explicit intention to do so.
Such influences include priming and performance on memory tasks, where
the person is unaware that memory is being tested, such as perceptual
identification or fragment–stem–completion tasks. The explicit memory
system is conceived of as being composed of the set of processes used during
active memory retrieval, such as recall or recognition. What distinguishes
the two mental systems is not the content of the information, but how it is
processed. In studies comparing amnesic patients with normal controls, it
has been found that the two groups of individuals did not differ on tasks
that used the implicit system, but did differ on tasks that used the explicit
system and the same experimental materials, thereby supporting the notion
that these are, in fact, two distinct mental systems.

The episodic–semantic distinction (Tulving, 1972, 1985, 1993) is another
popular distinction between multiple mental systems that illustrates how
different processing mechanisms are involved in each system. According to
this theory, the episodic and semantic systems store information in similar
representational forms. However, information that is processed in the
episodic system is operated on so that the information is related to an
individual's life experience (e.g., *when* the information was encountered,
where the information was encountered, etc.). In contrast, information that
is processed in the semantic system is handled with respect to how the
information relates to other information that is known about the world in
general. The critical feature that defines both the explicit–implicit and
episodic–semantic theories is how the information is processed with regard
to the functional operation of the system.

One aspect that all of the theories have in common, whether explicitly
stated or not, is the notion that these mental systems are arranged in a
hierarchical fashion, with more sophisticated or complex systems dependent, in some respect, on more primitive systems. The more sophisticated

systems are thought to have arisen over the course of evolution with an increase in specialization and to meet otherwise unmet needs (Sherry & Schacter, 1987). As such, the manner in which information becomes available to different mental systems, and how that information is shared by the different mental systems, is dictated to some degree by such a hierarchical structure.

How AST Differs From Other Theories

The AST model provides a framework composed of a complex of primary and secondary mental systems. Most of the primary systems can be identified with aspects of other theories, although there are clear differences. The sensory/perceptual system is identified explicitly in the modal model of information processing (Atkinson & Shiffrin, 1968), and is assumed to be operative in many of the other theories that distinguish multiple mental systems. The verbal system corresponds to the declarative systems, including semantic and episodic systems (e.g., Tulving, 1985). Finally, the action system bears a close correspondence to the procedural system (e.g., Zola-Morgan & Squire, 1988). Although none of the theories of mental systems mentioned here identifies a separate affective system, it is unlikely that most researchers would disagree with the notion that some specialized system for handling emotions does exist. Carlston also agrees with the other theories when he states that the AST model should suppose that information processed by the separate mental systems should have both a separate and unique representational form, as well as separate processing mechanisms.

One of the most striking differences between the AST model and the other multiple system theories I have described is the assumption that all of the systems covered by the theoretical model have equal status in processing. There is not the hierarchical structure that is stated or assumed by many of the other theories. Instead of a hierarchical organization of its mental systems, the AST model organizes its systems in terms of a two-dimensional plane, with concrete–abstract defining one dimension and self–other relevance defining the other. This organization presumably allows for a more even exchange of information across the systems.

In addition to this arrangement of the primary mental systems, the AST model asserts that there are other systems that can be derived through hybrid combinations of the primary systems. These hybrid systems necessarily arise from the interaction of two of the primary systems. However, none of these secondary systems has a clear counterpart in the other multiple system theories described here. Regardless of this fact, Carlston states that each of these secondary systems has its own unique set of representations and processes, and are unique systems in their own right. It is with these secondary systems that I take issue first.

The AST Secondary Systems

One troubling aspect of Carlston's AST model is that the secondary systems that he proposes do not seem to be systems at all. The primary systems are clearly different mental systems because they each derive from a separate set of input sources, operate on different contents, and require different mechanisms to process that information (Sherry & Schacter, 1987; Tulving, 1985). In contrast, the secondary systems (i.e., categorizations, evaluations, orientations, and behavioral observations) seem to be less mental systems and more the products of information processing.

For example, categorizations are a result of a classification mechanism. There is no evidence to support the notion that categories derive from a specific input source. The input for a categorization mechanism can come from any of the four primary systems, and does not need to be a combination of perceptual and verbal processing (we can categorize affect and actions quite well). In terms of representational form, there is not a specific category representational form much beyond some organization of existing representational forms, such as an arrangement of concepts in a network. In addition, it is unclear what specific processes would be involved in a categorization system, except the actual process of categorization. Although categorization is a unique process, that alone does not raise it to the status of a mental system. Specifically, it lacks independence from other mental systems, does not have a unique representational code, and can accept a variety of input and output sources. Similar arguments can be made for the other secondary systems.

One source of evidence presented by Carlston for the reality of the secondary systems are neurological studies of brain-damaged individuals. The neurological evidence for the mental systems proposed for the AST model shows some misunderstanding of these afflictions. First, Carlston conflates several types of unrelated amnesias that are a result of damage to a variety of different neurological substrates. For example, retrograde amnesia is typically caused by general cerebral or other physical trauma where a memory trace has not been allowed to consolidate, whereas anterograde amnesia is caused by damage to the hippocampus. Few researchers would be willing to say that these different types of amnesias are part of the same system. The disorders of categorization could be attributable to the sensory perceptual system alone, and the neurological evidence underlying the disorders of orientation are unclear as they are presented in the chapter. The aprosodias appear to be the only disorders in the secondary systems that fit well into the AST framework. Given the lack of theoretical justification and neurological support, it would be best to conclude that the secondary systems of the AST model are not systems at all, but the result of processing mechanisms on a variety of mental contents.

Does AST Need Multiple Systems?

Given the large amount of research and effort on the other multiple system theories, does the AST model's division of labor add anything new and of value? The secondary systems are not really systems at all, but certain functions that are identified as either being part of other systems or functions that cut across several systems. As for the primary memory systems identified by the AST model, there is nothing new here. All of the functions performed by these systems have been identified by other multiple system theories.

However, in fairness, AST's primary intention does not seem to be to provide an account of a new division of mental systems, but rather to provide an interpretation of how these systems relate and interact. The most novel aspect of the theory is its organization of the systems. Instead of the typical hierarchical arrangement, Carlston chose a cluster of the systems based on the nature of the information being processed. This choice is in the spirit of recent massively parallel and interactive systems, such as the parallel distributed processing (PDP) networks, in which information from several different sources or systems is available to all of the other systems at once. The arrangement of these systems in the AST model's organization is quite effective at capturing some relevant properties involved in the formation of impressions of other people, namely, whether the information is concrete or abstract, and whether the information pertains to the self or to some target other.

But is this multiple system organization needed? Probably not. Although it is clear that there are different kinds of information being processed, it is not clear that much is added to the predictive power of the AST model by supposing that different mental systems are involved. The notion that different types of information are subject to different types of processing can be made without supposing different mental systems. The need to suppose different mental systems occurs only when there is some functional incompatibility in the different processing mechanisms (Sherry & Schacter, 1987). For the AST model, there is always the common goal of forming an impression of a person. The remainder of the AST model, which follows from the description of the multiple systems, would not suffer much if the notion of multiple systems was abandoned in favor of a collection of processing mechanisms that operated with regard to the information's concreteness–abstraction, self–other relevance, and possibly even level of processing. The important distinctions among the processing mechanisms, in terms of the formation of impressions of other people, are based on these dimensions, not on whether there are actually separate memory systems.

Even when the multiple system notion is removed, the AST model does not introduce anything new in terms of dimensions on which people classify information. All of these dimensions are among the most well known to influence human memory and processing. This is evident by Table 1.1 in Carlston's chapter. Perhaps the only new thing that the AST model does provide in this vein is the manner in which these dimensions are identified, combined, and applied to situations where the formation of impressions of other people would occur.

REPRESENTATIONAL FORMS

As mentioned, if a theoretical model is going to specify the operation of a number of mental systems, it must specify the different representational forms employed by each of the systems. This allows the researcher to better understand how information is structured, and how the processes attributed to each system operate on that structure.

The Representational Forms of AST

One claim made by Carlston is that "AST focuses on forms of impression-related (or 'impressional') representations, rather than on their contents" (p. 2). This claim is in line with the notion that each of the systems in a theory should rely on a representational form that differs from the other systems. In this way, the needs of each system are met, in part, by the form of the representations used by that system. For example, the form of representation used in the sensory system should differ in substantial ways from the form of representations used in the affective system. The first should capture qualities and relations of the environment as they are experienced sensorily, whereas the second should capture the qualities of human emotion. This difference in representational forms is almost re-quired because of the vastly different nature of the information processed in each of the separate systems.

However, the AST model, as presented by Carlston, never stipulates what the different representation forms for each system are, nor is it specified how the representations would be required to differ from one another. Based on the claim cited in the preceding paragraph, the differentiation of different representational forms for each mental system would seem to be a requirement of a presentation of the model. Instead, all of the information that is assumed to be processed by the AST model is characterized by a single representational form—a network representation (either a proposi-tional or a PDP network). As such, what distinguishes the different mental systems in the AST model is not any difference in the representational forms, but is in the information content of each system, as well as the processing mechanisms assumed to operate in each of those systems. The representational forms in the AST model are identical in all of the systems — even the so-called secondary systems.

One of the identifiers of separate mental systems, aside from the use of different types of representations, is that each system is relatively independent of the others. However, as can be seen in Carlston's Fig. 1.5, the representation used for the impressions of *Ed* is a highly interactive network. The only identification of the different systems is that each of the boxes in which a concept has been graphed identifies in which system it is. Figure 1.5 also illustrates that the organization of systems and the description of how they interact by the AST model is violated by connections of concepts across nonadjoining areas, such as the link between *belligerent* and *yells a lot*, as well as *friend* and *likable*.

Realizing that there is no differentiation of representational form and little system independence brings up the issue raised in the last section: Is it necessary for Carlston to suppose multiple systems to explain the formation of impressions of other people? In the AST model, the differences among the various systems are primarily attributable to differences in information content. The difference in processing mechanisms that operate on the different types of information can be disregarded as a means to distinguish the different systems because the primary mechanisms involved in the AST model are general activation and inhibition mechanisms that operate on the entire impressional structure. In addition, any efficient single mental system should employ different mechanisms for a variety of information contents. Thus, little seems to be gained by actually specifying multiple mental systems to understand the formation of impressions of other people. Instead, as mentioned earlier, the important distinction the AST model seems to make is that the different types of information that are processed using these impressions of other people can be characterized by simply relying on two or three feature dimensions: concrete–abstract, self–other relevant, and possibly depth of processing.

Is a Network Representation Necessary?

Although the AST model does not contribute anything with regard to differences in representational form, and relies on only a single representational structure, it is necessary to assume some sort of representational structure in order to properly understand the mental processes involved in determining how people form impressions of others. The specification of a particular representational structure helps the researcher understand how information is organized in memory, how that information is retrieved, and how the activation or retrieval of some concepts prime or inhibit other related concepts. The network representational form presumed by the AST model can serve this function quite well. The selection of this representational form has the advantage that network structures are relatively well understood, and it gives memory the appearance of being a well-organized system with easily understood storage and retrieval properties.

However, the major contribution of the AST model is not in terms of representational form, but with how information is organized. Although a network structure provides a ready understanding of how such an organization could be accomplished, it is not the only type of representational form that can be considered. Other sorts of representational schemes can capture many of the same properties as network structures, as well as produce unique predictions concerning the nature and efficiency of mental processes (e.g., Hintzman, 1986; Radvansky & Zacks, 1991). One example of a nonnetwork representational scheme is multiple trace theory, such as the MINERVA 2 model (Hintzman, 1986, 1988). In a multiple trace theory, it is supposed that memory is an unorganized collection of memory traces. Each of these traces is the product of an external episodic experience or some internal mental processing. The organization that memory exhibits is a result of the manner in which these traces are accessed by the different processing mechanisms that access them. For example, memory traces that are used during the formation of impressions of other people, and related to visual appearance and a certain person, would appear to be organized if the traces were accessed by procedures that select out memory traces that have to do with the person and their appearance. One advantage of an alternative view, such as a multiple trace theory, over a network theory is that there is no need to specify how information from several sources is organized at encoding because the organization can occur at retrieval.

Because representational form is not central to the AST model, as outlined by Carlston, the model should be open to the possibility of other types of representational forms, although a network representation is just fine for developing some working assumptions of the processes that the model must be able to handle. The primary contribution of the AST model is in how the different types of information interact during the formation of impressions of other people, not how different types of information are represented. Focusing on determining a specific representational form only detracts from this effort.

PROCESS AND REPRESENTATION

The Distinction Between Process and Representation

There are two general goals in Carlston's AST model that typify much of the research in both social and nonsocial cognition. These are the goals of understanding the form of the representation in which information is stored, as well as the processes that operate on these representations. The concerns presented here echo those of Barsalou (1990) in an earlier volume in this series. Because mental representation and mental process are so intertwined, it is often extremely difficult to separate these two components from one another. Mental representation cannot be evaluated without considering the processes that act on it, and mental processes cannot be tested without some idea of the representations that are being processed. For a model of human cognition to succeed, the conjunction of mental representation and process must adequately describe the actual phenomenon.

Because of the inseparable nature of these two aspects of cognition, as well as a general desire for parsimony, a researcher should only include features into a model that provide some necessary contribution. The major contribution of the AST model, as described here, is in terms of the processes involved in the derivation and integration of information from several sources that can be used while forming an impression of a person. Little to nothing is gained through the supposition of several mental systems and their associated representations. The inclusion of such unnecessary components to the model leaves it weaker and obscures the contribution of relating how different types of information, so classified based on their content, may be related, and how these different types of knowledge and the processes that operate on them may interact. Because of these difficulties, perhaps it would be best to transform the AST model into an APT (Associated Processes Theory) that relates the different processes that operate on different information sources during the construction of a representation to be used in impression formation.

SUMMARY

The AST model presented by Carlston is an attempt to provide a framework for interpreting the representational forms and processes involved in the formation of impressions of other individuals in terms of the mental systems that the representations and processes originate from, as well as how they interact at higher levels of processing. The model supposes four primary systems and four secondary systems. The secondary systems are hybrid combinations of two primary mechanisms. I have argued that the secondary systems are not systems at all, but are the results of processing. The primary systems are generally accepted divisions of processing, but the unique contribution of the AST model is the conception of how these systems relate and interact during the formation of impressions of other people. I have argued that similar predictions can also be derived if the multiple system approach is abandoned and the model merely relates how information is processed with respect to where the information lies on the two or three feature dimensions that characterize the organization of the processing systems in the AST model. Finally, the AST model is presented as a theory that characterizes how developing an impression of another person is accomplished with regard to the form of the representation, rather than the information content. I have argued that the model does not specify any variations in representational form. Instead, all the differences in information processing during impression formation are due to the nature of the content of the information being processed.

REFERENCES

Anderson, J. R. (1983). *The architecture of cognition*. Cambridge, MA: Harvard University Press.

Atkinson, R. C., & Shiffrin, R. M. (1968). Human memory: A proposed system and its control processes. In W. K. Spence & J. T. Spence (Eds.), *The psychology of learning and motivation: Advances in research and theory* (Vol. 2, pp. 89–195). New York: Academic Press.

Barsalou, L. W. (1990). On the indistinguishability of exemplar memory and abstraction in category representation. In T. K. Srull & R. S. Wyer (Eds.), *Advances in social cognition* (Vol. 3, pp. 61–88). Hillsdale, NJ: Lawrence Erlbaum Associates.

Graf, P., & Schacter, D. L. (1985). Implicit and explicit memory for new associations in normal and amnesic subjects. *Journal of Experimental Psychology: Learning, Memory, and Cognition, 11*, 501–518.

Graf, P., & Schacter, D. L. (1987). Selective effects of interference on implicit and explicit memory for new associations. *Journal of Experimental Psychology: Learning, Memory, and Cognition, 12*, 45–53.

Hintzman, D. L. (1986). "Schema abstraction" in a multiple-trace model. *Psychological Review, 93*, 411–428.

Hintzman, D. L. (1988). Judgements of frequency and recognition memory in a multiple-trace memory model. *Psychological Review, 95*, 528–551.

Paivio, A. (1971). *Imagery and verbal process*. New York: Holt, Rhinehart & Winston.

Radvansky, G. A., & Zacks, R. T. (1991). Mental models and the fan effect. *Journal of Experimental Psychology: Learning, Memory, and Cognition, 17*, 940–953.

Sherry, D. F., & Schacter, D. L. (1987). The evolution of multiple memory systems. *Psychological Review, 94*, 439–454.

Tulving, E. (1972). Episodic and semantic memory. In E. Tulving & W. Donaldson (Eds.), *Organization of memory* (pp. 382–403). New York: Academic Press.

Tulving, E. (1985). How many memory systems are there? *American Psychologist, 40*, 385–398.

Tulving, E. (1993). What is episodic memory? *Current Directions in Psychological Science, 2*, 67–70.

Zola-Morgan, S., & Squire, L. (1988). Memory: Brain systems and behavior. *Trends in Neuroscience, 11*, 170–175.

7

Associated Systems Theory: If You Buy Two Representational Systems, Why Not Many?

Marilynn B. Brewer
Ohio State University

Six years ago, the editors of *Advances in Social Cognition* gave me the opportunity to write the lead article for the first volume in this series. It proved to be a valuable experience, permitting me to try out some new and (what seemed then) radical ideas about two separate representational systems for encoding and storing information about individual persons. I am pleased now to have a second opportunity to contribute to this series, this time in the role of commentator on an article that is yet more radical and far more elegant than the rough model I proposed in 1988. After reading Carlston's integrative chapter (this volume), I think it is safe to say we have come a long way in the last 6 years.

As Carlston acknowledges, in some respects Associated Systems Theory (AST) is an extension and elaboration of various dual-representation models proposed by myself (Brewer, 1988) and others (e.g., Andersen & Klatzky, 1987; Fiske & Pavelchak, 1986; Ostrom, Carpenter, Sedikides, & Li, 1993; Wyer & Martin, 1986). Although these prior models share the general idea that person information can be represented in different modes, each suggests a different basis for dichotomizing the primary representational systems. In effect, AST integrates different versions of dual-representation systems into a single multirepresentation framework. I hope to illustrate the value of this integrative effort by focusing on points of contact between AST and my own dual-process model—pointing out where the two models are mutually supportive, where AST can clarify and enrich concepts introduced in the earlier model, and where differences between the two approaches might suggest extensions and modifications of the AST framework.

141

USING THE AST MODEL TO CLARIFY CONCEPTUAL DISTINCTIONS

AST provides a basis for classifying person representations in terms of depth and breadth (the number and extent to which different mental systems are engaged), as well as form and content (which specific systems are involved in the associative network). This provides a language for clarifying (and ultimately operationalizing) several of the conceptual distinctions that were central to the dual-processing model, but only vaguely defined in the original presentation (Brewer, 1988). Among these are the distinctions between *identification* and *typing* as forms of person categorization, between *traits* and *prototypes* as systems of classification, and — most important — between *individuated* and *personalized* forms of mental representation of a single person.

Identification Versus Categorization

The dual-process model drew a distinction between identification and categorization (typing) as two different stages of the impression-formation process. Identification is an initial classification of a stimulus person associated with preconscious, automatic processes. Categorization, or typing, is a more elaborated, inferential level of processing associated with conscious, controlled processing modes. AST provides an alternative way to conceptualize this distinction in terms of level of activation of different response systems. Drawing on Fig. 1.1 from Carlston's chapter, *identification* can be defined as activation of either the verbal or perceptual response system as lower level representations prior to integration with other mental systems. *Categorization* is a higher level representation involving the combination of at least the visual and semantic systems, if not all four primary representational structures.

This distinction between categorization at different levels seems to me a useful one in distinguishing between *classification* and *stereotyping* as aspects of person perception. There is some confusion in the social cognition literature between the use of these terms — as if the act of placing an individual in a social category was equivalent to the use of category stereotypes. Yet the recognition that an individual has a category-defining feature, such as femaleness or black skin, does not necessarily imply that impressions of that individual are derived from category stereotypes.

Stereotyping may be a less effortful form of impression formation than piecemeal, trait-based impressions (Bodenhausen, 1990; Macrae, Hewstone, & Griffiths, 1993; Macrae, Milne, & Bodenhausen, 1994). But in the AST model, it is still a higher level representation engaging more associated systems and requiring more cognitive involvement than mere perceptual recognition or verbal labeling. Indeed, research on the "solo effect" suggests that category salience does not invariably lead to application of stereotypes (Oakes & Turner, 1986; Taylor & Falcone, 1982). Identification or classification as a preconscious, automatic process may prime access and utilization of associated category stereotypes, but both stimulus characteristics and perceiver goals can intervene at the level of conscious processing to sever the connection between classification and stereotyping (Bargh, 1989; Devine, 1989).

Further, the initial act of categorization may link into other associated systems besides stereotyping. For instance, categorization involves same-different judgments that, in the case of social categories, imply same as me versus different from me. Such ingroup–outgroup classifications may be more directly associated with the affective response system than with cognitive representations. AST helps articulate the idea that identification, ingroup–outgroup classification (prejudice), and stereotyping are conceptually distinct forms of representation that may be more or less closely linked for different individuals and different social categories.

Types Versus Traits

The AST model converges with the dual-process model in drawing a distinction between traits and categorizations as forms of person representations, with personality "types" falling somewhat ambiguously in between (see also Andersen & Klatsky, 1987). Regardless of whether verbal descriptors can be unambiguously classified as traits or types, the AST model provides a basis for distinguishing between the two in terms of which primary response systems are engaged. Category types should fall closer to visual representations than personality traits, which are verbal or semantic representations.

Support for this proposition comes from data collected by Brewer and Lui (1989) using a nonverbal picture-sorting task to assess different representational forms. Participants in this study were given 140 facial photographs to categorize by way of a free-sort procedure. The persons depicted in the photos varied systematically in age and sex, as well as many other visual features. For some subjects, the sorting instructions suggested that the faces should be grouped according to similarity of "psychological traits or states"; for others, the instructions indicated that similarity should be based on "character or personality type," and, for a third group, on "specific physical features."

The resulting clusterings of the 140 photographs (derived from aggregated co-occurrence matrices) differed as a function of the wording of the sorting instructions. Of particular importance for the present purposes, the values in the co-occurrence matrices produced by subjects in the physical feature and character-type instructional conditions were highly correlated with each other ($r = .75$), and corresponded much less with the sortings produced by subjects in the trait condtiion ($r = .44$ in both cases). (This was despite the fact that the stimulus materials were all visual rather than verbal.) Further, the sortings produced in both physical and character-type instructional conditions were hierarchically organized by age and gender; similarity in age and sex was the strongest predictor of the probability that two photos would be sorted into the same "character-type" group, suggesting that these person categories are subtypes of social categorizations based on age and gender. Sortings based on personality traits were less likely to be organized in accord with age or gender of the stimulus picture.

Following the sorting task in the Brewer and Lui study, all participants were asked to write brief verbal labels or descriptions for each of the groupings of photographs they had produced. For the most part, these verbal depictions were stongly influenced by the sorting instructions that had been given earlier. Verbal labels in the trait condition were largely personality trait terms (e.g., *friendly*, *intelligent*), those in the character-type condition were social types or roles (e.g., *hippies*, *frumpy housewives*), and those in the physical similarity condition were largely physical descriptors (e.g., *smiling*, *wearing glasses*, *heavy set*). However, although fully 93% of the photo pairings produced in the character-sorting condition were matched on age and gender (i.e., almost all of the photos grouped together were of the same gender and age), age and gender classifications were rarely explicitly mentioned as part of the verbal descriptions of the person categories. Gender was sometimes implicit in the labels (as in house*wives*), but the terms *young, old, male, female, man*, and *woman* seldom appeared (despite the fact that the photos being described were all young women). This finding reinforces the caution (also raised by Carlston) against relying exclusively on verbal statements to assess the forms in which persons are mentally represented.

Individuated Versus Personalized Impressions

Just as the AST model provides a system for conceptualizing the distinction between traits and types, it also provides a framework for distinguishing between person representations that have been derived from category-based individuating processes and those derived from personalized processing (Brewer, 1988). Of particular importance here is the distinction between representational forms that are produced by direct operation of a primary response system (e.g., trait representations generated from hearing or reading verbal descriptions of an individual, visual representations based on direct observation, etc.) and derivative forms generated by inference or association. According to the AST model, the final representation of any single person will be a combination of representational forms derived from the originating response system and those derived by addition or importation from associated systems (see Fig. 1.7).

Personalized and individuated impressions have different originating response systems, and they differ in the breadth and depth of the associated representational systems engaged in the final impression. To translate the original dual-process depiction (Brewer, 1988), personalized representations are more likely to originate with direct operation of the semantic or behavioral response systems; the final impressions are more abstract, more self-oriented, and more likely to combine behavioral, affective, and semantic response systems, compared with individuated impressions, which are more concrete and more limited to representations combining visual and semantic response systems. (From this perspective, Carlston's Fig. 1.5 depicts a highly personalized representation of a single individual.)

DIFFERENCES IN PERSPECTIVE: ARE ALL IMPRESSIONS FORMED BOTTOM-UP?

Despite the attention Carlston gave to multiple representational forms and systems, the AST model seems to rely almost exclusively on a single processing mode to characterize impression formation. Apart from the form and content of person representations, processing mode refers to the manner in which representations are achieved or developed.

Carlston's descriptions of the development of person representations are at least implicitly—and at times explicitly—bottom-up, in that final representations appear to be built, through processes of inference and abstraction, from pieces of information about or experiences with the target individual. For instance, observed behaviors are linked to traits through processes of extrapolation and "importation" of links from conceptual memory into the associative structure representing the individual person. Target-specific information is presumed to activate generic representations so that, over time, the person representation becomes more like those in conceptual memory.

Brewer's dual-process model postulates an alternative, top–down mode of impression formation, which begins with the generic representation and may be gradually modified as target-specific information is checked against the preexisting structure. Category-based impressions become individuated when specific features that do not match are incorporated as additions or alterations of the generic representation. The final representation, then, would be less like the initial generic representation. Top–down processing is characterized by comparison and differentiation, whereas bottom–up processing is characterized by inference, abstraction, and elaboration.

Differentiation and elaboration both lead to unique person representations, but are achieved through different routes. According to the dual-process model, the two processing modes produce structurally different person representations. Category-based, top–down processing leads to individuated impressions, whereas bottom–up processing results in personalized representations. As discussed previously, individuated impressions are more visual and concrete, and involve fewer associative links than personalized impressions.

Some evidence—albeit indirect—for the distinction between category-based and elaborative processing in person perception comes from research on the priming effects of stereotype labels on impression formation. For instance, a series of experiments by Macrae et al. (1994) demonstrates that trait information preceded by a category label (presented either subliminally or supraliminally) is processed with less effort and attention than the same information presented without a stereotype prime. In these experiments, participants formed impressions of four stimulus persons (each described by 10 personality traits) while simultaneously engaging in a prose-monitoring task. For half of the subjects, each target person was presented in association with a relevant category label (subliminal or supraliminal); for the other half, no label was provided. At the conclusion of stimulus presentation, subjects in the primed condition could correctly recall more trait items in a cued-recall task *and* performed better on the monitoring task than did nonprimed subjects. This evidence of cognitive-resource conservation is consistent with the idea that category-based processing consists of low-effort feature matching, in contrast to elaborative impression building.

As the Macrae et al. studies illustrate, the same information about a target individual could be processed in either mode. In the original presentation of the dual-process model (Brewer, 1988), the choice of processing mode was determined by perceiver motives and goals rather than by properties of the stimulus information. This idea could be incorporated into aspects of the AST model by modifying Carlston's Fig. 1.7 to insert a processing motive/goal factor early in the sequence (between the initial event-external stimulus and initial activities). The processing mode adopted would, in turn, influence which response systems were engaged in initial representations, and which representational forms were included in the final representation.

However, further integration of the AST and dual-process models might suggest a reciprocal relationship between processing mode and response system activation. Category-based processing may limit information search to the visual and verbal systems and associated representational forms (appearance, categorization, traits, and evaluations). Behavioral and affective responses would then be activated only after the final representation was achieved, as a consequence rather than a source of the composite impression. Personalized processing would extend the associative network to include affective and behavioral engagement at the initial representation stages. However, the initiating events may engage particular response systems that then determine which processing mode is adopted. The more response systems that are engaged directly by the stimulus presentation, the more likely it is that the impression formation will be personalized rather than category-based. By integrating the dual-process model with the AST framework, a dynamic and implication-rich conceptual system emerges.

REFERENCES

Andersen, S. M., & Klatzky, R. L. (1987). Traits and social stereotypes: Levels of categorization in person perception. *Journal of Personality and Social Psychology, 53*, 235–246.

Bargh, J. A. (1989). Conditional automaticity: Varieties of automatic influence in social perception and cognition. In J. Uleman & J. Bargh (Eds.), *Unintended thought* (pp. 3–51). New York: Guilford.

Bodenhausen, G. V. (1990). Stereotypes as judgmental heuristics: Evidence of circadian variations in discrimination. *Psychological Science, 1*, 319–322.

Brewer, M. B. (1988). A dual process model of impression formation. In T. Srull & R. Wyer (Eds.), *Advances in social cognition* (Vol. 1, pp. 1–36). Hillsdale, NJ: Lawrence Erlbaum Associates.

Brewer, M. B., & Lui, L. N. (1989). The primacy of age and sex in the structure of person categories. *Social Cognition, 7*, 262–274.

Devine, P. G. (1989). Stereotypes and prejudice: Their automatic and controlled components. *Journal of Personality and Social Psychology, 47*, 709–726.

Fiske, S. T., & Pavelchak, M. A. (1986). Category-based vs. piecemeal-based affective responses: Developments in schema-triggered affect. In R. Sorrentino & E. T. Higgins (Eds.), *Handbook of motivation and cognition* (pp. 167–203). New York: Guilford.

Macrae, C. N., Hewstone, M., & Griffiths, R. J. (1993). Processing load and memory for stereotype-based information. *European Journal of Social Psychology, 23*, 77–87.

Macrae, C. N., Milne, A. B., & Bodenhausen, G. V. (1994). Stereotypes as energy-saving devices: A peek inside the cognitive toolbox. *Journal of Personality and Social Psychology, 66*, 37–47.

Oakes, P., & Turner, J. C. (1986). Distinctiveness and the salience of social category membership: Is there an automatic perceptual bias towards novelty? *European Journal of Social Psychology, 16*, 325–344.

Ostrom, T. M., Carpenter, S. L., Sedikides, C., & Li, F. (1993). Differential processing of in-group and out-group information. *Journal of Personality and Social Psychology, 64*, 21–34.

Taylor, S. E., & Falcone, H. (1982). Cognitive bases of stereotyping: The relationship between categorization and prejudice. *Personality and Social Psychology Bulletin, 8*, 426–432.

Wyer, R. S., Jr., & Martin, L. L. (1986). Person memory: The role of traits, group stereotypes and specific behaviors in the cognitive representation of persons. *Journal of Personality and Social Psychology, 50*, 661–675.

8 Coherence Versus Ambivalence in Cognitive Representations of Persons

Galen V. Bodenhausen
Michigan State University

C. Neil Macrae
University of Wales, Cardiff

Don Carlston's Associated Systems Theory (AST), discussed in chapter 1, represents an ambitious attempt to come to terms with the fact that our mental representations of others are much more complex and multifaceted than most social psychological theories of impression formation and person memory have previously recognized. Drawing on recent developments in cognitive psychology and neuroscience, as well as social psychology, Carlston has devised a theoretical scheme that manages to address the inherent complexity of our cognitive representations of others with considerable elegance. AST represents a new way of looking at matters of long-standing concern in social cognition research, and it also raises a number of issues that will likely comprise the basis of future empirical efforts in this domain. As such, it holds the potential promise of setting the agenda for a new generation of impression-formation research. The comments that follow are intended to stimulate further consideration of some key aspects of the impression-formation process, in the hope of contributing to the identification of central issues for this agenda.

Of the many possible intriguing departure points for commentary, we have chosen to focus on a set of issues that seem particularly relevant to the type of mental representation that has been the focus of our own research; namely, representations of stereotyped outgroup members. One of the interesting qualities that characterize many people's reactions to members of minority groups is ambivalence. Several contemporary theories of intergroup relationships emphasize this fact. For example, Gaertner and Dovidio's (1986) aversive racism theory proposes that reactions to minorities typically consist of both negative affect and avoidance tendencies, as well as sincere egalitarian sentiments and favorable beliefs (Dovidio, Gaertner, Anastasio, & Sanitioso, 1992). Katz, Wackenhut, and Hass (1986) echoed these sentiments, characterizing intergroup attitudes as being composed of conflicting thoughts and feelings. More recently, Devine, Monteith, and their associates (Devine & Monteith, 1993; Devine, Monteith, Zuwerink, & Elliot, 1991) emphasized that, at least among low-prejudice individuals, automatized negative stereotypes and positive, sympathetic reactions to outgroup members co-exist. One potentially valuable aspect of Carlston's AST is that it provides a plausible theoretical vehicle for considering the nature of ambivalent representational structures such as the ones postulated in these theories of intergroup cognition. Indeed, because AST emphasizes the existence of semiautonomous representational systems serving the impression-formation process, it invites the consideration of the determinants and consequences of inter-representational conflict. In sketching out these considerations, we often make use of examples from the intergroup arena, while acknowledging that the ambivalence of representational structures is clearly a matter of more general importance (cf. Scott, 1968; Thompson, Zanna, & Griffin, in prep.).

HOW COHERENT IS THE COMPOSITE REPRESENTATION?

In Carlston's Fig. 1.7, we see a summary of numerous processes converging on an "experienced representation," which is a composite of the impressional outputs of the various representational systems. A critical question emerging from Carlston's analysis of mental life is exactly how this composite impression is experienced by social perceivers. Brown (1986) argued convincingly that we tend to produce coherent social impressions, and an impressive body of research supports the contention that perceivers actively strive for evaluatively coherent representations of others (e.g., Asch, 1946; Srull & Wyer, 1989; Wyer & Srull, 1989). Indeed, the social perceiver's need for consistency has been the hallmark of a wide variety of social psychological theories. This suggests, then, that the experienced impression of others is often a univalent, evaluative bottom line.

In Carlston's exposition of AST, surprisingly little was said about the nature of the experienced composite impression. Whereas past research has either explicitly or implicitly equated the concept of a global impression with evaluation, Carlston states that evaluations are only one part of this composite. Yet if the impression is experienced as a coherent bottom line, this suggests that the input of the representational systems is translatable into a common metric so that the various inputs can be consolidated into a unitary impression. It seems to us that the most plausible common metric would, in fact, be evaluative units. That is, perhaps it is the evaluative implications of visual appearance cues, categorizations, traits, affective responses, and all the other types of representational structures that are combined (in some as yet unspecified way) to produce the experienced composite impression. Even if one's impression of another person is ambivalent, as is sometimes the case, it is presumably necessary that the output of the various impressional systems receive some evaluative analysis in order for the nature of the conflict or ambivalence to be discerned or experienced. Given the central role of evaluation in the construction of meaning (Osgood, Suci, & Tannenbaum, 1957), it seems likely that the output of the various systems Carlston identifies are routinely channeled through the evaluative system en route to the construction of a composite impression (cf. Zanna & Rempel, 1988).

Given multiple, potentially conflicting systems, each a partially independent source of information about a social target, how is a composite impression constructed? Prior research on social impressions has addressed the issue of impressional coherence for the most part only within a given representational system (e.g., the trait system). Indeed, even when multiple systems have been methodologically implicated in a research paradigm, there has been little attempt to address the issue of impressional coherence when different systems furnish conflicting input into the composite impression. A notable exception to this trend, however, is research attempting to separate the impact of emotional and cognitive processes on attitudinal responses (e.g., Bagozzi, 1989; Breckler & Wiggins, 1989; Esses, Haddock, & Zanna, 1993). These researchers readily acknowledge that affective and cognitive responses can be at odds with each other, and they typically assume that whichever response is stronger will carry the day (usually by carrying greater weight in an aggregation of the outputs of the two systems). Thinking about the issue from the standpoint of AST suggests that there are many different ways in which conflict and contradiction could arise in our social representations of others. Consider the case of an individual whose membership in a stigmatized group is conveyed by visual cues, such as a physical handicap or disfigurement. If this person performs acts of kindness toward us, positive output may be produced from the behavioral observation system, and through translation processes such as trait inferences, affective, and evaluative responses as well. However, negative output may also result from processing of appearance cues and subsequent categorizations, affective, and evaluative responses. Carlston claims that when the various systems are simultaneously active, as in this example, they tend to produce consistent representations. What remains unclear, however, is specifically what processes operate to produce this interrepresentational consistency, and what the consequences are when such processes are unsuccessful.

PROCESSES PROMOTING REPRESENTATIONAL
COHERENCE

If we assume that people prefer consistency and coherence to conflict and ambivalence, it stands to reason that they will develop mechanisms to produce more internally consistent impressions. Some of these mechanisms may be automatized, occurring without conscious intent, whereas others may involve deliberate, controlled attempts to "manage" one's representations. We consider each type in turn.

One obvious strategy for minimizing interrepresentational conflict is to form simplified, unidimensional impressions. In many cases, such as those involving minimal interdependence between perceiver and target, a superficial impression will suffice (see Fiske & Neuberg, 1990). Stereotyping represents such a simplified strategy for impression formation. Categorization based on visual cues, with minimal initial activation of other impressional modes, may often produce a person representation that is adequate for the social perceiver's needs. Moreover, this mode of processing frees up resources for use on other potentially more important or rewarding tasks (Macrae, Milne, & Bodenhausen, 1994). Most important for the present purposes, if it becomes necessary or desirable to construct a richer sort of representation, other aspects of Carlston's impression matrix can be inferred on the basis of stereotypic knowledge through "translation" processes that access semantic and/or episodic memory. Under these circumstances, the representation is unlikely to contain discordant elements because much of it was inferred on the basis of the unitary initial impression.

When perceivers do engage more than one impressional system in forming a new impression, it is of course inevitable that these systems will sometimes initially produce inconsistent output, as in our earlier example of a helpful but disfigured person. What happens under such circumstances? One possibility is that a dominance hierarchy may be established among the systems, with the input from certain systems having preeminence over others. This sort of priority system could vary as a function of the person or the situation, but there might also be some general principles governing it. For instance, less involved forms of representation (see Carlston's Fig. 1.8) may carry less weight, whereas more abstract forms of representation may be seen as more informative and useful, and therefore carry more weight in any judgmental algorithm (see Carlston's Fig. 1.4). The nature of an impressional priority system of this sort is ultimately an empirical question. However, if such a system does operate, it could provide one (presumably automatic) mechanism for resolving or minimizing ambivalence in the representational structure: by emphasizing a subset of the total representation and using that subset as the primary basis for the translations and intermediate processes involved in impression formation, as articulated by AST.

It is clear that there are some circumstances under which we form impressions that are ambivalent and inconsistent, despite the potential operation of automatic processes designed to minimize the occurrence of such impressions. As we noted earlier, impressions of minority group members may represent one of the more common examples of this phenomenon. Of particular interest here is the aversive racist, who has lingering negative affect and avoidance tendencies toward minorities (because of socialization experiences in an historically prejudiced society), yet who also possesses sincere, positive beliefs about these groups (Gaertner & Dovidio, 1986). Does the aversive racist experience this ambivalence consciously? This is an important question that has not yet been fully resolved. Gaertner and Dovidio have shown that aversive racists attempt to justify their negative affect and behavior toward minorities as being due to factors other than minority group membership per se (so-called "nonracial justification factors"). If they are successfully able to engage in self-deception by invoking such factors, they may potentially avoid experiencing the ambivalence of their reactions to minority group members. Automatic, unintentional processes such as those outlined earlier may sometimes provide a means for resolving ambiguous representations before the conflict is consciously experienced. However, it must be noted that Devine et al. (1991) have clearly shown that sometimes we are acutely aware of inconsistent elements in our impressions of others. For example, many individuals are quite familiar with the discrepancies between their beliefs, feelings, and behavioral tendencies with respect to minorities such as African Americans and gay men and lesbians. How then does the social perceiver cope with this kind of ambivalence when it arises?

CONSEQUENCES OF IMPRESSIONAL AMBIVALENCE

Ambivalent and conflicting input into a composite impression is likely to create a kind of *metacognitive affective reaction* (for want of a better term) that is not an affective reaction to the target per se, but to the conflict arising in the process of forming a coherent impression of her or him. This "meta-affect" naturally would be unpleasant, and might motivate the perceiver to take actions that would reduce the impressional conflict. Two salient options open to social perceivers are: (a) to put the discordant impression out of mind, or (b) to attempt to "manage" their own impressions by consciously resolving the ambivalence. Along the latter line of thought, Devine and Monteith (1993) studied compunction as the affective motivation for controlled processing directed at eliminating unwanted stereotypic modes of thought. In this case, the source of the compunction is thought to lie in the perceiver's recognition that stereotypic thinking represents a contravention of his or her own personal nonprejudiced standards. In the more general case, the negative meta-affect, to which we alluded before, may be sufficient to provoke controlled attempts at resolving ambivalent impressions.

One possible way to conceptualize the controlled, metacognitive process of resolving inconsistent representations may lie in appealing to the "intermediate processes" postulated in AST. These processes (e.g., visual imagination, retrospection, verbal analysis) involve effortful activities that might be employed in the service of addressing impressional inconsistencies. In many cases, verbal thought may be the preferred mode for reconciling or rationalizing away these inconsistencies. Consider again the aversive racist who feels negative affect toward African Americans, yet who wants to think and act in nonprejudiced ways. In addition, consider an individual who desires to avoid stereotypic thinking, but who is aware of a target's group social membership, as well as individuating trait and behavioral information that is available (see Macrae, Bodenhausen, Milne, & Jetten, 1993). In such situations, there is conflicting input from different impressional systems: One type of input has attached to it some personal (in this case, moral) priority, whereas the other input is unwanted. There may be many other circumstances in which we desire to form certain kinds of impressions, yet not all of our impressional systems are producing output consistent with that desired end state. When this occurs, what is the perceiver to do about the inconsistent reactions that he or she is having?

One possible strategy, as Festinger (1957) noted, would be to mentally emphasize one subset of input and rationalize away the inconsistent input through verbal thought and analysis. In the case of the aversive racist, Gaertner and Dovidio expected that, under many circumstances, social perceivers will give in to the negative affective reactions they experience and rely on rationalization processes to bolster this negative impression and/or dismiss incompatible impressions. But Devine suggested a different process, at least among low-prejudice individuals. These individuals actively attempt to manage the impression-formation process by suppressing or inhibiting stereotypic or prejudiced modes of thought. This raises the interesting question of the extent to which the various impressional systems can come under executive control (Bargh, 1990; Uleman, 1989). One reasonable possibility is that the potential for executive control of impressional systems increases as the perceiver's level of involvement increases (see Carlston's Fig. 1.8). The success of this sort of metacognitive enterprise, however, may often be less than complete. For example, Wegner and Erber (1993) reviewed abundant evidence documenting that attempts at mental control often backfire. In our own research (Macrae, Bodenhausen, Milne, & Jetten, 1993, in press), we examined the consequences of attempts to avoid stereotypic modes of impression formation. In these studies, individuals attempted to not rely on categorical stereotypes while forming impressions of outgroup targets, instead basing their impressions on individuating behavioral information (i.e., they attempted to use the "behavioral observation" system, rather than the "categorization" system, to form an impression). The ironic consequence of this attempt to manage the impression-formation process was that, in devoting so much of their limited cognitive resources to the active suppression of their stereotypes, perceivers ended up paying less attention to the behavioral information on which they presumably wanted to base their impressions. Moreover, attempts at inhibiting stereotypic thoughts seemed to only make such thoughts hyperaccessible and likely to resurface later with greater vigor (see also Wegner & Erber, 1992).

If metacognitive strategies for impressional control fail, the perceiver may simply have to learn to live with ambivalent cognitive representations. Certain individuals may even prefer ambivalent structures (Kruglanski, 1989) because they fear the potential invalidity of their own conclusions if impressional closure is achieved. For such individuals, it is more comfortable playing both sides of the fence than risk being wrong. Langer (1993) argued that a tolerance for ambiguity and ambivalence may be adaptive, in that it may facilitate the identification of some new, viable options while minimizing the risk of prematurely foreclosing others. In any case, it is clear that Carlston's AST framework puts the issue of impressional coherence in a new light. It is our suspicion that empirical investigations of the intersystem coherence of impressions of persons and groups, inspired by the core ideas of AST, will reveal new and fundamental truths about the nature of humans' mental representations of their social worlds.

REFERENCES

Asch, S. (1946). Forming impressions of personality. *Journal of Abnormal and Social Psychology, 41,* 258-290.

Bagozzi, R. P. (1989). An investigation of the role of affective and moral evaluations in the purposeful behaviour model of attitude. *British Journal of Social Psychology, 28,* 97-113.

Bargh, J. A. (1990). Auto-motives: Preconscious determinants of social interaction. In E. T. Higgins & R. M. Sorrentino (Eds.), *Handbook of motivation and cognition* (Vol. 2, pp. 93-130). New York: Guilford.

Breckler, S. J., & Wiggins, E. C. (1989). Affect versus evaluation in the structure of attitudes. *Journal of Experimental Social Psychology, 25,* 253-271.

Brown, R. (1986). *Social psychology* (2nd ed.). New York: The Free Press.

Devine, P. G., & Monteith, M. J. (1993). The role of discrepancy-associated affect in prejudice reduction. In D. M. Mackie & D. L. Hamilton (Eds.), *Affect, cognition, and stereotyping: Interactive processes in group perception* (pp. 317-344). San Diego, CA: Academic Press.

Devine, P. G., Monteith, M. J., Zuwerink, J. R., & Elliot, A. J. (1991). Prejudice with and without compunction. *Journal of Personality and Social Psychology, 60,* 817-830.

Dovidio, J. F., Gaertner, S. L., Anastasio, P. A., & Sanitioso, R. (1992). Cognitive and motivational bases of bias: Implications of aversive racism for attitudes toward Hispanics. In S. Knouse, P. Rosenfield, & A. Culbertson (Eds.), *Hispanics in the workplace* (pp. 74–106). London: Sage.

Esses, V. M., Haddock, G., & Zanna, M. P. (1993). Values, stereotypes, and emotions as determinants of intergroup attitudes. In D. M. Mackie & D. L. Hamilton (Eds.), *Affect, cognition, and stereotyping: Interactive processes in group perception* (pp. 137–166). San Diego, CA: Academic Press.

Festinger, L. (1957). *A theory of cognitive dissonance.* Stanford, CA: Stanford University Press.

Fiske, S. T., & Neuberg, S. L. (1990). A continuum model of impression formation from category-based to individuating processes: Influences of information and motivation on attention and interpretation. In M. P. Zanna (Ed.), *Advances in experimental social psychology* (Vol. 23, pp. 1–74). San Diego, CA: Academic Press.

Gaertner, S. L., & Dovidio, J. F. (1986). The aversive form of racism. In J. Dovidio & S. Gaertner (Eds.), *Prejudice, discrimination, and racism* (pp. 61–89). Orlando, FL: Academic Press.

Katz, I., Wackenhut, J., & Hass, R. G. (1986). Racial ambivalence, value duality, and behavior. In J. Dovidio & S. Gaertner (Eds.), *Prejudice, discrimination, and racism* (pp. 35–59). Orlando, FL: Academic Press.

Kruglanski, A. (1989). *Lay epistemics and human knowledge.* New York: Plenum.

Langer, E. J. (1993, June). *The illusion of calculated decision.* Paper presented at the annual convention of the American Psychological Society, Chicago, IL.

Macrae, C. N., Bodenhausen, G. V., Milne, A. B., & Jetten, J. (1993). *On resisting the temptation for simplification: Cognitive costs of stereotype suppression.* Manuscript submitted for publication.

Macrae, C. N., Bodenhausen, G. V., Milne, A. B., & Jetten, J. (in press). Out of sight but back in mind: Stereotypes on the rebound. *Journal of Personality and Social Psychology.*

Macrae, C. N., Milne, A. B., & Bodenhausen, G. V. (1994). Stereotypes as energy-saving devices: A peek inside the cognitive toolbox. *Journal of Personality and Social Psychology, 66,* 37–47.

Osgood, C. E., Suci, G. J., & Tannenbaum, P. H. (1957). *The measurement of meaning.* Urbana, IL: University of Illinois Press.

Scott, W. A. (1968). Attitude measurement. In G. Lindsey & E. Aronson (Eds.), *Handbook of social psychology* (2nd ed., Vol. 2, pp. 204–273). Reading, MA: Addison-Wesley.

Srull, T. K., & Wyer, R. S., Jr. (1989). Person memory and judgment. *Psychological Review, 96,* 58–83.

Thompson, M. M., Zanna, M. P., & Griffin, D. W. (in prep). *Let's not be indifferent about (attitudinal) ambivalence.*

Uleman, J. S. (1989). A framework for thinking intentionally about unintended thoughts. In J. S. Uleman & J. A. Bargh (Eds.), *Unintended thought* (pp. 425–449). New York: Guilford.

Wegner, D. M., & Erber, R. (1992). The hyperaccessibility of suppressed thoughts. *Journal of Personality and Social Psychology, 63,* 903–912.

Wegner, D. M., & Erber, R. (1993). Social foundations of mental control. In D. Wegner & J. Pennebaker (Eds.), *Handbook of mental control* (pp. 36–56). Englewood Cliffs, NJ: Prentice-Hall.

Wyer, R. S., Jr., & Srull, T. K. (1989). *Memory and cognition in its social context.* Hillsdale, NJ: Lawrence Erlbaum Associates.

Zanna, M. P., & Rempel, J. K. (1988). Attitudes: A new look at an old concept. In D. Bar-Tal & A. Kruglanski (Eds.), *The social psychology of knowledge* (pp. 315–334). Cambridge, England: Cambridge University Press.

9 Attitudes in Associated Systems Theory

Russell H. Fazio
Indiana University

Carlston's Associated Systems Theory (AST; see chap. 1, this volume) provides an intriguing framework for considering the multiple representations that an individual can form of a target person. AST concerns the nature and source of these representations and, probably most importantly, their relations with one another. By postulating the existence of four primary mental systems—sensory, verbal, action, and affective—whose unique representations can combine to form hybrid representations, AST advances a 3 × 3 taxonomy. Representations vary from concrete to abstract along one dimension of the taxonomy (the columns in Carlston's Fig. 1.2). The other dimension involves representations that vary from a focus on the target to a focus on the perceiver's reactions to the target (the rows in Carlston's Fig. 1.2).

As one who has devoted much time to the study of attitudes, I find the lower right portion of the taxonomy (affective responses, evaluations, and orientations) especially interesting. This area includes relatively abstract representations of the perceiver's reactions to the target person. The focus is on the affective system and its hybrids. Thus, these reactions necessarily involve valence—positivity or negativity that the perceiver associates with the target. Essentially, then, the lower right portion of the taxonomy refers to representations of the perceiver's attitude toward the target person.

Carlston makes a number of provocative references to attitude theory and research at various points in his chapter. To emphasize the relationship between the attitude literature and AST more strongly, this chapter focuses on the attitude construct.

YES, AST CONCERNS ALL POTENTIAL ATTITUDE OBJECTS

AST need not and should not be restricted to cognitive representations of persons. In recognition of the generality of his model, Carlston suggests that AST can be extended to representations other than persons. I wish to reinforce this assertion in the strongest possible terms. The term *attitude object* traditionally has been employed in a very broad sense. The object can refer not only to a physical object, but also to a social issue, situation, event, or, especially relevant to AST, a person, or group of persons. Sensory, verbal, action, and affective systems are certainly involved in our representations of such broadly defined objects.

As my colleagues and I have noted elsewhere (e.g., Sanbonmatsu & Fazio, 1990; Sherman & Fazio, 1983), research on person perception and research on attitudes have needlessly developed as fairly independent traditions. Numerous parallels exist between these research domains. Both have been concerned with the integration of information—be it traits that a target person might possess or attributes that characterize an object—into a summary judgment (e.g., Anderson, 1981; Fishbein, 1963). Once formed, such summary judgments—be they impressions of a target person or attitudes toward an object or issue—are known to have the potential to color one's appraisals when the person, object, or issue is later encountered (e.g., Kelley, 1950; Lord, Ross, & Lepper, 1979). Regardless of whether they involve a target person, object, or issue, these summary judgments also share implications for memory processes (e.g., Carlston, 1980; Ross, McFarland, & Fletcher, 1981). Dual-process models that point to the importance of motivational factors in determining whether individuals will rely on such previously formed summary judgments when making a decision, as opposed to engaging in a more effortful, data-driven analysis of the available information, have achieved prominence in both literatures (e.g., Fazio, 1990; Fiske & Neuberg, 1990). In addition, questions have arisen in both literatures regarding the situational conditions and goals that prompt individuals to form such summary judgments (e.g., Fazio, Lenn, & Effrein, 1984; Wyer & Srull, 1986).

These are just some of the many parallels that exist between the person perception and attitude domains. My aim is not to enumerate such parallels, but merely to illustrate that the commonalities are more than sufficient to warrant linking these two literatures more closely. From my perspective, it would be very unfortunate if AST were to be viewed, tested, and developed solely as a framework for considering the impressions that perceivers form of target persons. AST has implications for issues central to the attitude literature, and also stands to benefit from consideration of issues that have arisen in the attitude literature.

ATTITUDES IN THE AST FRAMEWORK

As Carlston notes, AST relates to attitude theory and research in several significant ways. The points made by Carlston merit reiteration and elaboration. I also raise some additional issues concerning which AST and attitude work bear upon one another.

Hot Versus Cold Evaluation

In addition to employing the term *object* in a very broad sense, attitude researchers have used the terms *attitude, affect,* and *evaluation* broadly (and not necessarily consistently). Although terminology has varied, there appears to be considerable agreement that one's attitude toward an object may vary from a "hot," emotional response to the object to a "cold," more analytical judgment of the object (e.g., Abelson, Kinder, Peters, & Fiske, 1982; Fazio, Sanbonmatsu, Powell, & Kardes, 1986; Zanna & Rempel, 1988). AST provides a very useful perspective for considering the nature of the attitude that becomes associated with an object. An attitude can "reside" primarily within the affective system, in which case it represents a hot, emotional reaction to the object. However, AST postulates that the affective system may combine with the verbal system to form a hybrid representation that Carlston refers to as *evaluation.* Such a hybrid seemingly would involve a characterization of the affect that is likely to be produced by the attributes noted in the verbal system's representation of the object. Its link to the verbal system, and the resulting emphasis on the favorability of attributes possessed by the object, make an attitude of this sort "colder" than an attitude that emanates purely from the affective system.

This distinction between hot versus cold attitudes, affect versus evaluation, or whichever terms one prefers, may prove to be very important for attitude change and attitude–behavior processes. Both Edwards (1990) and Millar and Millar (1990) explored the question of social influence strategies that are best suited to altering attitudes of either type. Elsewhere, I have reported some evidence suggesting that hotter attitudes may generally be more accessible from memory than colder attitudes (Fazio, in press).

Basis for the Attitude

A second, but related, parallel between AST and recent attitude work mentioned by Carlston concerns the informational basis for an attitude. The AST perspective indicates that an attitude can be based on: (a) the affect that the object produces, (b) features that the verbal system associates with the object, or (c) past behaviors toward the object as represented by the action system. This view is harmonious with recent characterizations of the attitude construct by a number of attitude theorists. Most notably, Zanna and Rempel (1988) argued for a conceptualization of an attitude as not necessarily involving the affective, cognitive, and behavioral components postulated by the classic tripartite definition, but as evaluations of an object that can be based on affect, beliefs, and/or past behaviors.

This approach has two implications that merit discussion in the present context. First, it raises a provocative empirical question concerning the potential consequences of differential informational bases for an attitude. Generally speaking, some bases may lead to a stronger attitude than others. Elsewhere, I have suggested that individuals may be sensitive to the diagnosticity of the evidentiary base upon which they are relying to form an attitude (Fazio, in press). That is, through their previous learning, individuals may come to trust some classes of information as more indicative of their attitudes than other classes of information. I argued that freely chosen behavior toward an object and emotional reactions to the object may be viewed as especially informative and attitudinally diagnostic. As a result, the evaluation implied by such classes of information may be noted more readily, and the object and the evaluation more strongly associated in memory, producing a more accessible attitude (see Fazio, in press, for a review of relevant evidence).

It is interesting to consider this possibility in the context of AST. In the AST taxonomy, behavior and emotion differ from the verbal system in that the latter's focus is on the target, whereas the former both focus on the perceiver's reaction to the target. In other words, the behavior and emotion systems involve a greater self-orientation than does the verbal system. Past behaviors toward an object, and the emotions that an object provokes, may be viewed as attitudinally diagnostic precisely because they inherently involve this self-orientation. The self-orientation may enhance the ease with which individuals can create a summary attitudinal judgment of the object. In contrast, the verbal system provides only a description of the object's attributes, which the perceiver then needs to relate to the self. Such a difference may contribute to the strength of the resulting associations linking an object to a summary attitudinal judgment. Regardless of the validity of this specific reasoning, AST, like the Zanna and Rempel (1988) perspective, clearly encourages one to consider the differences that might exist among attitudes that stem from varying representational systems.

A second implication of this perspective on attitudes concerns the construction of attitudinal judgments. An attitude expression can be viewed as stemming from whatever particular information is available and salient at the moment of the expression's construction. This notion actually extends beyond a classification of the attitude as being affectively, cognitively, or behaviorally based. Even within a given class, the specific information that is relatively more accessible will exert greater influence on the attitude expression that is constructed. Experimental work has demonstrated that even subtle linguistic manipulations (e.g., "I did X 'because I . . .' vs. 'in order to . . .' ") can alter the manner in which individuals view their past behaviors, making the intrinsic or extrinsic value of an object differentially salient (e.g., Salancik, 1974; Seligman, Fazio, & Zanna, 1980). As a result, these different perspectives on one's behavior can influence attitude constructions. Considered in the context of AST, such findings suggest an intriguing and complex interplay among verbal, action, and affect systems. A verbal manipulation apparently produces differential representations of past behaviors toward the target object, which then form the basis for differing attitudinal assessments.

More recent research also has indicated that attitude expressions can be unduly influenced by momentarily salient attributes of an attitude object. Shavitt and Fazio (1991) found the consistency between attitudes and behavior predictions to be strongly influenced by the degree to which the attributes salient at the time of attitude expression and those salient at the time of behavior prediction corresponded. In this work, it was assumed that 7-Up and Perrier mineral water differ in the attribute dimensions on which they are naturally evaluated. 7-Up is typically evaluated on the basis of taste, whereas the trendiness of Perrier makes it more likely to be evaluated on the basis of the social impression it creates. Immediately prior to providing a favorability rating of one of these beverages, subjects completed a questionnaire intended to heighten the salience of either a taste or a social-impression dimension. Subjects rated either the taste of a number of food items or the extent to which each of a number of actions would make a good impression on others. A subsequent behavior prediction (likelihood of purchasing or drinking the target beverage in various specific situations) was made in the absence of any such contextual manipulation.

The manipulation apparently induced subjects to consider and weigh the target beverage's standing on the salient dimension more heavily than they typically would. The evaluations expressed by subjects corresponded closely with their behavior predictions when the attribute dimension whose salience was heightened by the questionnaire matched the one expected to be naturally salient for the target beverage (7-Up/taste, Perrier/social impression)—much more so than in the cases of a mismatch (7-Up/social impression, Perrier/taste). In these latter cases, attitude expressions appear to have been unduly influenced by the salient dimension. In the context of AST, such findings illustrate how alterations in the verbal system's representation of a target object can form the basis for different evaluative judgments.

It is important to recognize, however, that the malleability of attitudinal expressions, illustrated by the research mentioned previously, is not universally true of all attitudes of all individuals. Such malleability depends on the extent to which individuals are motivated by goal or task demands to construct an attitudinal evaluation on the basis of information available and salient at that moment in time. My colleagues and I have suggested that attitudes can be conceptualized along an attitude–nonattitude continuum (Fazio, 1989, in press; Fazio et al., 1986), representing the availability and accessibility of the attitude from memory. As noted originally by Converse (1970), *nonattitudes* refer to cases in which individuals provide responses to an attitude survey even though they have no preexisting evaluation of the attitude object available in memory. Essentially, the evaluation has to be constructed completely "on the spot"—on the basis of whatever relevant attributes might be available in memory or in the current situational context. As we move along the continuum, an evaluation is available in memory, and the strength of the associative connection in memory between the attitude object and the evaluation increases. Consequently, the attitude's capability for automatic activation increases. Thus, toward the upper end of the continuum is the case of a well-learned association—sufficiently so that the evaluation is capable of being activated automatically from memory upon mere observation of the attitude object.

According to this perspective, attitudes toward the upper end of the continuum (i.e., those characterized by relatively stronger object-evaluation associations in memory and, hence, greater accessibility) should display less malleability than those toward the nonattitude end of the continuum (Fazio, 1987). A variety of evidence supports this proposition. Attitude accessibility has been found to moderate the extent to which individuals are influenced by new information about the attitude object. More accessible attitudes are more resistant to counterinfluence and, hence, more persistent over time (see Fazio, in press, for a review). This relative stability provides one indication that accessible attitudes would be less sensitive to the momentary salience of a given attribute dimension or item of information.

Also relevant is a second experiment by Shavitt and Fazio (1991), which found the effects of attribute salience summarized previously to be moderated by the individual-difference measure of self-monitoring. High self-monitors displayed more sensitivity to the salience manipulation than did low self-monitors. High self-monitors are typically responsive to situational cues (Snyder & DeBono, 1989) and, hence, may have been more motivated to construct their attitudes on the basis of the salient-attribute dimension. Moreover, low self-monitors typically are guided by internal dispositions, and have been observed to hold attitudes of relatively greater accessibility, in general, than high self-monitors (Kardes, Sanbonmatsu, Voss, & Fazio, 1986). For either or both of these reasons, low self-monitors may have experienced less need to construct an attitude, as opposed to simply accessing a previously formed attitude, than did high self-monitors. Apparently, high self-monitors' reliance on an attitude-construction process led them to be unduly influenced by the contextually salient-attribute dimension.

The most direct evidence regarding the relationship between attitude accessibility and the malleability of attitude expressions as a function of information salience is provided by a recent study conducted by Hodges and Wilson (1993). Several weeks after having assessed subjects' attitudes toward then President Reagan, as well as the accessibility of subjects' attitudes, these investigators contacted subjects for participation in a phone survey. The subjects were asked to explain why they felt the way they did about various issues, including Reagan. As has been commonly observed in research concerned with the effects of analyzing reasons for one's attitude (Wilson, Dunn, Kraft, & Lisle, 1989), the reasons that subjects listed were not in perfect accordance with their previously measured attitudes. Subjects with attitudes of high or low accessibility tended to describe reasons that were equivalently discordant in this regard. That is, the correspondence between judges' rating of the attitude implied by the listed reasons and the prior attitude score did not vary as a function of attitude accessibility. Nonetheless, the impact of these now highly salient reasons upon subsequent attitude expressions did vary with attitude accessibility. Immediately after having generated their reasons, the subjects once again provided an evaluation of Reagan. Subjects whose attitudes were relatively low in accessibility (as assessed weeks earlier) more strongly based their evaluation on this momentarily salient set of reasons than did subjects with more accessible attitudes. Apparently, those with highly accessible attitudes could easily retrieve their previously stored, and strongly associated, evaluation of Reagan from memory. Not needing to construct an attitude on the spot, they were less influenced by the salient "reasons" information than were individuals for whom attitudes were less accessible from memory.

AST readily accommodates such findings. Relatively strong associations can be accessed easily. On the other hand, weak or nonexistent associations require the individual to construct an evaluative judgment on the basis of whichever representational system is engaged, and on the specific contents of the representation that are accessible for consideration.

Ambivalence

Sometimes a given object can produce both positive and negative affective responses from a given individual. Although long recognized as one of the reasons that individuals may rate an object at or near the neutral point of a bipolar scale (Kaplan, 1972), interest in such cases of ambivalence has enjoyed a recent resurgence among attitude researchers (Petty, 1993; Thompson, Zanna, & Griffin, in press). AST has some interesting implications for the consideration of ambivalence, and especially for the form that it may assume.

Carlston postulates that the activation of a concept may produce spreading inhibition, as well as spreading activation. Such spreading inhibition serves to suppress the activation of concepts that can be considered alternatives to the one that has been activated. At first glance, this theoretical premise would seem to imply that simultaneously experiencing positive and negative reactions to an attitude object is unlikely. However, Carlston's notion of spreading inhibition is more specific. He argues that the activation of any form of representation interferes "with retrieval of other alternate concepts *of that same form*" (p. 23, italics added). The implication is that ambivalence within the representation from any *given* mental system is unlikely. Hence, the affective system is not likely to react with both a positively and negatively valenced emotional response to an object.

This line of reasoning suggests that some forms of ambivalence may be more common than others. Ambivalence is more likely to stem from inconsistencies across mental systems (or their hybrids) than from inconsistencies within a given system. With respect to attitudinal reactions, these would be inconsistencies across the affective, evaluation, and orientation cells of the AST taxonomy. Intuitively, such forms of ambivalence do appear to be quite common. Emotional reactions to an object may differ in valence from the evaluations derived from the verbal system's representation of the attributes possessed by an object. Such cases as "going to the dentist" or "getting an injection" may evoke a negative emotion, while at the same time evoking a colder evaluation that recognizes the beneficial nature of the activity. Likewise, habitual orientations toward an object, as in the case of a cigarette smoker attempting to quit, may be inconsistent with evaluations based on an analysis of the consequences of cigarette smoking. Again, given that they "reside" in different representational systems, these inconsistent habitual orientations and evaluations may be experienced simultaneously.

To this point, I have considered attitudinal ambivalence as involving the simultaneous activation of positive and negative sentiments toward an object. However, there is a second perspective that also can be pursued — one that suggests that such simultaneous activation may be rather unusual. It is abundantly clear that, when asked to evaluate an object, a given individual sometimes associates both positive and negative evaluations with the object. That is, the individual often notes positively and negatively valued aspects of the object. When the object is encountered in a context that does not involve the deliberate goal of evaluating the object, however, it may be that only one of the two inconsistent evaluations (if any) is automatically activated from memory. Essentially, the differing evaluations may be associated with different categorizations of the attitude object, and the situational context may promote one categorization over another. Elsewhere I have discussed the possibility of an initial categorization stage (serving to identify the attitude object) preceding the automatic activation of any strongly associated evaluation of the object (Fazio, 1986). Thus, in the context of a peaceful stroll through the woods, a chain saw may be categorized as a noisemaker, automatically activating a negative evaluation. However, in the context of a large tree limb fallen against one's house, the chain saw may be categorized as a useful tool. Likewise, categorizations of a dentist are likely to vary in the context of a throbbing toothache versus an old filling that needs to be replaced.

This perspective views attitudinal ambivalence as stemming from multiple potential categorizations of an object — categorizations that vary in their affective associations. When people are asked to evaluate the object in the abstract, it may be their awareness and consideration of these multiple categorizations that prompt ratings indicative of ambivalence. However, in a specific situation, sufficient cues may exist to prompt identification of the object as an X, and only the affect associated with X may be activated.

Such a view appears consistent with the AST framework, in that AST allows for multiple categorizations of an object, which may themselves be associated with different affective reactions. The *categories* cell of the AST taxonomy, a hybrid of the perceptual system and verbal system, is obviously relevant in this regard. However, the *appearance* and *behavioral observations* cells are also relevant in that they too may involve what can be viewed as multiple categories (see Carlston's Fig. 1.5) — in these cases, categorizations of specific appearance cues (e.g., *good looking*) or common behavioral observations (e.g., *yells a lot*). The relevance of the cells in this upper left corner of the AST taxonomy (appearance, categories, and behavioral observations) may stem from their relatively concrete nature. As Carlston hypothesizes, seeming inconsistencies may be much more common (and less psychologically troublesome) at these concrete levels than at more abstract levels. To the extent that these multiple, relatively concrete categorizations are associated with affect of different valence, which categorization is more strongly activated by the specific context cues may be critical in determining the nature of the attitudinal reaction that is activated in that situation.

CONCLUSION

It appears evident that Carlston's AST framework and recent work concerning attitudes bear heavily on one another. For this reason, I hope that AST will be viewed and tested as a general model of representations —

one that extends beyond representations solely of other people. What is most appealing about AST is its integrative power. Its appeal and potential are only enhanced by its generalizability to cognitive representations of any broadly defined attitude object.

ACKNOWLEDGMENTS

Preparation of this commentary was supported by Research Scientist Development Award MH00452 and grant MH38832 from the National Institute of Mental Health.

REFERENCES

Abelson, R. P., Kinder, D. R., Peters, M. D., & Fiske, S. T. (1982). Affective and semantic components in political person perception. *Journal of Personality and Social Psychology*, *42*, 619-630.

Anderson, N. H. (1981). *Foundations of information integration theory*. New York: Academic Press.

Carlston, D. E. (1980). The recall and use of traits and events in social inference processes. *Journal of Experimental Social Psychology*, *16*, 303-328.

Converse, P. E. (1970). Attitudes and non-attitudes: Continuation of a dialogue. In E. R. Tufte (Ed.), *The quantitative analysis of social problems* (pp. 168-189). Reading, MA: Addison-Wesley.

Edwards, K. (1990). The interplay of affect and cognition in attitude formation and change. *Journal of Personality and Social Psychology*, *59*, 202-216.

Fazio, R. H. (1986). How do attitudes guide behavior? In R. M. Sorrentino & E. T. Higgins (Eds.), *The handbook of motivation and cognition*: *Foundations of social behavior* (pp. 204-243). New York: Guilford.

Fazio, R. H. (1987). Self-perception theory: A current perspective. In M. P. Zanna, J. M. Olson, & C. P. Herman (Eds.), *Social influence*: *The Ontario symposium* (Vol. 5, pp. 129-150). Hillsdale, NJ: Lawrence Erlbaum Associates.

Fazio, R. H. (1989). On the power and functionality of attitudes: The role of attitude accessibility. In A. R. Pratkanis, S. J. Breckler, & A. G. Greenwald (Eds.), *Attitude structure and function* (pp. 153-179). Hillsdale, NJ: Lawrence Erlbaum Associates.

Fazio, R. H. (1990). Multiple processes by which attitudes guide behavior: The MODE model as an integrative framework. In M. P. Zanna (Ed.), *Advances in experimental social psychology* (Vol. 23, pp. 75-109). New York: Academic Press.

Fazio, R. H. (in press). Attitudes as object-evaluation associations: Determinants, consequences, and correlates of attitude accessibility. In R. E. Petty & J. A. Krosnick (Eds.), *Attitude strength*: *Antecedents and consequences*. Hillsdale, NJ: Lawrence Erlbaum Associates.

Fazio, R. H., Lenn, T. M., & Effrein, E. A. (1984). Spontaneous attitude formation. *Social Cognition*, *2*, 217-234.

Fazio, R. H., Sanbonmatsu, D. M., Powell, M. C., & Kardes, F. R. (1986). On the automatic activation of attitudes. *Journal of Personality and Social Psychology*, *50*, 229-238.

Fishbein, M. (1963). An investigation of the relationship between beliefs about an object and attitude toward that object. *Human Relations*, *16*, 233-240.

Fiske, S. T., & Neuberg, S. L. (1990). A continuum of impression formation, from category-based to individuating processes: Influences of information and motivation on attention and interpretation. In M. P. Zanna (Ed.), *Advances in experimental social psychology* (Vol. 23, pp. 1–74). New York: Academic Press.

Hodges, S. D., & Wilson, T. D. (1993). Effects of analyzing reasons on attitude change: The moderating role of attitude accessibility. *Social Cognition, 11*, 353–366.

Kaplan, K. J. (1972). On the ambivalence-indifference problem in attitude theory and measurement: A suggested modification of the semantic differential technique. *Psychological Bulletin, 77*, 361–372.

Kardes, F. R., Sanbonmatsu, D. M., Voss, R., & Fazio, R. H. (1986). Self-monitoring and attitude accessibility. *Personality and Social Psychology Bulletin, 12*, 468–474.

Kelley, H. H. (1950). The warm–cold variable in first impressions of persons. *Journal of Personality, 18*, 431–439.

Lord, C. G., Ross, L., & Lepper, M. R. (1979). Biased assimilation and attitude polarization: The effects of prior theories on subsequently considered evidence. *Journal of Personality and Social Psychology, 37*, 2098–2109.

Millar, M. G., & Millar, K. U. (1990). Attitude change as a function of attitude type and argument type. *Journal of Personality and Social Psychology, 59*, 217–228.

Petty, R. E. (1993, August). *Attitudinal ambivalence.* Symposium presented at the annual meeting of the American Psychological Association, Toronto, Canada.

Ross, M., McFarland, C., & Fletcher, G. J. O. (1981). The effect of attitude on the recall of personal histories. *Journal of Personality and Social Psychology, 40*, 627–634.

Salancik, G. R. (1974). Inference of one's attitude from behavior recalled under linguistically manipulated cognitive sets. *Journal of Personality and Social Psychology, 10*, 415–427.

Sanbonmatsu, D. M., & Fazio, R. H. (1990). The role of attitudes in memory-based decision making. *Journal of Personality and Social Psychology, 59*, 614–622.

Seligman, C., Fazio, R. H., & Zanna, M. P. (1980). Effects of salience of extrinsic rewards on liking and loving. *Journal of Personality and Social Psychology, 38*, 453–460.

Shavitt, S., & Fazio, R. H. (1991). Effects of attribute salience on the consistency between attitudes and behavior predictions. *Personality and Social Psychology Bulletin, 17*, 507–516.

Sherman, S. J., & Fazio, R. H. (1983). Parallels between attitudes and traits as predictors of behavior. *Journal of Personality, 51*, 308–345.

Snyder, M., & DeBono, K. (1989). Understanding the functions of attitudes: Lessons from personality and social behavior. In A. R. Pratkanis, S. J. Breckler, & A. G. Greenwald (Eds.), *Attitude structure and function* (pp. 339–359). Hillsdale, NJ: Lawrence Erlbaum Associates.

Thompson, M. M., Zanna, M. P., & Griffin, D. W. (in press). Let's not be indifferent about (attitudinal) ambivalence. In R. E. Petty & J. A. Krosnick (Eds.), *Attitude strength: Antecedents and consequences.* Hillsdale, NJ: Lawrence Erlbaum Associates.

Wilson, T. D., Dunn, D. S., Kraft, D., & Lisle, D. J. (1989). Introspection, attitude change, and attitude-behavior consistency: The disruptive effects of explaining why we feel the way we do. In L. Berkowitz (Ed.), *Advances in experimental social psychology* (Vol. 19, pp. 123–205). Orlando, FL: Academic Press.

Wyer, R. S., & Srull, T. K. (1986). Human cognition in its social context. *Psychological Review, 93*, 322–359.

Zanna, M. P., & Rempel, J. K. (1988). Attitudes: A new look at an old concept. In D. Bar-Tal & A. W. Kruglanski (Eds.), *The social psychology of knowledge* (pp. 315–354). New York: Cambridge University Press.

10 AST Revisited: On the Many Facets of Impressions and Theories

Donal E. Carlston
Cheri W. Sparks
Purdue University

The diverse nature of these perceptive commentaries (see chaps. 2–9) reminds us of the poem about three blind men who encounter an elephant. As the reader may recall, one took hold of the trunk, one the tusk, and one the tail, and each described the same creature in starkly different terms. The poem is apropos whether one considers the elephant to represent intangible cognitive representations, or the more opaque facets of Associated System Theory (AST), because in either case it is hard to see these things clearly. Consequently, there are different ways to construe these "elephants," and at times different people may envision the same underlying creature in quite different ways.

We do not mean to imply that the commentators for this volume are blind or that their descriptions are in error. After all, in the poem, the various descriptions of the unseen elephant were essentially accurate, as far as they went. Similarly, the perceptions detailed in the various commentaries are, for the most part, quite insightful. Yet, in one way or another, we have all have managed to get a hold of something different. One challenge for this chapter is to show how the ideas touched on by commentators in the previous chapters fit together with the ideas that AST is groping to understand and explain. Perhaps by assembling and comparing these myriad insights, we can begin to piece together the nature of the illusive things that we are trying to describe.

The authors of most past target chapters have elected to organize their replies thematically, citing the commentaries at the various points where they became relevant. This has allowed them to organize their comments logically, and to proceed without tangent or redundancy through the points they wish to make. In Volume 4, McGuire and McGuire proved that a reply can be similarly coherent and intelligent when organized by commentary — a structure that simplifies the comparison of commentaries and replies. Here we try to follow McGuire and McGuire's example, proceeding through the commentaries one at a time.

The issues we focus on in the earliest chapters (Martindale, chap. 2; Van Manen & Fiske, chap. 3; Wyer, chap. 4) involve basic postulates and hypotheses underlying AST. These commentaries challenge us to clarify and justify different ideas from the target chapter; in attempting to do so, we hope to give readers a better sense of how we view the AST "elephant." The middle chapters (Fiedler, chap. 5; Radvansky, chap. 6) raise metatheoretical issues for us regarding the nature of AST's objectives and contributions. In replying to these commentaries, we try to differentiate AST from other approaches to cognitive phenomena. The final commentaries (Brewer, chap. 7; Bodenhausen & Macrae, chap. 8; Fazio, chap. 9) emphasize possible applications of AST to specific issues in social psychology. We find such efforts intriguing and flattering, although they do tempt us to go even further beyond our initial objectives than perhaps we should. At the risk of running this poor elephant metaphor into the ground, we might say that we have been seduced by these into climbing aboard to see where AST might take us when it is allowed to roam freely. As we make this trip, we must keep in mind that some uncertainty remains as to exactly what kind of creature we are riding, and how far we should allow it to take us before we jump off.

ON THE REPRESENTATION OF REPRESENTATIONS

Before addressing the specific concerns of various commentators (particularly those in chaps. 2–6), several general observations are in order. First, it should be openly acknowledged that the arrangement of systems and representations in AST could be in error. Several different theorists propose adjustments in this arrangement, and though we try to justify the structure currently hypothesized by AST, contrary evidence may ultimately prevail. When it does, the authors are prepared to modify the theory. This is not simply an admission of fallibility. Rather, we suggest that the particular structure that AST hypothesizes is less important than the basic theoretical postulates: (a) that social representations are represented multimodally, (b) that these representations are systematically related to basic mental systems and to each other, and (c) that this systematicity has important implications regarding the formation and utilization of these representations. A point-by-point listing of AST's central postulates is provided in our response to Wyer's commentary.

Second, as Carlston implies in the target chapter, the figural representations of AST are metaphorical. They are designed to convey some basic assumptions of AST, and an attempt has been made to achieve consistency with several existing models of mental organization and activity. However, the cones and matrices composing the figures clearly exist in the mind of the theorist, rather than in the brains of social perceivers. The figures are necessarily selective and oversimplified in that there are facets of cognitive organization that they represent better than others. Moreover, there are alternative ways to depict cognitive structure, such as those suggested in the commentaries by Martindale and by Van Manen and Fiske, that have different implications and lead to different conclusions. We concede that the choice of one metaphorical representation over others may have as much to do with art as with science. Consequently, although we attempt to clarify and justify our illustrations, we do not mean to imply that there is some extratheoretical truth regarding the shape and size of the cones, or the symmetrically rectangular arrangement of matrix cells.

Third, as described in the opening section of the target chapter, AST is centrally concerned with providing a theoretical integration of different kinds of social representations. Given this integrative goal, the structure shown in Fig. 1.2 (and related figures) is primarily intended to relate known representational forms to basic mental processing systems, and to arrange these forms in terms of various aspects of their similarity and dissimilarity. As the target chapter notes, the resultant organization is reasonably congruent with a rather diverse set of considerations. However, one must be careful not to exaggerate the implications of this organizational metaphor, especially when dealing with its less central aspects. Thus, for example, we have never viewed the depicted structure as characterizing a necessary progression in the generation or translation of representations: One can deduce traits from appearance without first "going through" categorizations.

Finally, AST necessarily involves particular definitions of social representations, generally derived from the social psychological literature. These definitions are briefly mentioned in the target chapter, and elaborated in more detail elsewhere (Carlston, 1992). We believe that the terms we use for different representations are generally congruent with common usage in social psychology, although some of these terms have somewhat broader referents outside of this field. Therefore, it is necessary to clarify certain definitions and constrain the discussion to the kinds of social representations implicated by AST.

CLARIFICATIONS OF BASIC THEORY

Thinking About Thoughts and Systems: Reply to Martindale

Martindale (chap. 2) justly notes that there are similarities between AST and his own model of general cognition. We especially recommend his 1991 volume, *Cognitive Psychology: A Neural-Network Approach*, for its clear elaboration of some of the theoretical underpinnings of AST, including the description of the internal, hierarchical organization of the perceptual, semantic, action, and episodic "modules," and his elaboration of ideas related to connectionism, lateral inhibition, and parallel processing. AST incorporates many such ideas in its attempt to provide a comprehensive model of the multimodal cognitive structure underlying social cognition. For the most part, however, the focus of this reply is on some of the issues where our views diverge.

Where We Don't Overlap.   In his commentary, Martindale suggests that the cognitive structure posited by AST is not quite right. In particular, he notes "that there is no overlap between the perceptual system and the affective system nor between the action system and the verbal system." He observes that visual appearance can evoke strong affective reactions, and that the verbal–semantic system may be necessary to interpret whether a touch is desired. He also suggests some other interactions among primary systems that he feels are inadequately represented by the structure depicted in Fig. 1.1. For example, he argues that semantic memory must play a role in the understanding of episodic events, and that some categorizations involve affect. He suggests several ways to modify Fig. 1.1 so that it incorporates the "overlap" in systems implied by such influences.

As implied earlier, the arrangement of representations in AST is primarily intended to reflect similarities between representations, rather than influences among them. Thus, in Fig. 1.1, the overlap between cones represents featural overlap, and the hybrid representations at these points of intersection are believed to embody features characteristic of both adjoining representations. Similarly, in Fig. 1.2, adjacent cells are assigned to forms of representation believed to relate to the same primary systems, and thus to have certain featural characteristics in common. Possible influences or associations between representations are diagrammatically represented not through spatial proximity, but through associative linkages of varying strength, as depicted in Fig. 1.5.

Admittedly, the target chapter does suggest that representations that are adjacent in Fig. 1.2 are more likely to be associatively linked than are more distant representations, and one might conclude from this that closely associated representations should be depicted as contiguous. However, as Carlston (chap. 1) attempted to illustrate with a geography analogy, there are probably many instances where stronger linkages exist between distant, unrelated forms of representation than between proximal, related forms of representation. One example provided in the target chapter involves the strong associations that can occur between physical appearance and affective reactions. This is one of the specific kinds of association that concerns Martindale, and, in a later commentary, Van Manen and Fiske. Consequently, the nature of such perception-affect associations are examined more fully in the following section.

On Liking What You See. It is undoubtedly true, as Martindale and others note, that the physical appearances of certain people provoke strong emotional responses in perceivers. Perhaps this linkage is so evident because it is easy to think of particular people whose very appearance prompts pleasant or unpleasant feelings. Moreover, in extreme cases, involving exceptional beauty or deformity, appearance cues may be capable of directly eliciting emotional responses. However, people who have such attributes probably represent a fairly small minority of those we encounter every day. The appearance characteristics of most people we interact with seem unlikely to provoke much of an emotional response. In general, appearance seems more likely to evoke categorizations or, with people we have encountered before, episodic memories. Furthermore, excluding the extreme cases described previously, our emotional reactions probably spring less from appearance per se than from cognitive appraisals (i.e., evaluations) or the general nature of our interactions (i.e., orientations). Those individuals about whom we feel strongly probably provoke a variety of associations, in addition to affect, and it may be that the affective response originated in earlier appraisals or interactions, but has now become automatized. Thus, as compelling as the notion of a general appearance-affect link may be, we maintain that associations between these representations are probably less common than other associations involving perception or affection, respectively.

This conclusion is supported by the multidimensional analyses described in the target chapter, which provide no evidence for close appearance-affect connections. Specifically, these results indicate that appearance characteristics and affective responses do not co-occur with any regularity, at least across written descriptions of an assortment of different target individuals. In this research, *affect* is operationally defined as a description of an explicit emotional reaction to a target individual. This can include statements of love, hate, disgust, good feelings, or whatever, provided that these are characterized as emotional reactions to the target. However, this definition excludes the affective tone that is sometimes inherent in other forms of representation, such as appearance descriptors (e.g., *beautiful*), traits (e.g., *brilliant*), evaluations (e.g., *wonderful*), or episodic descriptions (e.g., *he insulted me*).[1] Consequently, the kinds of affect examined in the

---

[1]Of course, other kinds of secondary implications are similarly overlooked by our focus on the central features of descriptors. Thus, we code *he punched a friend* as an episodic description even though it strongly implies hostile or aggressive traits, we code *beautiful* as an appearance descriptor even though it strongly implies evaluation, and so on. The central goal is always to infer the nature of the representation underlying each description by focusing on the principal features of each descriptor.

multidimensional analyses may be somewhat more limited than construed by Martindale or others.

It is certainly true that evaluative appearance or trait descriptors may betray an underlying affective reaction. However, such descriptors can also be used dispassionately, and characterizing all evaluative implications as affect would introduce a number of problems. For example, this would make it difficult to distinguish among affect, evaluations, and personality traits, all of which are almost always inherently evaluative. To permit the clear delineation of such forms, the AST coding system codes each descriptive "thought unit" only in terms of its principal features (e.g., appearance, traits, or affect), and codes its positive, neutral, or negative implications as the valence of that unit, rather than as a separate affective response to the individual. One benefit of this procedure is that it allows the evaluative implications of different impressional components to be compared as an index of ambivalence (see Bodenhausen & Macrae, chap. 8, this volume; Fazio, chap. 9, this volume; Carlston, 1992).

Although these distinctions make sense to us on practical grounds, we admit that affect appears to be a complex and pervasive form of representation, and that the AST conceptualization of its influence may be an oversimplification. Contemporary theories of emotion (e.g., Cacioppo, Klein, Berntson, & Hatfield, 1993; LeDoux, 1993) suggest that affect is introduced into cognitive processing at a number of levels, involving multilevel connections between the amygdala and other brain structures. The kinds of higher level affective representations that AST focuses on seem likely to implicate the bidirectional connections between the amygdala and the higher order (polymodal) association areas of the frontal, temporal, and parietal lobes. In contrast, connections between the amygdala and modality-specific neocortical association areas may serve to apprehend and record the affective significance of sensory stimuli, and such processes may underlie the kinds of basic or automatized appearance–affect associations that Martindale, and Van Manen and Fiske, mention.

A Few Words About the Semantic System.   Martindale suggests that the verbal–semantic system has an influence on a variety of forms of representation: examples include episodic memories, which need to be interpreted to be understood, and orientations, which similarly depend on real-world knowledge (he refers to the examples shown in Fig. 1.5). As a consequence, Martindale proposes expanding the overlap of systems in Fig. 1.1 so that episodic memories (behavioral observations) are located where the action, visual (perceptual), and semantic systems converge, and he suggests relocating orientations to this same area of the figure. His general point about the pervasive influence of semantic knowledge is well taken. Semantic knowledge is probably brought into play during the generation and storage of virtually every kind of higher order cognitive representation. Moreover, as the target chapter suggests (pp. 46–49), different kinds of representations also become jumbled together during retrieval processes, providing yet another opportunity for verbal–semantic knowledge to combine with different representational forms.

Nonetheless, we question whether these connections warrant reconfiguring the AST model. First, as already noted, the model is primarily intended to reflect featural similarity, rather than influence. To justify the kinds of alterations that Martindale proposes, we would want to be convinced that the verbal–semantic features of episodic or orientation representations are as vital as the other kinds of features that compose these representations. In the absence of such featural overlap, it may be more appropriate to represent semantic influence as associative connections between verbal–semantic representations and representations of other kinds. For example, behavioral episodes might be individually linked to propositions or labels representing actor intentions, desired outcomes, trait implications, and other such components of the semantic meaning of the events.

Second, we believe that our definition of the verbal–semantic system is probably more restrictive than Martindale's. Within the realm of person impressions, the verbal representations that we see as relevant to AST are personality traits, and the semantic knowledge relevant to these traits is perhaps best characterized as *implicit personality theory* (Rosenberg & Sedlak, 1972). This semantic knowledge involves perceived interrelationships among different trait concepts. Thus, the verbal–semantic system that AST is most concerned with pertains to verbal trait knowledge about other people, and the conceptual knowledge needed to extend and organize this trait knowledge into coherent impressions of an individual's personality characteristics. Martindale's implicit definition of *semantic knowledge* seems to be more encompassing, involving virtually all social knowledge. Such social knowledge is necessarily involved in the interpretation or utilization of any kind of social representation, as he implies. But much of this knowledge has little to do with the kinds of material that AST defines as integral to the verbal–semantic component of impressional representations.

We conceive of each primary system (and perhaps each subsystem as well) as involving its own specialized knowledge structure,[2] with all of these

---

[2]Consistent with this view, Zaidel (1994) argues that there is a "full-blown" meaning system in the nondominant hemisphere that specializes in the interpretation of nonlinguistic sensory (especially pictorial) data. Moreover, she suggests that "Language, however central, is but one feature of the meaning system in the left hemisphere" (p. 8). Such views are not prominent in psychology, where language and meaning are generally viewed as inextricably intertwined. We have therefore chosen to refer to the system involved in the processing of verbal, trait information as the verbal–semantic system, but not to presume that this particular system is involved in all interpretive analysis.

knowledge structures linked together to form a knowledge network that we refer to as *conceptual social memory* (Carlston & Skowronski, 1988; Hastie & Carlston, 1980). As discussed in the target chapter (pp. 35–36), conceptual social memory thus represents perceived relationships among all different forms of representation. From this perspective, the interpretive influence of semantic knowledge implicates this all-encompassing network of conceptual social knowledge, but not our more narrowly circumscribed verbal–semantic system.

Extending the Cones and the Theory.   Martindale suggests that greater interconnectivity among systems could be illustrated in Fig. 1.1 by extending the cones representing different systems so that they overlap more. Interestingly, one of the original versions of Fig. 1.1 included such extensions. This version is shown in Fig. 10.1 to illustrate Martindale's suggestion. The simpler version was presented in the target chapter primarily because Fig. 10.1 is complex and raises some additional issues, which we briefly attempt to address here.

The premise underlying Fig. 10.1 is that cognitive representations are probably not experienced in the pure, clearly delineated forms suggested at the level labeled *impressional associations.* As stated in the target chapter, "the different kinds of representations that are retrieved may not be readily discriminable to the perceiver who is searching memory. Instead, the memories may surface as an amalgam of representational features that blend together, with no clear demarcation between one representation and another" (p. 47). To illustrate this "blending together" of different forms of representation, Fig. 10.1 extends the system cones to a level that might represent the conscious experience of retrieved information. Some of the material at this upper level could reflect a blending of all forms of representation, whereas other material might represent overlap among only two or three different systems, and some peripheral material might actually reflect a single, relatively pure form of representation.

Martindale proposes that the regions where three systems overlap may better characterize episodic memories and orientations than the regions where only two systems overlap. As indicated earlier, we disagree with this particular proposal because we believe episodic memories and orientations primarily reflect the pairs of systems suggested by AST. However, the proposal is nonetheless consistent with the basic logic of AST, which states that combinations of representations may be viewed as new representations (p. 7). It may be that the higher level representations involving greater system overlap can be meaningfully identified as unique forms of representation. Nonetheless, we demur from this exercise at present because the principal goal of AST was to integrate those forms of representation that

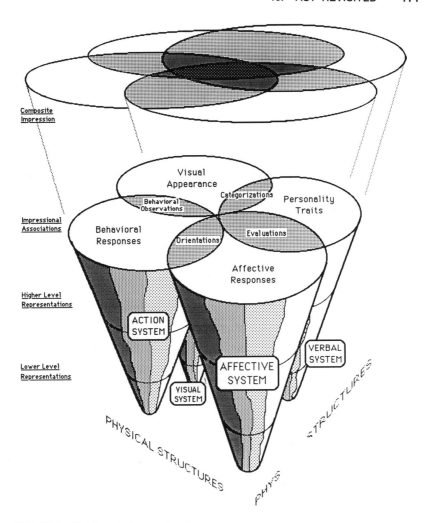

FIG. 10.1.   Version of Fig. 1.1 showing increased overlap of system representations when the system cones are extended to the level of the composite impression.

have been of most theoretical interest to social psychologists, and these are already represented within AST.

Martindale also tries to extend AST in some other interesting directions by relating it to some of his own eclectic research interests. He proposes that the involvement of basic mental systems in both social and nonsocial representational processes may set up trade-offs between these. For example, according to Martindale, people who have elaborate representations of other people may have "less space left for knowledge of nonsocial objects," and highly creative people may have "sketchy or impoverished" representations of other people (p. 84). Much of his discussion seems to relate more to individual differences in the contents of particular systems (or perhaps in the contents of all systems combined) than to issues regarding the form in which relevant representations are stored, or the extent to which one system rather than another is implicated in creative processing.

In contrast, the AST approach suggests a focus on people's use of different systems or different forms of representation. Thus, for example, scientifically creative people may be those who have well-developed systems for perceiving, analyzing, and cataloging things, but less well-developed systems for dealing with affect or for interacting in suitable ways with other people. This implies that such individuals may rely more on target-based forms of representation and less on self-referent ones. Artistic creativity may be a different matter altogether, perhaps reflecting particular strengths in the sensory and affective domains. Some similar ideas on individual differences in representational use were discussed in the target chapter (pp. 59–62).

Fishing for the Right Metaphor: Reply to Van Manen and Fiske

Van Manen and Fiske (chap. 3) state that they "approach AST with a mixture of appreciation and apprehension" (p. 87). We appreciate the appreciation, particularly as we count Fiske and Cox (1979) and Fiske and Taylor (1991) among the seminal writings that influenced the initial formulation of AST. However, given space limitations, we focus primarily on Van Manen and Fiske's apprehensions, hoping to clarify aspects of the theory that they find troublesome. Borrowing their fishing net analogy, we hope to show that AST is not quite so full of holes as it may at first appear to be.

Acting Like Your Self.   We begin with Van Manen and Fiske's suggestion that the action system is redundant with a self-system. Clearly, within AST, action representations (behavioral responses) are self-related, as are affect representations and the action–affect hybrid (orientations). This premise is evident in our characterization of these representations as self-referent. However, our early efforts to extend AST to self-descriptions (p. 30) suggest that the self may also encompass other identified representational forms, including appearance (the self-image), categories (self-identification), traits (self-concept), evaluation (self-esteem), and behavioral observations (biographical memory). Thus, we do not equate the action system alone with the entire self-system.[3]

---

[3]On the other hand, given their especially self-referent nature, we might grant that action and affect representations provide a linkage between representations of self and of others.

Similarly, we would not equate the action system with the affective system, as Van Manen and Fiske suggest. They wonder whether "covert" responses such as increased heart rate belong to the action or the affective system, question how to draw the line between the two when characterizing emotional behaviors such as crying, and are troubled by their perception that responses are output from single systems. We believe the action and affect systems are conceptually and physically distinct, although this may reflect definitional nuances that were described in more detail in Carlston (1992) than in the target chapter. At one level, changes in heart rate involve the autonomic nervous system, and seem readily distinguishable from behavioral responses, which involve the peripheral nervous system. However, our derivations of *systems* really depend on functional and conceptual considerations, rather than on physiological ones. Therefore, we suggest that the action system is best conceived as a system for the execution and representation of complex behavioral sequences (see our reply to Wyer later in this chapter), and the affective system as a system for the creation and representation of emotional states. From this standpoint, crying probably has more to do with the latter than the former. But, of course, the operations of different mental systems are generally coordinated, and some emotional behaviors might best be viewed as outputs from both the action and the affective systems. Contrary to the singularity assumed by Van Manen and Fiske, we suggest that many internal and external events influence several or all of the primary systems (pp. 30–35). Thus, several systems could be implicated in any observed output, such as crying.

However, this does not suggest that it is meaningless to make distinctions between acts and affects. For example, an individual may reach out to fix a stray curl on a loved one's brow—an action that after many repetitions becomes strongly associated with feelings of tenderness and affection. The action and the feelings may tend to co-occur from that time forward, but that does not make hair tinkering an affect or tenderness an action. The reliable relationship between the two would simply be characterized in AST as an automatized translation from one kind of representation to another.

Can One Make a Habit of Crying?   Van Manen and Fiske question how visual and affective representations can become linked through automatization, as AST implies, when emotional responses appear to become habituated with repeated access. For example, they note that one might cry after first rediscovering a photo of a (lost?) loved one, but that one would be less likely to do so on subsequent occasions. This sort of phenomenon seems to suggest that the link between appearance and emotional responses might actually weaken with repeated use, making repetition an unlikely mechanism for the creation of strong associations between perceptions and affect.

In the situation that Van Manen and Fiske describe, the person who rediscovers the photograph presumably cries because of a flood of emotions and thoughts associated with the person who is pictured. Why might this response diminish upon subsequent exposures to the photograph? Possibly one reason is that the photograph becomes progressively more associated with the context in which it is viewed and handled, creating a "fan" of associations (see Anderson, 1983), and diminishing the relative retrievability and influence of the emotional associations contributing to the original response. More generally, the habituation of responses to photographs may occur because the associations built up while viewing, handling, and storing photos ultimately supplant those based on photographic content. Another possibility relates to the "caricaturization" of incompletely retrieved memories discussed in the target chapter (p. 44). Unless the perceiver wallows in sadness with each viewing of the photo, these emotional responses may be experienced less fully each time, just as episodic memories may be recalled less fully each time. Eventually, the prominent (and probably mostly cognitive) features of the emotional response predominate, and the experience becomes a mere caricature of the original emotional experience. This may be more of a description of habituation than an explanation, but it does emphasize that the phenomenon may hinge on cursory and incomplete retrievals characteristic of an inadvertent, and perhaps unwanted, memory.

Now consider a different situation, where a perceiver is "falling in love" with another person. Repeated exposure to this other person produces a positive affective response, which becomes associated with that individual's presence. Unlike a photo, the actual target of affection is not viewed, handled, or treated in ways that compete with this positive response. Moreover, the felt emotions are likely to be experienced fully, and perhaps even compounded by feelings of self-conscious nervousness that sometimes accompany infatuation. In time, the association between appearance and affect may become so strong that the perceiver has an affective response toward others who simply look like the target of affection (see Fiske, 1982). Similar dynamics may also underlie negative responses — when they are accompanied by enough fear or anxiety that the affect is reexperienced at a relatively undiminished level. The mechanisms underlying these sorts of conditioning phenomena have been rather thoroughly discussed in the literature (e.g., Ohman, 1993). Under these circumstances, repetition of associations between representations may strengthen these and lead to more reliable and rapid translations of one into the other, as suggested by AST.

Getting Concrete About Abstraction.   Van Manen and Fiske note that there seems to be a contradiction between the assumption that the four primary systems are hierarchically organized and the premise that the representational products of these systems differ in levels of abstraction. They suggest that this seeming contradiction creates several implausibilities. For example, if the overall structure is metaphorically represented as a table (more on this shortly), then the four legs of the table must differ in length because some necessarily stretch over a larger range of abstractions than others. This threatens to upset the simple organizational elegance that we claim as an attribute of the theory.

AST does assume that the primary systems are hierarchically organized, in keeping with a vast amount of research and theory on the organizational structure of mental systems (e.g., Glass & Holyoak, 1986; Izard, 1993; Konorski, 1967; Martindale, 1991). The most basic cognitive units within any system detect or represent simple features, with higher level units combining such inputs into more complex and general representations until, at the highest levels, material is represented in terms of the kinds of general concepts of interest to social and cognitive psychologists. Thus, the lowest levels of each system can be characterized as simple, primitive building blocks that are closely related to the physical structures involved in perception and response, and the highest levels can be characterized as abstract constructs that are utilized in complex cognitive processes. The intermediate levels are probably the hardest to characterize with any confidence, except that it is evident that they must progressively build the basic units into the higher order units (see Martindale, 1991, for an attempt to specify the intermediate levels of systems similar to those posited by AST).

When AST suggests that higher order cognitive representations differ in abstractness, this refers to something quite different from these hierarchical levels within mental systems. Unfortunately, the target chapter is fairly vague in defining the *abstraction dimension* (see p. 14), contributing to the confusion in the Van Manen and Fiske commentary, as well as in Fiedler's (chap. 5) later commentary. Basically, we suggest that there are two primary differences between the concrete representations depicted on the left side of our figures and the abstract ones depicted on the right side. First, representations on the left side tend to have temporal and contextual features that give them specificity. Representations of appearance or behavior generally include time and place markers, or at least did so at one time. However, recalled traits, evaluations, and affect generally lack such markers, and thus they lack the same degree of detail and concreteness.

Of course, there are times when behaviors are described abstractly, without any real contextual referents, and there are times when traits are qualified temporally or contextually. To reflect such variations, the Carlston and Sparks coding scheme, depicted in Fig. 1.4, assigns such abstract behaviors and concrete traits to more intermediate positions along the concreteness–abstraction dimension. However, this is really just an attempt to characterize descriptions that may be incomplete or that may be confoundings of several different kinds of representation. At a conceptual level, we still allege that pure and complete forms of these different representations tend to differ in the manner we have described.

The second primary difference between the representational forms on the left of the figures and those on the right is their numerousness. We argue that there are more different ways of looking (appearance representations) and acting (behavioral responses and observations) than there are distinguishable trait concepts or emotional states. Of course, the contextual and temporal markers already mentioned help to delineate different behaviors, and the absence of such markers makes it more difficult to distinguish abstract concepts, such as traits, from each other. In addition, representations to the right of our figures tend to summarize groups of those on the left, so that there are generally fewer such representations needed as one moves from left to right. For example, categorizations (e.g., *professors*) tend to group a number of distinguishable appearances or behaviors together, and traits (e.g., *intelligent*) tend to summarize or characterize a number of distinguishable categories.

However, it must be emphasized that the *abstraction* label for the horizontal dimension of our figures is simply our characterization of apparent differences among the representations that we have identified. These characterizations are interpretive, the labels used for the dimensions are arbitrary, and the resultant two-dimensional spatial representation is merely a theoretical convenience. This is a point to which we return later (see our reply to Radvansky). Here we simply argue that the attempt to characterize differences among higher level representational forms is conceptually unrelated to the hierarchical, building-block organization assumed within different mental systems, even though both can be discussed using the term *abstraction*.

Tabling the Cone Metaphor.   As noted earlier, Van Manen and Fiske view the AST structure, as depicted in Fig. 1.1, through a *table* metaphor. The legs of the table represent the four primary systems, and the table top represents the region where higher order products of the systems interact. This analogy suggests several issues to them. First, because table legs are separate and independent, the metaphor implies that systems do not interact at more primitive levels than that represented by the table top. This, in turn, suggests that abstract representations (i.e., higher order representations within a system hierarchy), which are already at the level of the table top, should be translated more quickly and readily into other forms of representation than should lower order representations. Finally, this analogy poses problems for the interpretation of simple phenomena such as observational learning and conditioning, which arguably do not implicate higher level representations.

Actually an early version of Fig. 1.1, which was never circulated publicly, did look a lot like a table, and it could have been construed as having some of the implications that Van Manen and Fiske mention. For precisely this reason, the figure was redrawn as shown in the current Fig. 1.1. A Purdue graduate student, Scott Phillips, suggested that these overlapping cones better reflect the likelihood that mental systems also interact at some levels that are more basic and primitive than the higher level representations embodied in AST. The figure is thus intended to illustrate that the representations within any system become more abstract and elaborated toward the top of each cone, and that as the cones merge together these representations begin to blend with cognitive material from other systems. This is consistent with neurological models described by Damasio (1989) and others (e.g., Kolb & Whishaw, 1990) that suggest a progression from lower level (or "first-order") association areas, which combine relatively similar kinds of material, to higher level association areas (the multimodal cortex), where material from altogether different systems is combined. Although these complexities are reflected in Fig. 1.1, they are not really relevant to the kinds of phenomena that AST was designed to deal with, and thus are not much emphasized in the target chapter model.

If systems are assumed to interact at lower levels, it is not necessarily true that more abstract representations must be translated more quickly, nor is it necessary for basic processes like observational learning and conditioning to implicate higher level representations. Thus, some of Van Manen and Fiske's general concerns dissipate. Actually, we believe that AST can accommodate such phenomena. But because we concur with Van Manen and Fiske that "AST was not intended to address" such issues, we do not attempt to do so here. Broad theories, like fishing nets, are susceptible to overstretching.

Ruminating About What Might Have "Bin": Reply to Wyer

As the first author's mentor, and the second author's academic grandfather, Wyer has had an extensive, albeit general, influence on our thinking about social cognition issues. The associative-network processing metaphor used in AST derives from a similar, although more basic, model outlined by Wyer and Carlston (1979) in *Social Cognition, Inference, and Attribution* — one of the early tomes in this area. Our thinking about social cognition has diverged somewhat from Wyer's since that time, although an attempt was made to reintegrate these recently, in Wyer and Carlston (1994). Working on that chapter and on this reply reminded the first author just how interesting, creative, and intellectually challenging his mentor can be.

Wyer's detailed commentary (chap. 4) first suggests that AST is difficult to translate into specific theoretical premises—a challenge that we address in the next section of this reply. Then the commentary raises some definitional issues regarding the action system, similar to those raised by Martindale, and Van Manen and Fiske. Next, Wyer makes some interesting points about the interrelationships among different representational forms in AST, providing us with the opportunity to clarify some of our assumptions about mental organization. Finally, some empirical findings are discussed that Wyer feels fall beyond the scope and competence of AST, but not of the person memory (bin) model. The divergence in viewpoints noted earlier is probably most evident here. Thus, our challenge, in the limited space available, is to justify the target chapter's assertion that AST provides a complementary, rather than an alternative, approach.

Taking Inventory of the Premises. Wyer states that he was unable to "identify a set of premises that would permit the generation of predictions outlined in the chapter" (p. 101). Although he politely suggests that it might be premature to expect this level of precision from AST, we nonetheless find it discouraging that such premises were not clearer from the target chapter. At least this gives us an excuse to outline AST's premises and hypotheses AST in a more systematic fashion than was done originally (see Table 10.1). However, given the complexity of the theory, and our desire not to restate the entire target chapter, we found it necessary to simplify and even omit some premises in this overview. Therefore, we caution against using this summary table as a definitive substitute for the theoretical narrative provided by the chapter (and by Carlston, 1992).

Getting Action. Like the previous commentators, Wyer raises questions about the exact nature of particular systems. One of his basic concerns is whether the "language" underlying behavioral representations is proprioceptive or cognitive, and whether this language is the same for both behavioral responses and behavioral observations. Van Manen and Fiske raised a related issue in wondering whether there is really any difference between watching another person's foot step and watching one's own (p. 95).

Standard descriptions of the action system (e.g., Gallistel, 1980; Martindale, 1991; Shallice, 1978) suggest a hierarchical structure that includes (or is linked to) motor neurons at the most primitive level. These motor units are linked to layers of progressively more complex functional units that ultimately combine into units representing discrete actions. These, in turn, are linked to layers of units representing meaningful behavioral sequences,

TABLE 10.1
Summary of AST Premises and Hypotheses

A. Philosophical Premises
1. A comprehensive theory of social cognition should provide an integrated account of social categorization, trait inference, affect, and other forms of social representation.
2. Social cognition theories ultimately need to articulate with work on brain function and organization, just as they have with theories of cognitive process and organization.

B. Central Premises
1. Cognitive representations derive from the operation of one or more basic mental systems.
   a. Each representation therefore possesses features determined by the nature of the basic mental systems from which it derives.
   b. Each representation also plays a special, mediating role between higher level cognitions and the inputs or outputs associated with the corresponding system.
2. The basic systems of the human mind include visual/sensory systems, a verbal-semantic system, an affective system, and a system for the production of behavior.
   a. Each mental system is organized hierarchically, with primitive units necessary for system inputs and outputs combined into progressively higher order units.
   b. The cognitive representations of interest to social cognition researchers are among the highest level units within each system.
3. The cognitive representations implicated by different systems are linked together in an associative network at higher cognitive levels (with some linkage at lower levels, as well).

C. Derivative Premises
1. In the social domain, the characteristic representations associated with the basic systems relate to appearance images, personality traits, affective responses, and behavioral responses.
2. Additional forms of social representation combine features of these primary representational forms.
   a. Social categorizations combine features of visual appearance and personality traits, evaluations combine features of personality traits and affective responses, and episodic memories (behavioral observations) combine features of visual appearance and behavioral production.
   b. Moreover, the combined features of the affective and behavior production (action) systems can be construed as an additional form of representation (orientations), which roughly corresponds to the "relationship" representation recently identified by some researchers.
3. These "hybrid" forms of representation relate to both of the mental systems from which they derive features.

D. Organizational Premises
1. Figure 1.2 summarizes the hypothesized organization of representational forms in terms of featural overlap and relationships to primary processing systems.
2. In general, those forms of representation shown toward the top of the figure can be characterized as more target-referent, and those shown toward the bottom can be characterized as more self-referent.
3. In general, those forms of representation shown on the left of the figure can be characterized as more concrete, in that they include temporal and contextual detail, are more numerous, and are more distinguishable; whereas those on the right of the figure can be characterized as more abstract, in that they lack detail, are less numerous, and possess fewer distinguishing characteristics.

(continued on next page)

TABLE 10.1 (*continued*)

E. Organizational Hypotheses
  1. Concrete forms of representation may be more difficult to freely recall (but easier to recognize), less consistent with other concepts, yet more influential when recalled than more abstract forms of representation.
  2. Self-referent forms of representation may be more contingent on the self-concept, more stable, and more often perceived as idiosyncratic (and less often perceived as objectively or consensually true) than more target-referent forms of representation.
F. Generational Premises
  1. Representations relating to a given person are likely to be generated during activities involving that individual.
  2. The likelihood that a perceiver will have a representation of a particular form in regards to a particular target person depends on the nature of past interactions with that person or with others who are similarly perceived.
G. Generational Hypotheses
  1. Simple observation of a target is likely to foster the generation and use of appearance representations (and related forms, such as episodic memories and categorizations).
  2. Thinking about a target is likely to foster generation and use of trait representations (and related forms, such as categorizations and evaluations).
  3. Emoting about a target is likely to foster generation and use of affective representations (and related forms, such as evaluations and orientations).
  4. Interaction with a target is likely to foster generation and use of behavioral representations (and related forms, such as episodic memories and orientations).
  5. The recent use of a mental system for an unrelated purpose may increase the likelihood that representations relating to that system are subsequently accessed and used.
  6. The preoccupation of a mental system for an unrelated purpose can interfere with the retrieval or use of representations involving that same system.
H. Structural Premises
  1. The associative linkages among higher level concepts of all representational forms can be suitably modeled using an elaborated associative network metaphor.
      a. One useful elaboration involves the spread of inhibition, as well as excitation, through the network of associated concepts.
  2. Associative links between concepts become strengthened with use.
  3. Two representations of an individual are more likely to become linked if both are related to the specific mental systems engaged by activities regarding that individual.
I. Structural Hypotheses
  1. The activation of one form of representation can prime associated representations of other forms.
  2. In general, factors that affect one form of representation will also affect other, related forms of representation in the same way.
  3. In general, the use of different representations that relate to the same systems will tend to be correlated.
  4. Two forms of representation are more likely to have consistent implications if the two have tended to be activated at the same time in the past.
J. Automaticity Premises
  1. When two concepts become so strongly associated that one is consistently recoded as the other, this recoding may become automatized.
  2. When a well-learned association generalizes across multiple actors or circumstances, this association becomes a part of the conceptual knowledge that is brought into play in generating new representations from old ones.

TABLE 10.1 (*continued*)

K. Automaticity Hypotheses
1. Automatic translations from a given initial representation to another target representations should be more likely for frequently encountered initial representations, frequently generated target representations, and, especially, frequently made translations.
2. Automatic translations are more likely to proceed from concrete initial representations to abstract target representations than the other way around.

L. Output Hypotheses
1. Judgments, behaviors, affects, and imagination will tend to be influenced by extant verbal, action, affective, and visual representations, respectively.
2. All forms of output will also tend to be influenced by those specific representations that are most salient.
3. Different kinds of judgments may reflect particular forms of representation, as suggested in Table 1.2.
4. Different kinds of behaviors may reflect particular forms of representation, as suggested in Table 1.3.

M. Individual-Difference Hypotheses
1. Individuals may differ in the extent to which they characteristically generate or utilize different forms of representation.
2. Such individual differences should relate in predictable ways to standardized measures that tap into visual or verbal orientations, affective styles, need for cognition, and self-monitoring.

and ultimately to higher level behavioral representations such as scripts, plans, goals, and the like. The "language" of such a system might be characterized as proprioceptive at the lowest levels, and as progressively more cognitive at higher levels. The most primitive functional units, which are involved in the generation of behavior, are presumably less relevant to the encoding of other people's behaviors than of one's own, whereas the more cognitive levels would seemingly be relevant to both. Additionally, according to AST, memories of others' behaviors probably have more salient visual components than do memories of one's own. Consequently, behavioral observations and behavioral responses do partly rely on different languages, with responses having stronger links to motoric structures and observations having stronger links to perceptual structures; but they also rely partly on the same language, namely the more cognitive representations characterizing upper levels of the action system.

Does this imply that watching one's own foot step involves a different system than watching someone else's foot step—a conclusion that Van Manen and Fiske characterize as unlikely? Strictly speaking, "watching" anything involves the visual system. However, the "watching" or visual component is unlikely to be of much importance in representations of one's own experiences. In fact, people's memories of their own acts are frequently viewed from an outside vantage point, rather than from a first-person perspective, suggesting that these are not actual perceptual encodings at all, but constructions based on other forms of representation such as those involved in the action system. This may primarily involve "cognitive" concepts, such as plans, goals, and scripts, but it can also involve more primitive, motoric representations, to which these are connected. These latter components can be particularly evident in memories of physical or athletic behaviors. For example, when describing their athletic exploits, athletes often physically mimic the shot or throw about which they are speaking.

Does AST suggest that different aspects of an interaction are independently encoded and stored by the sensory and action systems, a possibility that Wyer describes as unlikely? We think not. As noted earlier, all of the different processing systems necessarily function in a well-coordinated fashion, and the material they encode is undoubtedly linked together in a manner that provides coherent representations of people and events. This possibility is explored more fully in the next section.

Some Eventful Associations. Wyer questions the AST premise that similar representations tend to be more closely associated than representations differing more in form (see also Radvansky, chap. 6, this volume). He interprets this premise as meaning, for example, that a single appearance representation must be more closely linked to other appearance images than to other forms of representation stemming from the same observation or interaction. In disagreement, he observes that "it seems intuitively clear that the features that compose each recalled experience, although in different forms, are all much more closely associated with one another than they are with the similar forms that compose the other experience" (p. 105). Wyer is probably correct that all of the representational components of a single experience are likely to be associated with each other, at least initially and to some degree. A vivid memory may well encompass appearance images, verbal conclusions, affective responses, and other forms of representation that were produced during the initial experience (Neisser, 1982). It makes sense that when different mental systems are engaged by a single encounter, the products of all of these systems will be linked to form a single, integrated representation (Johnson, 1992). Furthermore, Wyer may be correct that the within-episode associations embodied in this integrated representation are stronger than the associations among similar forms of representation from different episodes.

However, granting that representations from a single episode may be closely linked, AST implies that similar representations from a single episode will be even more closely related than dissimilar representations from a single episode. For example, recall of another individual's appearance on some occasion should be closely linked to recall for their behavior on that same occasion, and this in turn should be closely linked to recall for one's own behavior on that occasion. Moreover, similar representations from different episodes should be more closely related than dissimilar representations from different episodes. For example, a person's appearance on one occasion should be more closely associated with their appearance, behaviors, or category assignments on other occasions that it is with dissimilar material, such as evaluations or trait inferences, from other occasions.

These comparisons allow for the possibility that similarity and episodic relatedness have independent effects on the associations among representations. Although Wyer interprets AST as suggesting that knowledge is organized by representational form rather than by experience, we do not see these as mutually exclusive alternatives. Instead, featural overlap and temporal contiguity may be construed as two different factors that influence strength of association among different concepts. Under different circumstances, one or the other of these influences may predominate, although in general the two probably operate in tandem. Similar conclusions are suggested by Barsalou's (1988) theory of episodic recall.

As an illustration of how different representations relating to a single event tend to be associated, Wyer gives an example from the first author's days in graduate school at Illinois. Wyer suggests that he remembers a meeting in his office one afternoon, and that his memory includes details of Carlston's appearance, as well as his own feelings and trait conclusions, all stored separately from other memories that he has of Carlston. Given the flattering nature of the example, we are reluctant to challenge its accuracy. However, it seems likely that the various representations that Wyer describes are actually samples or distillations from numerous different events. Wyer and Carlston met frequently to discuss attribution theory and the newly emerging field of social cognition. Possibly Wyer's episodic memory is not of a single one of these meetings, but rather a blend of several such meetings. Moreover, the visual image that accompanies this memory seems likely to be a composite based on repeated (and possibly more recent) observations, rather than on observations made during one such meeting. The reported trait characterization may have been made at another time altogether, possibly during the preparation of a letter of recommendation, rather than during the described meeting. Finally, the feelings that Wyer describes may actually be current emotions, or may be a current reconstruction of difficult to recall emotions, rather than veridical reports of the emotions experienced in his office. There is certainly ample evidence for these kinds of reconstructive blendings of recall (e.g., Barsalou, 1988; Loftus, 1975).

If these speculations are correct, then Wyer's example does not really illustrate the linking together of different representations from a single event, although such linkages certainly occur. It has been suggested that the kind of integrated event representation that Wyer postulates is most likely to be maintained when the constituent representations are regularly retrieved and rehearsed together (Johnson, 1992; Neisser, 1982). However, because infrequently used links degrade with time, and because "unlinked" representations may tend to blend with similar representations of other events, the kind of mixture that we have described may become more likely over time. Ultimately, as links between contemporaneous representations degrade, the primary basis for organization of different representations may simply be their common association with the target individual.

Does AST Have Explaining to Do?   The final sections of Wyer's commentary raise metatheoretical issues, providing a segue into the next two commentaries, which are similarly oriented. Wyer states that a new theory of person impression formation should "incorporate the processes postulated by previous models or . . . explain the same phenomena implied by these models in different ways" (p. 107). He suggests that AST may not do this, and he describes several phenomena that "appear to be outside the range of those for which the present model has clear implications," including the incongruity effect and conversational effects on social cognition.

However, AST was not intended to provide an alternative explanation for many social cognition phenomena, but rather to be "integrative, supplementary, and sometimes even complementary to other theories" (p. 64). AST's processing assumptions are perfectly compatible with many existing social cognition theories, and, in some cases, these other theories adopt similar assumptions (e.g., Fazio, 1989; Higgins, Rholes, & Jones, 1977; Srull, 1981). It therefore seems superfluous to describe or reinterpret all such phenomena in terms of AST. To illustrate, consider the incongruity effect. As Wyer notes, superior recall for behaviors that are incongruent with expectations has generally been interpreted in terms of inconsistency-resolution processes. People either pay more attention to incongruent information (Hastie & Kumar, 1979) or they mull it over, establishing linkages between incongruent items and other items that enhance subsequent retrieval (Srull, 1981). Both the proposed attentional and linkage mechanisms could easily be accommodated within the general structure and processes assumed by AST. However, simply importing these mechanisms into the theory would do little, by itself, to clarify either the incongruity phenomenon or AST.

A more elaborate integration of incongruity work with AST principles *might* lead to some novel hypotheses. For example, it is possible that inconsistencies will be less noticed among self-referent than target-referent representations because perceivers may resist viewing their own behaviors or feelings as inconsistent. However, once such inconsistencies are noticed, perceivers may be more likely to engage in resolution processes because of the need to eliminate conflicts relevant to their self. Inconsistencies may also tend to be more noticeable among abstract than concrete representations because a certain amount of variability is expected in concrete realms such as appearance and behavior. On the other hand, inconsistency resolution may be easier for more concrete representations because they tend to be more ambiguous (Stangor & McMillan, 1992).

Inconsistencies may also be more noticeable, and reconciliation processes more common, among morphologically similar representations than among morphologically dissimilar ones. Thus, if a perceiver possesses trait representations of an actor, the most bothersome inconsistencies may involve other trait material, followed by categorizations and evaluations that have different trait implications, and finally by other kinds of inconsistent representations. However, effects such as these may be contradicted by the greater salience of inconsistencies that violate well-learned associations in conceptual social memory, and these well-learned associations do not always involve similar forms of representation. In any case, speculations like these take us rather far afield, and their disconfirmation would not necessarily infirm the central premises of AST. Hence, it may be premature for AST to extend itself this far, as Wyer acknowledges from time to time in his commentary.

Finally, Wyer asks what AST accomplishes that the Wyer and Srull person memory model does not, "and what empirical phenomena it can explain that the latter model cannot address" (p. 111). A partial answer to these questions is provided in Table 10.1. Although the Wyer and Srull model incorporates several alternative forms of representation, just as AST does, and although it includes a number of processing mechanisms, probably more than AST does, few of the central premises or hypotheses of AST outlined in this table could be directly derived from that model. For example, AST integrates all of the different forms of representation that social cognition theorists have studied, describes how these may relate to each other and to various basic mental systems, suggests how they are affected by different kinds of interactions and processes, and speculates about how they may influence different kinds of behaviors and judgments. This is not to say that the Wyer and Srull model "cannot address" such issues any more than the AST model "cannot address" incongruity or communication phenomena. However, the Wyer and Srull model does not currently incorporate such phenomena. Moreover, if it were to be extended to deal with such issues, this would seem to confirm the heuristic and complementary nature of AST.

METATHEORETICAL ISSUES

Ecological Validity and Valid Ecology: Reply to Fiedler

Fiedler's commentary (chap. 5, this volume) raises a variety of interesting issues about the nature of the whole AST enterprise. He first outlines the goals and benefits of macrotheories like AST, making several excellent points. He suggests that such theories help to overcome uncertainty about whether processes or factors identified by microtheories will exercise the same influence in contexts that might involve other kinds of processes or factors as well. Moreover, he notes that the integration of principles from different microtheories may reveal new principles and insights that exceed those apparent from the individual theories. Although AST aspires to make such contributions (at this point, emphasizing the latter over the former), Fiedler appears uncertain that it does so.

Fiedler's primary concerns relate to the general issue of whether AST reflects reality or itself. Does AST's two-dimensional classification of representations describe cognitive organization, or does it mistake semantic relationships for empirical truth? Does this two-dimensional structure represent real, rather than merely convenient, distinctions between abstract and concrete representations? Do the multidimensional scaling analyses shed light on objective relations among representations, or merely reflect the taxonomic scheme used to code the underlying data? After trying to address such specific concerns, we close this section by considering Fiedler's more global views regarding the importance of social ecology.

Seeing Structure in the Cosmos or Scratches on the Lens?   We must concede that there is some validity to Fiedler's general concerns about the interplay between theory and data. As those who philosophize about science constantly remind us (Gergen, 1982; Gergen & Gergen, 1984; Kuhn, 1970), theorists and researchers view the empirical world through lenses that are shaped by the assumptions of their era and distorted by the language and methods they employ. There is always the danger that they will mistake language for logic, or the structure of their theories for the structure of reality. In fact, we acknowledged at the beginning of this chapter that the cones and matrices depicted in AST's graphical representations exist in the mind of the theorist rather than in the brains of social perceivers. Still, there is a clear implication in AST that these structures do reflect important characteristics of the actual cognitive structure, and so we must consider the specific arguments that underlie Fiedler's metatheoretical skepticism.

First, Fiedler warns that there is a danger of "reifying" semantic concepts as brain systems. More specifically, he suggests that "For any verbal label denoting a psychological system, a center or pathway can be localized in the brain" (p. 118); moreover, he argues that "As long as there is no compelling independent evidence from brain research and cognitive psychology, and as long as brain research is not shown to disconfirm competing systems approaches, the brain systems can be suspected as reflecting the very semantic concepts that have guided brain research" (p. 118). We suspect that this rather overstates the subjectivity of neuropsychology, although it may well apply to the selective interpretation of brain research by theories such as AST. The evidence provided by neuropsychology is "independent" of AST, and, in most cases, has been obtained by researchers whose orientation (and "semantic concepts") differ markedly from that adopted in AST or other social cognition theories. Moreover, this research provides rather clear evidence regarding the general nature of major functional systems. In general, the convergence of work from dissimilar areas and orientations contradicts Fiedler's argument that all such evidence suffers from semantic subjectivity.

Of course, the manner in which some of this work is interpreted in the target chapter may be subjective, speculative, or even incorrect, particularly in the attempt to tie particular functional systems to particular social representations. We note again that the primary purpose of the target chapter was to provide a systematic integration of known forms of social representation, rather than a systematic integration of social cognition and neuropsychology. In fact, AST was never exclusively a "bottom–up approach" (p. 115) to theory development in the sense of beginning with physiology and ending with derivative forms of mental representation. Rather, AST began with conceptions of social representation, and then worked back and forth between the apparent features of these representations and the apparent nature of basic mental systems. This comparison process suggested ways of construing the structural interrelationships among social representations, as well as ways of relating these to basic functional systems. However, given the synthetic nature of the process, some subjectivity in the interpretation and use of the neuropsychological evidence was probably inevitable.

Whether this evidence is really more supportive of AST than other "competing systems approaches" is difficult to say because the present authors are not aware of any competing systems approaches that address the same sorts of issues. Perhaps such approaches will emerge; if they are more consistent with the neuropsychological evidence than is AST, this would be a point in their favor. We will then take a certain amount of satisfaction in having fostered such comprehensive approaches to social representation. Ultimately, however, different theories in this area will be judged on their consistency with the evidence that is generated to test their premises and hypotheses, rather than on their consistency with brain research. Thus, philosophical arguments about the inherent subjectivity of theory-building processes are likely to assume less importance as data begin to accumulate.

Fiedler's second point is that there is a certain arbitrariness in the classification of social representations as relatively concrete or abstract. We clarified the definition of the concreteness–abstraction dimension in our reply to Van Manen and Fiske, emphasizing the existence of temporal and contextual markers in concrete representations and the summary nature and numerousness of abstract representations. These distinctions may still be arbitrary, in the sense that they simply reflect our characterization of the primary differences among different representational forms. However, these sorts of distinctions are empirically tractable. For example, Klein, Loftus, Trafton, and Fuhrman (1992) recently demonstrated that traits tend to summarize groups of related behaviors. Similarly, one could show that people can generally differentiate among more different appearances or behaviors than they can among different traits or affects. Alternatively, one could verify whether appearance and behavioral memories are more likely to co-activate contextual features than are trait or affective memories.

Fiedler also questions the self-reference dimension, wondering "in what respect 'personality traits' are located in the target, whereas 'affective responses' reside within the subject" (p. 119). We perceive physical appearance, category membership, and personality traits as being inherent characteristics of the target, which in principle are objectively true, regardless of whether there is even an observer. On the other hand, without an observing self, there would be no self-perceived behavioral responses, orientations, or affect toward the target. Of course, this raises difficult philosophical issues regarding the existence of objective reality and whether a falling tree makes noise in the absence of an observer. However, the critical issue here would seem to be the extent to which naive perceivers are likely to view different representations as inherent characteristics of the target or as subjectively self-referent observations. In other words, what makes representations self-referent is perceivers' awareness that these reflect as much on them as on the target being described. This could be easily assessed by asking subjects to generate descriptions of each type (e.g., appearance, traits, affect, etc.), and then to indicate the extent to which each descriptor is revealing about themselves, or the extent to which each is objectively true or would be confirmed by other informants. Consequently, although there may be a certain arbitrariness in our descriptions of these dimensions, the resultant distinctions among representations seem to be logical and testable, and to provide a "sound basis for comparing such intrinsically different things" (p. 119) as different forms of representation.

Putting the Coding System Under the Microscope. The multidimensional scaling analyses reported in the target chapter provide considerable support for the structural arrangement theorized by AST. As shown in Fig. 1.6, two different studies have revealed interrelationships among the descriptors that subjects use in describing others that closely approximate the patterns predicted by the theory. However, Fiedler raises an important issue in suggesting that these results could reflect the coding system, rather than the actual structure of social cognitions: "Because the coders actually utilize the taxonomy to classify the verbal materials, it is no surprise that the same verbal–semantic structure will be rediscovered in multivariate analyses of the coded data" (p. 118). In general, such concerns are valid: If coders expect two things to be related, this expectation may color their codings, biasing the results toward the anticipated effects.

However, we doubt the relevance of such concerns to our analyses. The multidimensional scaling (MDS) analyses rely on the pattern of intercorrelations among 8 different forms of representations encoded in terms of 25 discreet coding categories. Our coders did no more than note the occurrence of each coding category as it appeared in the written descriptions, and their data consisted only of the resultant category assignments. The computer then totaled these assignments into frequencies per description, calculated the intercorrelations among these frequencies, and input these into the IND-SCAL analysis. No relational ratings or encodings were made by the coders, and the computed MDS structures therefore reflect only the empirically determined co-occurrence of taxonomic categories within people's descriptions. It makes no difference to the computer whether these categories are adjacent in the AST coding scheme because this information is not input in any way; all the computer "knows" is the similarity or dissimilarity in the frequencies with which different categories are used. To the extent that increases in the use of one category are associated with increases in the use of another category in the same description, the MDS analysis views the two as similar and plots the two more closely in the two-dimensional space.

We have some doubt that a coder could figure out how to purposefully influence such results, let alone do so inadvertently. However, let us suppose that a bias was somehow introduced, such that two categories of descriptors that are not really related appeared to co-occur, or that two categories that are actually related appeared not to co-occur. To erroneously produce the overall patterns revealed by the MDS analyses, coders would need to engage in a number of systematically related biases that produce just the right patterns of intercorrelations. Such systematic biases can only occur in this paradigm by miscoding individual items in a way that increases or decreases their correlation with items in another category. In other words, the miscoding of individual items must somehow be influenced by the presence or absence of other material in the same description.

We previously calculated reliabilities that revealed high agreement between two different coders using the AST taxonomy. Overall, the coders assigned items to the same one of the 25 taxonomic classifications over 74% of the time, and to classifications that were within a single row or column of each other 94% of the time. In other words, the few differences of opinion were over distinctions finer than those differentiating the eight basic forms of representation, with only 6% of the codings differing enough to implicate different representational forms. However, this does not preclude the possibility that both coders were systematically influenced in the same way by the overall description, leading them to make the same coding "errors." To examine this possibility, 223 descriptors were randomly drawn from descriptions written by 223 different subjects and transcribed, out of context, onto typewritten sheets. These were then coded by an individual who had never seen these descriptions before, who was unaware of the remaining portions of each description, and who therefore could not possibly be influenced by the other material in any description. This "blind" coder produced the same codings as the original coder over 81% of the time, and classifications that were within a single row or column of the original codings 95% of the time. In other words, only 5% of the codings differed enough to involve different basic forms of representation. These data indicate that the codings were so little influenced by contextual information that it is difficult to see how miscodings could have systematically produced the patterns of correlation revealed by the MDS analyses. Hence, it does not appear that the coding system could have artificially produced the relationships apparent from the MDS analyses.

Preserving the Social Ecology. Fiedler commends the target chapter's suggestion that experiential and ecological factors influence the forms of representation that people generate about others. As he notes, many kinds of environmental influence have been neglected during the recent social cognition era. However, Fielder argues that the target chapter does not go far enough, in that environmental influences may substantially determine many of the judgmental phenomena of interest to social psychologists. In this section, we briefly reconsider the AST arguments concerning ecological influence, and then examine the more radical views proposed by Fielder.

From the perspective of AST, the form in which social information is observed or experienced is an important influence on the form in which it is represented cognitively. Different kinds of interactions (e.g., in role vs. emotionally involving) and communications (e.g., descriptive vs. judgmental) implicate different mental systems and provide the perceiver with different kinds of input. Similarly, different kinds of situations demand different kinds of output from perceivers. Finally, experience in dealing with different kinds of information is likely to facilitate the proceduralization of the cognitive routines involved in storing, translating, and outputting such material. These ideas are central to the process model spelled out in the target chapter (see especially pp. 32–39).

This aspect of AST has a number of implications regarding the study of social cognition phenomena. For example, this perspective suggests that social cognition researchers need to do more to: (a) examine the frequencies with which different kinds of interactions and communications occur in the social environment; (b) determine the kinds of behavioral, judgmental, and communicative demands placed on people by the social environment; (c) investigate the linkages between social interaction and social representation; and (d) detail the relationships between individual social histories and experiences, and preferences for different forms of cognitive representation. Thus, as Fiedler notes, AST does emphasize the importance of the social ecology in social representation, arguing, in essence, that social cognition researchers should focus on the "social" as well as the "cognitive" in social cognitive phenomena.

In some respects, these arguments are consistent with Fiedler's views regarding the interactions between communicative language and cognitive representation. However, Fiedler's approach goes considerably beyond such ecological arguments to the more radical view that "many findings of biased social representations can be explained without recourse to biased or selective processing, just by considering the density and distribution of stimuli in the environment" (p. 123). For example, Fiedler argues that phenomena as different as illusory correlation and the extremity shift can be explained simply in terms of the distribution of events or opinions to which people are exposed. His arguments are complicated and fall somewhat outside of the scope of AST, so we shall deal with these only briefly.

First, at a metatheoretical level, we are not completely comfortable with the idea that there are "representations outside the individual," or that cognitive phenomena can be adequately explained in terms of "an external world obeying completely different laws and requiring a new class of theoretical concepts" (p. 125). Target-based cognitive representations may be similar in form or content to material "outside the individual," but it is nonetheless necessary to specify the mechanisms by which such material comes to be internally represented. Self-referent representations cannot really be described as existing outside of the individual at all. At a metatheoretic level, the specification of extrapersonal laws and concepts may be useful in describing certain kinds of sociological or interpersonal phenomena, but this represents an entirely different level of analysis than the social cognition perspective adopted here. Like most social cognition theorists, we prefer to focus on intrapsychic principles and causes, even though we recognize that the real world impinges on these in important ways.

Second, at a more concrete level, no distribution of environmental cues can, by itself, lead to biases or distortions in judgmental processes. Random sampling from a distribution will, on average, simply produce a new distribution with the same mean as the original. Implicit in Fiedler's argument is the assumption that a sampling mechanism exists that tends to overweight majority cues at the expense of minority cues. However, this mechanism cannot be in the environment; rather, it must reflect the operation of as-yet-unspecified cognitive procedures that tend to overemphasize particularly salient forms of information. Therefore, it would seem necessary to focus on how the environmental cues are perceived, processed, represented, retrieved, and used. This, of course, brings us back to the information-processing perspective of social cognition models such as AST (see Schneider, 1991).

Systematically Different Approaches to Mental Systems: Reply to Radvansky

Radvansky (chap. 6, this volume) approaches AST from a different perspective than that adopted by Carlston in the target chapter, or by the more social psychological commentators. His perspective involves not only somewhat different concerns and interpretations, but also different definitions and goals than those described in the target chapter. Thus, although we attempt to resolve some fairly specific disagreements, we acknowledge that most of these points of contention reflect far more general differences in orientation between Radvansky and AST. Therefore, the overall value of this particular dialogue may lie less in the details than in the metatheoretical issues that are raised regarding the proper relationship between approaches that derive from altogether different research fields.

Some Systematic Misunderstandings   One central and recurrent concern in Radvansky's commentary involves the nature of the *systems* posited by AST. Radvansky suggests that AST claims the existence of 8, or perhaps 25, different forms of representation that have "equal status" in processing, with secondary systems serving as "a bridge across which the information from the separate systems can be shared." He then questions whether the secondary systems should be described as systems at all, suggests that a hierarchical arrangement of systems is more likely, and argues that the kinds of associative structure depicted in Fig. 1.5 contradict the organization implied by AST.

The target chapter is actually quite specific in proposing the existence of only four primary mental systems, which deal with visual, verbal, affective, and behavioral activities, respectively. These four systems are represented by the four cones in Fig. 1.1 and by the four corner circles in all other pertinent figures (i.e., 1.2, 1.3, and 1.5). Radvansky acknowledges the existence of these systems, stating at one point that "the primary systems are clearly different mental systems because they each derive from a separate set of input mental sources, operate on different contents, and require different mechanisms to process that information" (p. 134). The target chapter also refers to "secondary" or "hybrid" systems, which are described as deriving both content and function from pairs of primary systems (p. 7). However, contrary to Radvansky's description, these systems are never characterized as having equal status with the primary systems, nor is it ever suggested that they are independent of other systems, have their own input or output sources, or require different mechanisms to process information. In fact, their derivative nature generally suggests the opposite, and the target chapter states that where the primary systems merge together "common principles of organization and process are assumed to operate" (p. 7). Thus, most of Radvansky's criticisms of the secondary systems stem more from his misinterpretation of their nature than from any substantive disagreement.

However, Radvansky's principal objection to the characterization of these secondary systems as *systems* probably stems from the way in which this term is used in cognitive psychology. In cognitive psychology, different memory systems are generally defined as involving discrete and separable processes and are identified through dissociations in the effects of different manipulations. Radvansky extols this definition and cites as "successful" examples the distinctions between procedural and declarative knowledge, between episodic and semantic knowledge, between implicit and explicit memory, and between the visual and verbal codes in Paivio's dual-code model. It should be noted that each of the distinctions that Radvansky mentions has actually proved controversial (see Anderson, 1978, 1979; Commentary, 1986; Pylyshyn, 1973; Schacter, 1987; Tulving, 1972), suggesting that what constitutes a system is a little elusive, even within cognitive psychology.

In any case, there is a fundamental difference between the objectives of cognitive theories such as those Radvansky mentions and of AST. The end goal in cognitive psychology is to identify and describe different memory and processing systems; given this goal, there is obviously a need for stringent criteria regarding what constitutes a separable system. However, the primary goal in AST is to characterize the likely interrelationships among previously identified forms of social representation. Given this objective, it is somewhat more arbitrary whether one labels the processes relating to different representational forms as *systems* or as something else. The target chapter does occasionally use the term *systems* in connection with secondary representations as well as primary ones. However, the careful reader will note that the narrative always specifies whether the systems being referred to are primary mental systems or secondary systems of representation. Furthermore, the target chapter never refers to 25 systems, or even to 25 different forms of mental representation. The AST taxonomy does distinguish among 25 different forms of descriptors that people use in describing other people, but emphasizes that the real goal is simply to "classify the kinds of descriptors obtained from subjects in a manner that reflects the likely contributions of the 8 basic representational forms" (p. 25).

Space limitations preclude extensive consideration of Radvansky's observations about the organization of mental systems. The commonly posited hierarchical structure of cognition is assumed by AST to operate within the primary mental systems, although we do not presume that major systems are hierarchically related to other major systems. In addition, as noted earlier, we do not view the arrangement of representations in Fig. 1.2 as reflecting a necessary progression among systems, and thus we would not be comfortable characterizing secondary forms of representation as a "bridge" between primary forms of representation. Finally, as already mentioned, the structural model in AST primarily reflects the characteristics of representations, rather than their connectivity, with the latter being modeled with a network representation that is influenced, but not determined, by the systemic structure. Consequently, we do not believe that the AST model is "violated by connections of concepts across nonadjoining areas" (p. 137).

Other Defining Issues. In several other instances, Radvansky's comments reflect definitional disagreements more than substantive ones. This may reflect a pervasive problem in trying to transport theories from one subfield of psychology to another. The same term can have rather different meanings across different fields, and even within a field, it is often necessary to extend or restrict a term from its conventional meaning. The target chapter attempted to explicate the meaning of key terms, but sometimes did so through reference to literatures with which all readers may not be familiar. Therefore, we elaborate here on the definitions of several key terms.

In his criticism of the secondary systems in AST, Radvansky argues that categorizations do not have a unique representational code, that "categorization mechanisms can come from any of the four primary systems," and that "we can categorize affect and actions quite well" (p. 134). All of this may be quite true, but it is also quite irrelevant because AST only refers to *categorizations* as a specific form of social representation that has been examined by Cantor and Mischel (1977), Klatzky and Anderson (1988), and others (see Carlston, 1992, for a more extensive definition of *categorizations*, as well as the other forms of social representation). Classic examples include ethnic, role, and gender classifications, as well as personality categories such as *slob* or *extrovert*. Based on previous definitions and research in social cognition, we stand by the target chapter's assertion that these social categorizations can best be understood as involving both visual and verbal components (see Brewer, 1988).

Radvansky also takes issue with the target chapter's assertion that "AST focuses on the forms of impression-related (or impressional) representations, rather than on their contents" (p. 2). He argues that the model actually deals with only "a single representational form, a network representation" (p. 136), and that "differences among the various systems are primarily attributable to differences in information content" (p. 137). These arguments rely on radically different definitions of content and form than those assumed by AST. The target chapter's assertion regarding form and content continues as follows: "In other words, the theory does not directly specify when one is likely to feel positive or negative about others, when one will think this or that about them, or whether one will act one way or another toward them. . . . In essence, the concern is not with *what* people think about others, but *how* they think it" (p. 2). This phrasing was intended to differentiate AST from other social cognition theories that focus on one particular form of representation and examine the nature of the contents that are represented in that form. For example, interpersonal attraction theories (Berscheid, 1985) focus on affective or evaluative responses, and specify when these responses will be positive or negative; the Hastie–Srull model (Hastie & Kumar, 1979; Srull, 1981) focuses on episodic memories, and predicts when these memories will be congruent or incongruent with expectations; and Higgins' work (Higgins et al., 1977) on priming focuses on trait attributions, and details the role of accessibility in the utilization of one trait concept over another. AST does not directly address such content issues, although it aspires to complement these theories by raising and addressing issues relating to multiple forms of representation.

The definition of *representational form* inheres in the various specific social representations described in AST. There are extensive literatures dealing with most of these forms, and these literatures detail the informational features, operating characteristics, influencing factors, and phenomenological experiences that distinguish one from another. A more general definition might be that unrelated forms of representation tend to involve essentially different kinds of informational features, and may be experienced in fundamentally different ways (see p. 48). Such a definition places the most emphasis on the kinds of differences likely to be important to interpersonal judgment, communication, and interaction, but steers away from issues regarding underlying representational codes. Controversies regarding the codes underlying representations have been persistent in cognitive psychology, but have been less relevant to the concerns of social cognition.

In asserting that the *network representation* is the only representational form in AST, Radvansky equates *form* with organizational structure — a definition that we do not see as either common or useful in this domain. We prefer to characterize the network representation as a structural or organizational model, rather than as a form of representation. Perhaps this is simply a matter of preference, as we recognize that terminologies differ from discipline to discipline. Even so, forcing the concepts and ideas from one discipline into the uncomfortable language of another runs the risk of obscuring underlying issues, rather than clarifying them.

Should We Forget About Amnesia?   Radvansky suggests that the target chapter shows "some misunderstanding" of clinical syndromes, with the primary illustration being that:

> Carlston conflates several types of unrelated amnesias that are a result of damage to a variety of different neurological substrates. For example, retrograde amnesia is typically caused by general cerebral or other physical trauma where a memory trace has not been allowed to consolidate, whereas anterograde amnesia is caused by damage to the hippocampus. Few researchers would be willing to say that these different types of amnesias are part of the same system. (p. 134).

Actually, anterograde and retrograde amnesia are both defining characteristics of the amnesic syndrome — an affliction that stems from a wide range of aetiologies, including head injury, cerebral infarction, Wernicke's disease, and other disorders. The two forms of amnesia not only co-occur in the purer forms of amnesic syndrome, but their severity is often correlated, especially in diencephalic cases (Parkin & Leng, 1993). This has led some theorists to propose common underlying mechanisms, such as deficits in the processing of contextual information (Mayes, 1988). Consequently, a number of researchers might grant that these different amnesias are part of the same system, if *system* is used in a general way.

However, the only claim that the target chapter made was that both retrograde and anterograde amnesias could be viewed as deficits in the episodic memory system.[4] AST is centrally concerned with functional systems, and both anterograde and retrograde amnesia reflect disruptions with episodic memory functions. Radvansky's objections to these claims probably stem again from his desire to define *systems* differently — in this case, in terms of particular physical brain structures. Because anterograde and retrograde amnesia can occur independently, given damage to thalamic or temporal lobe structures, his viewpoint argues that these deficits must

---

[4]Actually, there is some debate over whether amnesic deficits only involve episodic memory, as narrowly defined by Tulving (1972), and some have suggested that the deficits might better be characterized as involving explicit, as opposed to implicit, memory (Parkin & Leng, 1993). Nonetheless, in general, major forms of amnesia can be viewed as involving episodic knowledge to a greater extent than alternative forms of representation.

involve different systems. However, even if the underlying mechanisms could be so easily localized and delineated, this would not preclude viewing episodic memory as a functional system, or amnesias as dysfunctions in that system, as the target chapter did.

Shooting at the Wrong Goal.   Radvansky's unique perspective not only led him to adopt different definitions for AST's primary terms, but to approach the theory with an entirely different set of expectations and goals. From the vantage point provided by cognitive dual-memory models, he is disappointed to discover that AST describes no previously undiscovered memory systems: "As for the primary memory systems identified by the AST model, there is nothing new here. All of the functions performed by these systems have been identified by other multiple system theories" (p. 135). He similarly notes that the AST taxonomic scheme incorporates many forms of description that relate to previous taxonomies, and concludes that "the AST model does not introduce anything new in terms of dimensions on which people classify information" (p. 135). He does concede at one point that "in fairness, it does not seem to be the primary intention of the AST model to provide an account of a new division of mental systems" (p. 135), but he nonetheless chastises the model repeatedly for failing to make any contributions of this type.

Such complaints overlook the stated integrative objective of AST. As discussed in the opening paragraphs of the target chapter, the goal of AST is to provide a comprehensive integration of previously studied forms of social representation that "suggests both the origins and the consequences of impressions differing in representational form" (p. 1). This approach does not disavow known representational forms or suggest that these be replaced with novel and previously unknown constructs. Doing so would forfeit the stated integrative goal of AST, as well as the considerable knowledge already accumulated about social representation (not to mention the indulgence of many readers). To the contrary, the target chapter notes that most of the representational forms with which it deals "have been individually studied within social cognition, or within psychology more generally" (p. 1), and it provides a brief review of such work (see also Carlston, 1992). However, the chapter goes on to point out that "little attention has been paid to the manner in which these diverse impression-related contents are organized, how they evolve or interact, or how they ultimately influence various interpersonal responses". Therefore, AST was designed to foster the simultaneous consideration of these various forms of representation, and to address new issues that arise from such a multimodal view.

The paucity of novel descriptors in the AST taxonomy is also a logical consequence of the integrative nature of AST. Both the theory and the other descriptive taxonomies build on research on interpersonal perception, and it is logical that both end up incorporating important forms of social representation. The AST scheme does include both affective and behavioral response descriptors, unlike most other schemes. Nonetheless, as the target chapter proudly points out, "It is evident that most, though not all, of the AST representational forms recur regularly across these different taxonomies" (p. 16). Does this mean, as Radvansky suggests, that the AST scheme "does not introduce anything new?" We think not. The AST taxonomy has a number of significant advantages over previous schemes, including greater breadth and structure, specification of relationships among classifications, potential for computation of summary indices, and linkages both with theory and with commonly studied interpersonal responses.

In summary, then, Radvansky adopts the view that AST should describe new and different representations, whereas the actual goal of the theory was to provide an integrative account of known forms of representation. As noted earlier, this difference in expectations for the theory may stem partly from the different general objectives of the fields of cognitive psychology and social cognition. The former emphasizes the discovery and delineation of basic mental processes, whereas the latter has historically been more derivative, attempting to use cognitive concepts to explain interpersonal phenomena.

In any case, we believe that the contributions of AST are better assessed in terms of its stated goals than in terms of the goals of other disciplines. It is true that, even on these terms, Radvansky seems to find AST wanting. However, his conclusion that "little seems to be gained by actually specifying multiple mental systems to understand the formation of impressions of other people" (p. 137) seems to derive entirely from the cognitive concerns already discussed, rather than from explicit consideration of impression-formation processes or phenomena. As already noted, Radvansky's interpretation of these issues is colored by different concept definitions and theoretical objectives than those described by AST. It might be unrealistic given our fundamental differences in approach, but we would like to think that he would find AST more useful if he considered it on its own terms. In any case, we turn now to several commentators whose definitions and goals overlap more with AST, and whose social psychological approaches seem more complementary to our own.

AST: EXTENSIONS AND APPLICATIONS

Multiple Views of Multiple Representations: Reply to Brewer

In their preface to the first volume of this series, the editors characterized Brewer's target chapter as "perspicacious and intrepid" (Vol. 1, p. xi). This is high praise indeed (we checked a dictionary to make sure), and it sets a lofty standard for subsequent target chapters. We are therefore especially gratified to have Brewer pronounce AST to be even "more radical" than her original model. We are also flattered and intrigued by her efforts to merge some of the ideas from that original chapter with aspects of the AST model. In commenting on these efforts, we attempt to highlight some of the ways in which we have been influenced by her original target chapter and by her commentary in this volume.

More Than One Way to Skin a Categorization.   Brewer (chap. 7, this volume) notes that AST provides a useful framework for thinking about some of the concepts from her dual-processing model and from related work on intergroup attitudes. For example, different writers have tended to use terms relating to categorization, stereotyping, and prejudice in different ways, creating some uncertainty regarding the similarities and differences among such concepts. Brewer suggests that "AST helps articulate the idea that identification, ingroup–outgroup classification (prejudice), and stereotyping are conceptually distinct forms of representation that may be more or less closely linked for different individuals and different social categories" (p. 143). In fact, AST implies that there could be a variety of different kinds of intergroup impressions that reflect the differential engagement of different systems, and that incorporate correspondingly different forms of representation. The simplest of these might only involve the perception of physical features, as Brewer suggests (p. 142). Two other processes — categorization and stereotyping — seemingly reflect greater involvement of other kinds of representations. The perceiver may categorize individuals, ascribing special importance to their membership in a social or occupational group, and thus cognitively equating them with others in that same group. Going one step further, the perceiver may attribute personality characteristics to individuals based on their categorization. Such *stereotyping* is usually defined as involving all three of these representational forms: appearance features, categorizations, and trait attributions.

From the perspective of AST, stereotyping thus reflects target-based forms of representation with little self-reference or engagement. When intergroup impressions also involve behavioral or affective components, the result might be characterized as a more self-referent and involving form of prejudice. The target chapter speculated that behavioral and affective representations "implicate the self, a relatively stable structure for most perceivers (Kihlstrom & Cantor, 1984)," and thus "may be more difficult to influence or change" (p. 14) than representations of other forms. Consequently, full-blown, multirepresentational prejudices that involve affect and behaviors, as well as stereotypes, may be particularly difficult to influence or eliminate (Katz, 1960).

It may also be useful to think about intergroup impressions in terms of variations along the concreteness dimension. Some people may fall into prejudiced patterns of interactions with members of identifiable groups, without concomitant negative beliefs or feelings. In essence, this kind of rote prejudice may reflect thoughtless habits or adherence to social norms, rather than stereotypical beliefs or ill will. A good example might be the inadvertently sexist behaviors of traditionally reared males who sincerely espouse egalitarian views, but have not successfully altered their styles of interacting with females. From the point of view of AST, such prejudice arguably reflects the more concrete representations of appearance, categorization, action, and orientation in the absence of abstract representations such as traits and affect. Thus, this prejudice differs in important ways from more full-blown forms of chauvinism, which implicate stereotypes and affective responses as well.

This analysis suggests that AST may be able to add some precision to concepts such as *categorization* and *prejudice*, and may provide a system for delineating different kinds of prejudice. Whether this will lead to new and novel insights about intergroup relationships is not evident at this point. In any case, it seems useful to try to firm up the meaning of constructs such as *stereotype*, and to relate them to more general ideas about the engagement of different cognitive systems and representations. We appreciate Brewer's suggestion that AST may provide a useful tool in this effort.

Up the Down Staircase.   Brewer states that, in AST, impressions are constructed from the bottom–up, through observation of stimuli, inference processes, and the importation of links from conceptual social memory into the impressional structure. She argues that this seems to disregard the importance of top–down processes such as comparison and differentiation. Moreover, she suggests that bottom–up processes produce impressions that become progressively more like those in conceptual memory, as more generic material is imported, whereas top–down processes produce impressions that become progressively less like those in conceptual memory, as more individual aberrations are noted. Finally, she relates these differing processes to her concepts, personalization, and individuation, arguing that each of these results in a different kind of associative structure.

Looking back over the target chapter, it is evident why Brewer concluded that AST is a bottom–up approach. Figure 1.7 depicts impression formation as a progression through stages that begin on the left with the external stimulus, followed by translation processes and other cognitive activities, and ending on the right with judgment and response processes. All arrows in the figure point from left to right, and thus all influence seems to move from the stimulus through cognitive mediation to the ultimate response. If one assumes that conceptual processing is introduced somewhere during the stages of cognitive mediation, the logical conclusion is that impressions become more like conceptual memory as one moves from left to right in the figure.

Figure 1.7 notwithstanding, we actually perceive every stage of impression formation as dependent on the interplay between certain inputs and relevant knowledge structures. Initial cognitive representations derive from the match between external stimuli and known patterns in conceptual social memory. Secondary translations involve the "importation" of well-learned associations that determine how the initial representations are elaborated cognitively. Intermediate processes are instigated when the patterns of activated concepts stimulate the execution of different cognitive procedures. Finally, judgments and other overt responses eventuate when the overall pattern of activated material matches the triggering conditions for these activities. Thus, all cognitive activity would seem to inherently involve both top–down and bottom–up processes.

This view is reflected in the parallel distributed processing (PDP) model of conceptual memory described in the target chapter:

> The pattern of activation that represents an actual behavior may sufficiently approximate a generic pattern to cause or allow the activation of generic representations in conceptual memory. Once these new forms of representation are activated, they can become associated directly with the actor. In other words, the activation pattern that constitutes our impression of someone is likely to encompass these new feature nodes, representing material "imported" from conceptual social memory, as well as old feature nodes representing the prior impression. (p. 37)

In other words, the features composing an impression at any time are likely to reflect a mixture of those derived (in bottom–up fashion) from the stimulus and those derived (in top–down fashion) from conceptual representations that approximately match the patterns of material activated in cognition.

Does this view imply that impressions will progressively become more and more like the generic representations in conceptual memory? Probably not. The target chapter does suggest that individual representations (e.g., an episodic memory or a trait inference) tend to become more like their generic or schematic forms over time, as they degrade. In contrast, overall impressions seem likely to change from the generic to the ideosyncratic as additional information accumulates. The relatively impoverished patterns of observation that contribute to initial impressions seem more likely to match the generic patterns in conceptual memory than the complex and idiosyncratic patterns that build up after extended interaction and involvement. Thus, general conceptual knowledge seems more likely to be imported and incorporated into initial impressions than into later ones, just as Brewer assumes in her own model. On the other hand, there is no guarantee that such individuation processes will occur, because individuating information may be ignored or misinterpreted, and the resultant representations may ultimately be relatively less salient than the implications of particularly strong stereotypes or other forms of generic knowledge. Even so, in general, Brewer is probably correct that impressions come to look less like our conceptual stereotypes over time. Moreover, Brewer's model may be viewed as an attempt to explain when such individuation is likely to occur, given different stimulus characteristics and perceiver motives (see also Fiske, 1988; Fiske & Pavelchak, 1986).

If all cognitive processing is both bottom–up and top–down, as we have argued, does it make sense to differentiate the impressions resulting from these processes in the manner that Brewer does? For example, in her target chapter, Brewer characterized *individuation* as a process in which people come to be viewed as special instances of the more general categories to which they have already been assigned, whereas she defined *personalization* as the process of forming impressions bottom–up from the characteristics of the individuals. She argued that these two processes result in distinguishable cognitive structures, with individual features subordinated to categorizations in the former instance, and features of the category subordinated to characteristics of the individual in the latter instance.

We have never been completely sure about this provocative suggestion, despite the evidence that Brewer marshalled in its support. One possible interpretation of the proposal is that it matters how an impression was developed, independent of the particular representations that it ends up containing. For example, if we have similar representations of Doug and Gary, these impressions are supposed to be organized quite differently if Doug was initially categorized as a member of some group and Gary was initially viewed as an individual. However, our intuition is that, as we get to know Doug, his initial categorization may become rather less relevant and accessible, and that as we get to know Gary, we might conceivably view him as fitting some category type better than we first realized. At that point where our impressions of the two consist of equivalent representations, the ontogeny of these impressions would not seem to matter anymore.

In any case, Brewer's commentary suggests a way to cast these suppositions in a somewhat different light. Brewer states that "individuated impressions are more visual, more concrete, and involve fewer associative links than personalized impressions" (p. 146), and furthermore, that cognitive processes relating to individuated impressions may focus on "the visual and verbal systems and associated representational forms (appearance, categorization, traits, and evaluations)" (p. 146). This is consistent with AST's implication that, when we categorize an individual, our initial impression of that person will probably include other representations that are closely related to categorizations (i.e., appearance and traits). Moreover, Brewer suggests, behavioral and affective responses should then become linked to the impression only later, after the final representation is achieved, whereas these representations are included in personalized impressions from the very start. This also seems consistent with the AST argument that secondary representations derive from translation of initial ones. Thus, when a person has been categorized or stereotyped, subsequent behavioral and affective responses should be dictated by these initial representations. In other words, we respond to this person in ways that are characteristic of our responses to other individuals who we categorize similarly.

On the other hand, when our initial impression lacks such strong categorical determinants, our behavioral and affective responses are more likely to be "personalized" in response to idiosyncratic features or behaviors of the other person. The more target-based representations that we eventually develop may then derive from our response representations, rather than the other way around. The individuated categorical impression and the personalized impression may therefore comprise different representational forms, as Brewer suggests, or they may be equivalent in form, but differ in specific content, depending on which representations coalesced first. Thus, from this point of view, the important difference between individuation and personalization is that they are likely to result in different representations, rather than that they simply result in differing organizations of the same representations.

Sorting It All Out.   One of the challenges for representational theories (and for the field of social cognition, more generally) is to develop methodologies suitable for examining concepts and processes that are not readily observable. It is particularly difficult to examine the organizational structure underlying cognitive representations, for which reasons we are constantly on the lookout for methods that we can adapt to our purposes. Multidimensional scaling of free descriptions provides one such method, as previously described in the target chapter. However, as noted both in the target chapter and in Brewer's commentary, there is some danger in relying exclusively on subjects' verbal statements in assessing cognitive representations or their interrelations.

Brewer and Lui (1989) developed a different method that we believe has considerable potential in this area. In their procedure, subjects were instructed to sort people into different groups based on one or another kind of representational characteristic. The researchers instructed subjects to sort photographs in terms of "specific physical features," "character or personality type," or "psychological traits or states." Coincidentally, these instructions correspond closely to our definitions of the appearance, categorization, and trait representations depicted in the top row of Fig. 1.2.

Consistent with AST, analyses indicated that sortings in response to the appearance and categorization instructions were more similar than sortings in response to the appearance and trait instructions. However, sortings in response to categorization and trait instructions were no more similar than sortings in response to appearance and trait instructions, which may seem contrary to AST. There is evidence in the study that subjects in the categorization condition used visually definable categorizations (e.g., age and gender) rather than appearance-independent groupings (e.g., status, occupation, or personality types such as *introvert*), which is understandable, given that subjects were sorting photographs of strangers and would have lacked information about any appearance-independent groupings. This bias presumably inflated the similarity between appearance and categorization sortings, and decreased the similarity between categorization and trait sortings.

In our adaptation of this method, subjects first write the names of a disparate group of friends, acquaintances, and celebrities on index cards. They then engage in eight (randomly ordered) sorting tasks, corresponding to the eight assumed forms of social representation. In addition to appearance- and trait-based sortings, like those Brewer used, subjects are instructed to sort the index cards into piles of individuals who are similar in terms of social group memberships (categorizations), likability (evaluations), gut reactions (affect), relationship (orientations), behaviors (behavioral observations), and treatment by the subject (behavioral responses). Although we have no data to report as this book goes to press, the pattern of results that we are hoping for should be obvious. We expect to find that instructions describing forms of representation that are related in AST will result in highly similar sortings.

Brewer and Lui's sorting task may overcome some of the potential shortcomings of free-description methods. For example, the method de-emphasizes communication conventions that may lead subjects to include or exclude different kinds of material from their public descriptions. It also allows subjects to deal with forms of representation that are largely nonverbal (e.g., behavioral and affective responses), making comparisons along lines that would be difficult for them to articulate. We are also working to adapt other methods, including, for example, the task-facilitation paradigm recently described by Klein et al. (1992), and the savings method utilized by Carlston and Skowronski (1994). The point is that creative methods such as these permit determination of the organizational structure underlying impressional representations, making even these difficult aspects of AST subject to experimental confirmation or disconfirmation.

An Ambivalent Approach to Ambivalence: Reply to
Bodenhausen and Macrae

Like Brewer, Bodenhausen and Macrae (chap. 8, this volume) attempt to
integrate AST with their own approach and concerns in social cognition.
The result is a thoughtful and provocative discussion of the role that
multiple representations may play in feelings of interpersonal ambivalence.
In many respects, the ideas raised complement our own, although once
again we focus more on disagreements in this chapter. In any case, we are
enthusiastic about Bodenhausen and Macrae's effort, and are only concerned that, in our excitement, we may be tempted to pontificate about
matters outside our expertise.[5]

Phenomenological Phenomena.   Bodenhausen and Macrae note that the
target chapter says "surprisingly little" about how composite impressions
are "experienced by social perceivers" (p. 150). What little the target chapter
does say could probably use clarification, so we welcome this opportunity
to speculate about the phenomenology of impressions. What chapter 1 says
is that "impressions may often be experienced as undifferentiated amalgams
of representational features, rather than as discrete representational forms"
(p. 9). It later adds that "the overall representation or impression of an
individual is probably experienced as a flood of associations, rather than in
terms of discreet representational components" (p. 16). The intended
implication is that cognition consists of material drawn from all different
representational forms, mixed together without regard to systemic origin,
and experienced as an amorphous collection of interrelated features. In
other words, perceivers seem likely to be indifferent to the systematic
structure that we see underlying impressional representations. Instead, the
phenomenological experience of the impression is likely to simply be a
mental mixture of all those representational features that are accessible. Of
course, this experience may change from moment to moment as different
associations rise to consciousness.

We suggested earlier that different representational forms "tend to
involve essentially different kinds of informational features, and may be
experienced in fundamentally different ways" (p. 201). Thus, the phenomenological experience associated with an impression will differ, depending
on the different kinds of representations that are most salient at any
moment. My impression of a friend can consist at one time of a facial image
and a couple of personality traits, and at another time of an episodic
memory with associated affect and perhaps a behavioral intention or two.
Each of these impressions will be experienced a little differently, with the

---

[5]Cynics may suggest that it is a little late to develop such scruples.

most fundamental differences occurring when lower level representations also become activated within the different systems. Then the impressions will vary not only in terms of abstract, higher level thoughts, but also in terms of the images that are seen, the feelings that are felt, and the actions that are initiated.

As noted in the target chapter, featural and phenomenological differences among different forms of representation may help people to differentiate among these components of their impressions under some circumstances. However, we assume that people rarely have cause to stop and sort out their feelings from their images, or their memories from their inferences. In general, the ways that people think and act are predicated on the overall pattern of representations that are activated, rather than on the separate implications of individual representations of one or another form. Consequently, there is probably little need to partial certain representations out of the mix, and the overall experience simply involves an amalgamation of thoughts and feelings, as suggested earlier.

Bodenhausen and Macrae suggest that for impressions to be "experienced as a coherent bottom line," it is necessary for the inputs from the different systems to be "translatable into a common metric" (p. 150). We suspect that perceivers ordinarily do experience their impressions as coherent, in that all of the different representational components probably seem to fit together and to work together reasonably well. However, the need for a "common metric" may be less acutely felt by the social perceivers who have impressions than by the social psychologists who wish to characterize these in terms of some singular dimension. Perceivers probably respond to people in terms of the overall pattern of representations that are activated, or possibly in terms of those representations that are most closely related to the response being made. If the overall pattern adequately matches the preconditions for a cognitive procedure, that procedure can initiate the response. For example, if one is struck by a fellow player during a pickup basketball game, if that player is a friend, and if that player is known to be careful and considerate, then one will overlook the foul and continue playing. However, if the offending player is disliked, looks angry, and is known to be aggressive, the more likely response is retaliation. In such cases, there is no need to reduce the amalgamation of experienced representations to a common metric such as evaluation in order to produce a response.

This is not to say that we disagree with Bodenhausen and Macrae's general remarks about coherence and ambivalence. On the contrary, we agree with much of their analysis, and would actually expand it in ways to be suggested later. However, we do not believe that impressions are experienced primarily in terms of any singular metric, and thus we would not characterize feelings of coherence and ambivalence simply in terms of inconsistencies in evaluative implications. Rather, ambivalence may be said to exist whenever one subset of activated cognitions precipitates a response that is incompatible with implications of a different subset of activated cognitions.

Consistency by Coincidence. A second area where our view differs somewhat from Bodenhausen and Macrae's regards the causes of "interrepresentational consistency." They observe: the following: "Carlston claims that when the various systems are simultaneously active . . . they will tend to produce consistent representations. What remains unclear, however, is specifically what processes operate to produce this interrepresentational consistency, and what the consequences are when such processes are unsuccessful" (p. 151). The target chapter actually proposes that simultaneous activation of various systems produces consistent representations more or less through coincidence, rather than as a result of specific cognitive processes. To be more precise, the argument is that coincident representations are more likely to influenced by similar factors, and are more likely to influence each other, than representations produced in different situations or at different times. As a result, images, thoughts, feelings, and acts that stem from the same event or events are likely to have rather similar implications. On the other hand, images, thoughts, feelings, and acts that eventuate from different situations may have rather different implications.

For example, consider the impressions formed by a search committee chairperson who first reads a young man's reference letters, then talks to him on the telephone, and finally meets and interacts with him during the job interview. Possibly the letters describe the candidate as warm and personable, whereas the phone call is somewhat awkward and formal, and the personal interactions are actually unpleasant. The different representations composing the chairperson's impressions will undoubtedly diverge considerably in their implications. In contrast, the impressional representations of another professor, who only interacts with the candidate during the interview, are likely to be more consistent and coherent. Her trait impressions, feelings, and actions are likely to be generated coincidentally with, and perhaps even from, each other. Of course, inconsistencies may occur because the candidate's appearance, words, and actions may prompt representations with somewhat different implications. However, it is likely that, during the course of the episode, the professor's actions will be shaped by her thoughts, feelings, and so on, ensuring that all of these forms of representation are ultimately coordinated and consistent.

In summary, "different representations are likely to be consistent with each other to the extent that they have grown up together and are products of similar events" (p. 55), and they are more likely to be inconsistent with each other to the extent that they derive from dissimilar events.

However, this argument rests on the coincidence of the representations, rather than on motivations or mechanisms by which perceivers bring discordant representations into harmony. Such motivated efforts toward consistency are another matter altogether, and Bodenhausen and Macrae's intuitions about these raise some interesting possibilities, as discussed in the next section.

Different Sides of Ambivalence.   Bodenhausen and Macrae suggest that if people generally "prefer consistency and coherence to conflict and ambivalence" (p. 152), they will have developed either automatic or deliberate mechanisms to maintain the consistency of impressional representations. Among the possibilities they discuss are overreliance on singular forms of representation; suppression of discordant representations; and reconciliation of inconsistencies through imagination, retrospection, or other intermediate processes postulated by AST. They note that these latter possibilities are reminiscent of Festinger's (1957) dissonance theory, extending that theory beyond attitudes and behavior to additional forms of cognitive representation. Finally, they note that attempts to repress discordant representations can fail, sometimes due to capacity limitations, and that people may therefore need to learn to live with ambivalent cognitions.

These are interesting and useful insights. Certainly, when representations with strongly discrepant implications are contained within the same impression, this may create stresses that need to be dealt with. Bodenhausen and Macrae suggest a number of ways by which perceivers might attempt to deal with such stresses. One particularly rich suggestion is that these attempts may involve the various intermediate processes shown in Fig. 1.7. Of these, the role that verbal thought and analysis play in reconciling divergent cognitive representations has probably been most emphasized by cognitive consistency theories of one sort or another (see Abelson, et al., 1968). However, AST highlights the possibility that visual imagination, emotivity, retrospection, and rehearsal can also be used to alter the "metacognitive" angst that inconsistent cognitions may engender. For example, an individual guilty of mistreating a friend may: (a) picture that person smirking in ways that justify the behavior, or smiling in ways that say that all is forgiven; (b) misrecall the friend's prior behaviors or their own, or the mistreatment itself; (c) plan ways to redress the mistreatment or to explain it; (d) redefine their relationship with the friend; (e) focus on the anger that precipitated the mistreatment (and which now justifies it); or (f) attribute traits and evaluations to the friend that explain the mistreatment, or that reassure the perceiver that friends forgive and forget. In addition, the guilty party may adopt coping strategies such as distraction and suppression that serve to make alternative representations of one kind or another more salient. As Bodenhausen and Macrae note, these diversionary strategies can backfire (see especially Wegner, Schneider, Carter, & White, 1987), as can the earlier ones. Nonetheless, such alternative strategies are suggested by the framework provided by AST.

However, much of the time we suspect that perceivers simply do not see the inconsistencies between different representational forms because these do not rise simultaneously to the level of consciousness. For example, the traditional male described in our reply to Brewer may be totally unaware that his manner of interacting with females is incongruent with his professedly liberated views. Nonetheless, even if the inconsistencies do not become conscious, the individual's impression might be viewed as containing interrepresentational discrepancies or ambivalences. These presumably will not create the kind of stress or angst to which we already alluded, but they are nonetheless important because they can create variability in the perceiver's judgments and behaviors. We pursue the implications of this further in our response to Fazio's commentary, which deals most explicitly with the relevant issues.

When are perceivers likely to notice and confront inconsistencies that may exist among their images, beliefs, feelings, and behaviors regarding a target person? First, cognitive material may have to be represented at higher levels for it to be consciously attended and compared to other forms of representation. Second, as discussed earlier, the discrepant representations may have to be activated simultaneously for any inconsistencies to be noted. AST suggests that these preconditions may relate to the nature of the perceiver's past and present involvements with the target person or similar persons. More specifically, it is most likely that higher level representations will exist if the perceiver has employed the relevant system or systems during past involvements with the target, and that incongruent representations will be activated simultaneously if the perceiver's current involvement engages those relevant systems.

Bodenhausen and Macrae suggest further that "the potential for executive control of impressional systems increases as the perceiver's level of involvement increases" (p. 154; see Carlston's Fig. 1.8). This may suggest that the more the perceiver focuses on a particular system, and perhaps the more developed that system has become through past involvements, the greater control the perceiver should have over representations associated with that system. If we are interpreting this premise correctly, it raises some provocative possibilities. However, one might also hypothesize that the more a particular system is currently engaged, the less readily it can be controlled by the perceiver. Thus, for example, strong feelings of affect, well-rehearsed memories, or salient trait attributions may each interfere with attempts to access alternative representations of the same form (see p. 23). Consequently, remediation of the conflict may involve representational systems that are involved, but not too involved.

The perceiver's level of involvement can also be viewed in more general terms, as the overall level of engagement in the task at hand. This general level of involvement may also relate to people's detection of representational inconsistencies. For example, uninvolved individuals may tend to utilize those mental systems most necessary in any situation, at relatively primitive levels, without retrieving or considering higher level representations at all. Alternatively, they may simply operate on the basis of whatever kinds of higher level representations happen to be most accessible at the moment. In contrast, highly involved individuals may be more likely to engage in search processes that access a variety of different forms of representation (see Van Manen & Fiske, chap. 3, this volume), and that compare and combine these in systematic ways (Chaiken, 1980). Therefore, in general, more highly involved people seem more likely to notice inconsistencies among different forms of representation than less involved people.

The detection of representational inconsistencies may be affected by other individual differences as well. Carlston suggested that "people may differ in representational complexity, with some tending to rely primarily on one salient form of representation, and others tending to use a variety of different forms of representation" (p. 62). Because representationally simple individuals function primarily on the basis of one form of representation, other components of their impressions may simply reflect translations from this form, resulting in a high degree of representational consistency. If inconsistencies do occur (perhaps due to external pressures), representationally simple individuals may be less likely to notice these because they rarely attend to different forms of representation at once.

Once again, these speculations take us rather far afield. However, they do suggest the richness of the possibilities that Bodenhausen and Macrae raise in their commentary. If AST does not actually succeed in "setting the agenda for a new generation of impression-formation research" (p. 149), we hope that it at least stimulates a few other researchers to be as creative in reframing the issues that concern them.

Attitudes Toward AST: Reply to Fazio

In relating AST to his own research interests, Fazio (chap. 9, this volume) reiterates the target chapter's argument that AST should be extensible to impressions that are more commonly thought of as attitudinal. These might include attitudes toward physical objects, social issues, situations, events, or groups of people, with the latter extension being the easiest and most obvious. He suggests further that AST is useful in distinguishing among different kinds of attitudes, and relates aspects of the theory to issues regarding the accessibility and construction of attitudes, as well as contributing to the discussion of attitudinal ambivalence begun by Bodenhausen and Macrae. He concludes that the appeal and potential of AST lie in its integrative power and generalizability.

Given the target chapter's modest efforts to integrate attitudinal work in general, and Fazio's work in specific, we are especially pleased to have elicited encouragement, rather than dismay, from an attitude theorist of such note. Fazio's ideas on attitude accessibility are threaded throughout AST, and his research on attitude–behavior relationships underlies much of our thinking about interrepresentational consistency (see pp. 54–56, as well as Carlston, 1992). We are happy to acknowledge our intellectual debt, although we retain responsibility for any inadvertent misappropriation of this work.

Attitudinal Systems Theory?   Fazio suggests that AST is useful in delineating various basic kinds of attitudes. He notes that the perceiver's attitude toward a target person is reflected in AST's three affect-related representational forms (orientation, affect, and evaluation), and that the latter two forms correspond to the common distinction between *hot* and *cold* attitudes. He also delves into some of the important issues surrounding stored versus constructed attitudes, both of which are implicitly dealt with in AST. We are in substantial agreement with most of these observations, and elaborate these a little further here in an effort to make AST's viewpoint more explicit.

Suppose that an individual is asked about his attitudes toward some social group, perhaps journal editors. AST would seem to suggest that this attitudinal inquiry can be answered in two ways. First, the respondent can retrieve an existing cognitive representation that corresponds to the kind of attitudinal information being solicited. Alternatively, the respondent can retrieve those cognitive representations that are most accessible, and construct a response from these. The first of these processes involves what Fazio referred to as a *summary-based* judgment, and what social cognition theorists have termed a *memory-based* judgment (Hastie & Park, 1986). The second relates to Fazio's concept of a *nonattitude*, and to what social cognition theorists call *on-line processing* (Hastie & Park, 1986). This adds yet another parallel to Fazio's list of similarities between research on attitudes and person perception.

The kinds of summary representations that AST identifies include orientations, affects, and evaluations. All of these implicate the affective system, but orientations have more of an action component, consistent with definitions of attitudes as "predispositions to respond," and evaluations have more of a cognitive component, consistent with definitions of attitudes as "evaluative responses" or summaries of beliefs (see p. 29). All of these forms of representation can presumably be created and stored in the course of certain activities, and can then be retrieved in response to attitudinal inquiries. In terms of our example, this retrieval might correspond to the instant realization that one likes or dislikes editors, the reexperience (possibly at a superficial level) of emotions associated with editors, or the sense that one generally has a good or a bad relationship with editors. By translating these direct retrievals into the form required by the attitudinal inquiry, the respondent can describe the attitude without engaging in additional mental computations.

When no summary representation is stored, the respondent must construct an attitude through the retrieval and combination of other forms of representation. All forms of representation potentially have attitudinal implications, as well as implications for other kinds of judgments. Given the pervasive nature of affect, the attitudinal implications may have special importance, for which reason the AST coding scheme separately encodes the valence of each descriptor. In any case, those representations that are most salient will be retrieved, combined, and translated into the form required for response. These computations take time and are likely to result in attitudinal responses that vary from occasion to occasion, depending on which representations are used (Millar & Tesser, 1986; Wilson & Dunn, 1986).

Although it is conceptually useful to make a distinction between retrieved and computed attitudes, the same fundamental process may underlie both. In other words, the attitudinal inquiry prompts a search of memory for response-related material, and the result is a flood of the most accessible associations to the search probes. The respondent sorts through this material as well as possible, and constructs a response from those representations that seem most applicable and appropriate.[6] When a previously stored attitudinal representation is particularly salient and accessible, this representation is likely to dominate the response, so that one can reasonably refer to the response as *memory based* or *precomputed*. When such representations are not particularly accessible, the response will be based more on less relevant representations such as episodic memories, categorizations, and so on, and it reasonable to refer to an on-line or computed judgment. As this account emphasizes, however, intermediate forms of attitudinal response are also possible, such that preexisting attitudinal representations contribute to the judgment response along with other, less relevant, but more accessible forms of representation.

To some extent, this account is simply a rehashing of points that Fazio makes in his commentary and elsewhere (1989). What AST contributes might be viewed as embellishments that follow from its integrative systematicity and its emphasis on multiple representations. For example, AST provides a systematic framework for defining and comparing different

---

[6]Details of such search and judgment processes are provided in the target chapter.

kinds of attitudes. Additionally, AST suggests new approaches to attitudinal phenomena that derive from one or another proposal in the theory. For example, the AST speculation that mental systems can be preoccupied by competing activities suggests that a respondent who is engaged in demanding physical activities may have trouble accessing orientations or affects, and may need instead to compute attitudes from other cognitions. Similarly, a respondent who is engaged in demanding mental activities may have trouble accessing evaluations, or trouble sorting through and combining multiple forms of representation, and may therefore simply respond with gut feelings. As Fazio notes (p. 160; see also Bodenhausen & Macrae, chap. 8), people may develop a priority system, relying more on self-referent or abstract attitudinal representations, perhaps particularly when cognitively overloaded.

AST further suggests that all of those forms of attitudes that derive from the affective system (i.e., orientations, affect, and evaluations) are likely to have fairly similar implications, whereas those that derive from completely different systems (e.g., the visual) may result in rather different responses. It implies that, of all the stored forms of attitudinal representation, orientations may be most related to behaviors, and evaluations may be most related to verbal judgments and communications. Moreover, it suggests that different kinds of judgments may draw differentially on different kinds of existing representations (see Table 1.2). At least a few of these suggestions may prove to be mistaken, but it nonetheless seems fruitful to consider ways of combining the knowledge that has been gained in different (and, all too often, separate) research areas, such as person perception and attitudes.

More Ambivalent Thoughts.   Fazio expands on some of the ideas about ambivalence that were touched on in chapter 8. He observes that ambivalent feelings involving the simultaneous activation of evaluatively inconsistent representations may occur infrequently, except perhaps when the perceiver is called upon to construct an evaluative response: "When the object is encountered in a context that does not involve the deliberate goal of evaluating the object, however, it may be that only one of the two inconsistent evaluations (if any) is automatically activated from memory" (p. 164). Fazio goes on to suggest that inconsistent representations often seem to involve different interpretations or uses for the same attitude object.[7] Because only one of these interpretations is likely to be engaged at any time, the evaluations associated with that representation are unlikely to conflict with those associated with alternative interpretations.

---

[7]Fazio refers to these as different *categorizations*, but we prefer to steer away from this term in this context, so as to avoid confusion with the representational form that we label with this term.

To draw the argument a bit more broadly, inconsistent representations seem most likely to develop when different situational contexts and demands place rather different pressures on the perceiver. For example, a perceiver may learn racist beliefs from family and friends, but work in a situation where egalitarian norms are enforced. The negative stereotypes toward African Americans that develop in the first context are likely to be incongruent with the civil behavioral responses that develop in the other. Most often, the cues provided by family and friends will activate one set of representations, and the cues provided by the workplace will activate the second. In Fazio's terms, the perceiver's impression of African Americans hinges on two differing interpretations: as a group to be reviled with friends, and as colleagues to be accommodated at work. As long as only one of these interpretations is salient at a time, the perceiver can probably function adequately in each group. However, problems seem likely to arise when: (a) the perceiver is cued to think about workplace activities while with friends and family, (b) the perceiver is cued to use stereotypic cognitive representations while interacting at work, or (c) the perceiver is in a situation that cues both the cognitive stereotypes and the behavioral civility.

This illustration was structured so that the different contexts emphasize different representational systems. As Fazio notes, AST argues that representational inconsistencies are probably more likely across different systems than within them. One could plausibly construct a scenario where the different contexts engage the same mental system, but, in rather different ways, creating within-system inconsistencies. For example, a TV personality might be friendly to co-workers on the air, but act belligerently once the cameras go off. As Fazio again notes, AST suggests that such inconsistencies may be more common in concrete forms of representation than in abstract forms. People do look and act differently at different times, but it is less common (though not unheard of) for people to have conflicting trait attributes, to be perceived as both good and bad, or to be both hated and loved.

When AST is applied to groups of people, rather than to individuals, it may be easier to envision single forms of representation with seemingly inconsistent implications. We love some actors and hate others, we are friendly to some waiters and curt to others, or we may see some politicians as honest as others as dishonest. In fact, however, such examples do not reflect inconsistent representations toward single attitude objects, because the referents are clearly differentiated into subgroups. In other words, the actors we love undoubtedly fall into a different psychological category than the actors we hate. Here again, the inconsistencies among representations seem to reflect different interpretations of the attitude object, as Fazio suggested.

Just as inconsistent representations are theorized to result from the different pressures put on perceivers by different situations, consistent representations are thought to result from experiences that place coherent demands on perceivers' different mental systems. As discussed earlier, AST suggests that mental representations are more likely to be consistent when they have developed together and been subject to the same kinds of influences. This proposal is actually an extension of Fazio's (e.g. Fazio, Chen, McDonel, & Sherman, 1982; Fazio, Powell, & Herr, 1983) theorizing about the effects of direct experience on attitude–behavior consistency. In that specific instance, experiences that allow the simultaneous engagement of the action and affect systems encourage the development of harmonious behavioral and attitudinal representations. More generally, AST proposes that experiences that involve multiple systems encourage the development of corresponding representations that are consistent with each other. This once again illustrates both the overlap and the symbiosis between the attitude and person perception areas to which Fazio alludes in his commentary.

CONCLUDING REMARKS

AST was designed to provide an integrative and heuristic account of the different forms of social representation that have been studied in social psychology. It begins with the premise that mental representations reflect the operations of different mental systems; provides an account of how the visual, verbal, affective, and action systems produce basic forms of social representation; and then suggests a conceptual structure that summarizes some of the interrelationships among these. AST includes a process model that combines common information-processing and associative-network assumptions, accommodates the notion of multiple representation, and relates the representational system to judgmental and behavioral outputs. Although it ties in work from such realms as neuropsychology, PDP models, and attitudes research along the way, its primary goal is simply to suggest "both the origins and the consequences of impressions differing in representational form" (p. 1).

Given the integrative nature of AST, it is appropriate that the eight commentaries in this volume reflect such a variety of different viewpoints. The first three commentaries – by Martindale, Van Manen and Fiske, and Wyer – invite clarification of the theory by raising issues regarding different systems, representations, or processes. The next two – by Fiedler, and Radvansky – challenge AST at more fundamental levels, questioning either the objectivity or the objectives of the approach. The final three commentaries – by Brewer, Bodenhausen and Macrae, and Fazio – expand the theory by suggesting ways in which it relates to their areas of expertise. All make interesting points, and we appreciate their thoughtful and helpful attention to the nuances of this complex model.

We began this chapter with the tale about the three blind men who took hold of different parts of an elephant and then could not agree about the nature of the beast they were holding. One underemphasized implication of this story is that, by comparing and contrasting their different perspectives, the three blind men could have arrived at a much clearer conception of the elephant, which none could fully apprehend by himself. Perhaps combining all of the different viewpoints in this volume will also help readers to see things a little more clearly.

REFERENCES

Abelson, R. P., Aronson, E., McGuire, W. J., Newcomb, T. M., Rosenberg, M. J., & Tannenbaum, P. H. (Eds.). (1968). *Theories of cognitive consistency: A sourcebook*. Chicago: Rand McNally.

Anderson, J. R. (1978). Arguments concerning representations for mental imagery. *Psychological Review, 85*, 249–277.

Anderson, J. R. (1979). Further arguments concerning representations for mental imagery: A response to Hayes-Roth and Pylyshyn. *Psychological Review, 86*, 395–406.

Anderson, J. R. (1983). *The architecture of cognition*. Cambridge, MA: Harvard University Press.

Barsalou, L. N. (1988). The content and organization of autobiographical memories. In U. Neisser & E. Winograd (Eds.), *Remembering reconsidered: Ecological and traditional approaches to the study of memory. Emory symposia in cognition, 2* (pp. 193–243). New York: Cambridge University Press.

Berscheid, E. (1985). Interpersonal attraction. In G. Lindzey & E. Aronson (Eds.), *Handbook of social psychology* (pp. 413–484). New York: Random House.

Brewer, M. B. (1988). A dual process model of impression formation. In T. K. Srull & R. S. Wyer, Jr. (Eds.), *Advances in social cognition* (Vol. 1, pp. 1–36). Hillsdale, NJ: Lawrence Erlbaum Associates.

Brewer, M. B., & Lui, L. L. (1989). The primacy of age and sex in the structure of person categories. *Social Cognition, 7*, 262–274.

Cacioppo, J. T., Klein, D. J., Berntson, G. G., & Hatfield, E. (1993). The psychophysiology of emotion. In M. Lewis & J. M. Haviland (Eds.), *Handbook of emotions* (pp. 119–142). New York: Guilford.

Cantor, N., & Mischel, W. (1977). Traits as prototypes: Effects on recognition memory. *Journal of Personality and Social Psychology, 35*, 38–48.

Carlston, D. E. (1992). Impression formation and the modular mind: The Associated Systems Theory. In L. L. Martin & A. Tesser (Eds.), *The construction of social judgments* (pp. 301–341). Hillsdale, NJ: Lawrence Erlbaum Associates.

Carlston, D. E., & Skowronski, J. J. (1988). *Trait memory and behavior memory: II. The effects of conceptual social knowledge on impression judgment response times*. Unpublished manuscript, University of Iowa, Iowa City, IA.

Carlston, D. E., & Skowronski, J. J. (1994). Savings in the relearning of trait information as evidence for spontaneous inference generation. *Journal of Personality and Social Psychology, 66*, 840–856.

Chaiken, S. (1980). Heuristic versus systematic information processing and the use of source versus message cues in persuasion. *Journal of Personality and Social Psychology*, *39*, 752–766.

Commentary on Endel Tulving precis of *Elements of episodic memory*. (1986). *Behavioral and Brain Sciences*, *9*, 566–577.

Damasio, A. R. (1989). The brain binds entities and events by multiregional activation from convergence zones. *Neural Computation*, *1*, 123–132.

Fazio, R. H. (1989). On the power and functionality of attitudes: The role of attitude accessibility. In A. R. Pratkanis, S. J. Breckler, & A. G. Greenwald (Eds.), *Attitude structure and function* (pp. 153–179). Hillsdale, NJ: Lawrence Erlbaum Associates.

Fazio, R. H., Chen, J., McDonel, E. C., & Sherman, S. J. (1982). Attitude accessibility, attitude-behavior consistency, and the strength of the object-evaluation association. *Journal of Experimental Social Psychology*, *18*, 339–357.

Fazio, R. H., Powell, M. C., & Herr, P. M. (1983). Toward a process model of the attitude-behavior relation: Accessing one's attitude upon more observation of the attitude object. *Journal of Personality Social Psychology*, *44*, 723–735.

Festinger, L. (1957). *A theory of cognitive dissonance*. Palo Alto, CA: Stanford University Press.

Fiske, S. T. (1982). Schema-triggered affect: Applications to social perception. In M. S. Clark & S. T. Fiske (Eds.), *Affect and cognition: The 17th annual Carnegie symposium on cognition* (pp. 55–78). Hillsdale, NJ: Lawrence Erlbaum Associates.

Fiske, S. T. (1988). Compare and contrast: Brewer's dual process model and Fiske et al.'s continuum model. In T. K. Srull & R. S. Wyer, Jr. (Eds.), *Advances in social cognition* (Vol. 1, pp. 65–76). Hillsdale, NJ: Lawrence Erlbaum Associates.

Fiske, S. T., & Cox, M. G. (1979). Person concepts: The effects of target familiarity and descriptive purpose on the process of describing others. *Journal of Personality*, *47*, 136–161.

Fiske, S. T., & Pavelchak, M. A. (1986). Category-based vs. piecemeal-based affective responses: Developments in schema-triggered affect. In R. M. Sorrentino & E. T. Higgins (Eds.), *Handbook of motivation and cognition* (pp. 167–203). New York: Guilford.

Fiske, S. T., & Taylor, S. E. (1991). *Social cognition*. New York: McGraw-Hill.

Gallistel, C. R. (1980). *The organization of action: A new synthesis*. Hillsdale, NJ: Lawrence Erlbaum Associates.

Gergen, K. J. (1982). *Toward transformation in social knowledge*. New York: Springer-Verlag.

Gergen, K. J., & Gergen, M. M. (1984). *Historical social psychology*. Hillsdale, NJ: Lawrence Erlbaum Associates.

Glass, A. L., & Holyoak, K. J. (1986). *Cognition* (2nd ed.). New York: Random House.

Hastie, R., & Carlston, D. E. (1980). Theoretical issues in person memory. In R. Hastie, T. Ostrom, E. Ebbesen, R. Wyer, D. Hamilton, & D. Carlston (Eds.), *Person memory: The cognitive basis of social perception* (pp. 1–53). Hillsdale, NJ: Lawrence Erlbaum Associates.

Hastie, R., & Kumar, P. A. (1979). Person memory: Personality traits as organizing principles in memory for behavior. *Journal of Personality and Social Psychology*, *37*, 25–38.

Hastie, R., & Park, B. (1986). The relationship between memory and judgment depends on whether the judgment task is memory-based or on-line. *Psychological Review*, *93*, 258–268.

Higgins, E. T., Rholes, W. S., & Jones, C. R. (1977). Category accessibility and impression formation. *Journal of Experimental Social Psychology*, *13*, 141–154.

Izard, C. E. (1993). Four systems for emotion activation: Cognitive and noncognitive processes. *Psychological Review*, *100*, 68–90.

Johnson, M. K. (1992). Mechanisms of recollection. *Journal of Cognitive Neuroscience*, *4*, 268–280.

Katz, D. (1960). The functional approach to the study of attitudes. *Public Opinion Quarterly*, *24*, 163–204.

Kihlstrom, J. F., & Cantor, N. (1984). Mental representations of the self. In L. Berkowitz (Ed.), *Advances in experimental social psychology* (Vol. 17, pp. 1–47). New York: Academic Press.

Klatzky, R. L., & Andersen, S. M. (1988). Category-specificity effects in social typing and personalization. In T. K. Srull & R. S. Wyer (Eds.), *Advances in social cognition: A dual process model of impression formation* (Vol. 1, pp. 91–102). Hillsdale, NJ: Lawrence Erlbaum Associates.

Klein, S. B., Loftus, J., Trafton, J. G., & Fuhrman, R. W. (1992). Use of exemplars and abstractions in trait judgments: A model of trait knowledge about the self and others. *Journal of Personality and Social Psychology, 63,* 739–753.

Kolb, B., & Whishaw, I. Q. (1990). *Fundamentals of human neuropsychology* (3rd ed.). San Francisco: Freeman.

Konorski, J. (1967). *Integrative activity of the brain.* Chicago: University of Chicago Press.

Kuhn, T. S. (1970). *The structure of scientific revolutions.* Chicago: University of Chicago Press.

LeDoux, J. E. (1993). Emotional networks in the brain. In M. Lewis & J. M. Haviland (Eds.), *Handbook of emotions* (pp. 109–118). New York: Guilford.

Loftus, E. F. (1975). Leading questions and the eyewitness report. *Cognitive Psychology, 7,* 560–572.

Martindale, C. (1991). *Cognitive psychology: A neural-network approach.* Pacific Grove, CA: Brooks/Cole.

Mayes, A. R. (1988). *Human organic memory disorders.* Cambridge, England: Cambridge University Press.

Millar, M. G., & Tesser, A. (1986). Effects of affective and cognitive focus on the attitude-behavior relation. *Journal of Personality and Social Psychology, 51,* 270–276.

Neisser, U. (1982). Snapshots or benchmarks? In U. Neisser (Ed.), *Memory observed: Remembering in natural contexts* (pp. 43–48). San Francisco: Freeman.

Ohman, A. (1993). Fear and anxiety as emotional phenomena: Clinical phenomenology, evolutionary perspectives, and information-processing mechanisms. In M. Lewis & J. M. Haviland (Eds.), *Handbook of emotions* (pp. 511–562). New York: Guilford.

Parkin, A. J., & Leng, N. R. C. (1993). *Neuropsychology of the amnesic syndrome.* Hillsdale, NJ: Lawrence Erlbaum Associates.

Pylyshyn, Z. W. (1973). What the mind's eye tells the mind's brain: A critique of mental imagery. *Psychological Bulletin, 80,* 1–24.

Rosenberg, S., & Sedlak, A. (1972). Structural representations of implicit personality theory. In L. Berkowitz (Ed.), *Advances in experimental social psychology* (Vol. 6, pp. 235–297). New York: Academic Press.

Schacter, D. L. (1987). Implicit memory: History and current status. *Journal of Experimental Psychology: Learning, Memory, and Cognition, 13,* 501–518.

Schneider, D. J. (1991). Social cognition. In M. R. Rosenzweig & L. W. Porter (Eds.), *Annual review of psychology* (Vol. 42, pp. 527–561). Palo Alto, CA: Annual Reviews.

Shallice, T. (1978). The dominant action system: An information-processing approach to consciousness. In K. S. Pope & J. L. Singer (Eds.), *The stream of consciousness: Scientific investigations into the flow of human experience* (pp. 117–157). New York: Plenum.

Srull, T. K. (1981). Person memory: Some tests of associative storage and retrieval models. *Journal of Experimental Psychology: Human Learning and Memory, 7,* 440–463.

Stangor, C., & McMillan, D. (1992). Memory for expectancy-congruent and expectancy-incongruent social information: A review of the social and social developmental literatures. *Psychological Bulletin, 111,* 42–61.

Tulving, E. (1972). Episodic and schematic memory. In E. Tulving & W. Donaldson (Eds.), *Organization of memory* (pp. 381–403). New York: Academic Press.

Wegner, D. M., Schneider, D. J., Carter, S. III, & White, L. (1987). Paradoxical effects of thought suppression. *Journal of Personality and Social Psychology, 53*, 5-13.

Wilson, T. D., & Dunn, D. S. (1986). Effects of introspection on attitude-behavior consistency: Analyzing reasons versus focusing on feelings. *Journal of Experimental Social Psychology, 22*, 249-263.

Wyer, R. S., Jr., & Carlston, D. E. (1979). *Social cognition, inference, and attribution.* Hillsdale, NJ: Lawrence Erlbaum Associates.

Wyer, R. S., Jr., & Carlston, D. E. (1994). The cognitive representation of persons and events. In R. S. Wyer & T. K. Srull (Eds.), *Handbook of social cognition* (2nd ed., Vol. 1, pp. 41-98). Hillsdale, NJ: Lawrence Erlbaum Associates.

Zaidel, D. W. (1994). Worlds apart: Pictorial semantics in the left and right cerebral hemispheres. *Current Directions in Psychological Science, 3*, 5-8.

Author Index

A

Abelson, R. P., 8, *67,* 108, *112,* 159, *166,* 214, *222*

Alba, J. W., 47, 49, *67*

Allen, R. B., 49, *70*

Allport, G. W., 82, *85*

Anastasio, P. A., 150, *156*

Andersen, S. M., 8, 63, *67, 73,* 141, 143, *147,* 200, *224*

Anderson, J. R., 5, 7, 37, *67,* 106, 107, *112,* 131, *140,* 180, 199, *222*

Anderson, N. H., 16, *67,* 158, *166*

Anderson, R. A., 10, 13, *67*

Anderson, R. C., 47, *67*

Anderson, S. W., 10, 13, *67*

Anshel, M. H., 59, *67*

Armbruster, T., 124, *126*

Aronoff, J., 8, *68*

Aronson, E., 214, *222*

Asch, S. E., 82, *85,* 99, *112,* 150, *155*

Assor, A., 8, *68*

Atkinson, R. C., 131, 133, *140*

B

Bachelard, G., 82, *85*

Baer, J. S., 42, *72*

Bagozzi, R. P., 151, *155*

Baldwin, M. W., 55, *69*

Bargh, J. A., 22, 37, 38, 42, 49, *67, 68, 72, 74,* 99, 104, *112,* 143, *147,* 154, *155*

Barsalou, L. W., 139, *140,* 189, *222*

Bassili, J. N., 35, 37, *67*

Battistich, V. A., 8, *68*

Beach, L., 16, 18, *68*

Bem, D. J., 51, 55, *68,* 103, *112*

Bem, S. L., 48, *71*

Berntson, G. G., 174, *222*

Berscheid, E., 61, *76,* 93, *97,* 201, *222*

Bissonnette, V., 35, *72*

Blank, A., 37, *73*

Bodenhausen, G. V., 142, 146, *147,* 152, 154, *156,* 170, 174, 211–217, 219

Bond, R. N., 38, 57, *67*

Boring, E. G., 29, *68*

Bormann, C., 39, *76*

Bower, G. H., 22, *68*

Bradshaw, J. M., 47, *69*

Breckler, S. J., 8, 29, *68,* 151, *155*

Brewer, M. B., 8, 22, 63, *68,* 92, *97,* 110, 141–146, *147,* 170, 200, 204–206, 208–211, *222*

Briggs, M. A., 60, *73*

Briggs, S. R., 60, 62, *68*

Bromley, D. B., 16, 18, *74*

Brooks, L. R., 58, *68*

Brown, R., 42, *68,* 150, *155*

Brunswik, E., 121, 124, *126*

Bryden, M. P., 57, *68*

227

Subject Index